T0210897

IFIP Advances in Information and Communication Technology 417

Editor-in-Chief

IFIP – The International Federation for Information Processing

IFIP was founded in 1960 under the auspices of UNESCO, following the First World Computer Congress held in Paris the previous year. An umbrella organization for societies working in information processing, IFIP's aim is two-fold: to support information processing within its member countries and to encourage technology transfer to developing nations. As its mission statement clearly states,

> IFIP's mission is to be the leading, truly international, apolitical organization which encourages and assists in the development, exploitation and application of information technology for the benefit of all people.

IFIP is a non-profitmaking organization, run almost solely by 2500 volunteers. It operates through a number of technical committees, which organize events and publications. IFIP's events range from an international congress to local seminars, but the most important are:

- The IFIP World Computer Congress, held every second year;
- Open conferences;
- Working conferences.

The flagship event is the IFIP World Computer Congress, at which both invited and contributed papers are presented. Contributed papers are rigorously refereed and the rejection rate is high.

As with the Congress, participation in the open conferences is open to all and papers may be invited or submitted. Again, submitted papers are stringently refereed.

The working conferences are structured differently. They are usually run by a working group and attendance is small and by invitation only. Their purpose is to create an atmosphere conducive to innovation and development. Refereeing is also rigorous and papers are subjected to extensive group discussion.

Publications arising from IFIP events vary. The papers presented at the IFIP World Computer Congress and at open conferences are published as conference proceedings, while the results of the working conferences are often published as collections of selected and edited papers.

Any national society whose primary activity is about information processing may apply to become a full member of IFIP, although full membership is restricted to one society per country. Full members are entitled to vote at the annual General Assembly. National societies preferring a less committed involvement may apply for associate or corresponding membership. Associate members enjoy the same benefits as full members, but without voting rights. Corresponding members are not represented in IFIP bodies. Affiliated membership is open to non-national societies, and individual and honorary membership schemes are also offered.

Jonathan Butts   Sujeet Shenoi (Eds.)

Critical Infrastructure Protection VII

7th IFIP WG 11.10 International Conference
ICCIP 2013
Washington, DC, USA, March 18-20, 2013
Revised Selected Papers

 Springer

Volume Editors

Jonathan Butts
Air Force Institute of Technology
Wright-Patterson Air Force Base
Dayton, OH 45433-7765, USA
E-mail: jonathan.butts@afit.edu

Sujeet Shenoi
University of Tulsa
Tulsa, OK 74104-3189, USA
E-mail: sujeet@utulsa.edu

ISSN 1868-4238   e-ISSN 1868-422X
ISBN 978-3-662-52543-2   e-ISBN 978-3-642-45330-4 (eBook)
DOI 10.1007/978-3-642-45330-4
Springer Heidelberg New York Dordrecht London

CR Subject Classification (1998): K.6.5, J.7, K.4, I.6, D.4.6, K.5.1, C.2, H.4, H.3, K.6

Typesetting: Camera-ready by author, data conversion by Scientific Publishing Services, Chennai, India

Printed on acid-free paper

Springer is part of Springer Science+Business Media (www.springer.com)

Contents

Contributing Authors

Saed Alajlouni is a Researcher in the Department of Electrical Engineering at Texas Tech University, Lubbock, Texas. His research interests include cyber-physical systems security, control systems, autonomous systems, industrial automation, renewable energy systems and power electronics.

Abdullah Alsubaie is a Ph.D. student in Electrical Engineering at the University of British Columbia, Vancouver, Canada. His research interests include power systems operation and critical infrastructure simulation.

Aaron Alva is a J.D. candidate and an M.S. student in Information Management at the University of Washington, Seattle, Washington. His research interests include cloud forensics, digital evidence admissibility and legal barriers to critical infrastructure resilience.

Tara Anderson is a member of the Senior Professional Staff at the Johns Hopkins University Applied Physics Laboratory in Laurel, Maryland. Her research interests include information security, modeling and simulation, and mission risk assessment.

Daniel Arnaudo is a Senior Research Fellow at the Jackson School of International Studies, University of Washington, Seattle, Washington. His research interests include Internet governance, information assurance and Brazilian telecommunications policy.

Damindra Bandara is a Ph.D. student in Computer Science at George Mason University, Fairfax, Virginia. Her research interests include the security of software-defined radios and wireless-controlled trains, and protocol verification.

Andre Bondi is a Senior Staff Engineer at Siemens Corporate Technology, Princeton, New Jersey. His research interests include computer performance engineering, modeling and simulation.

Mike Burmester is a Professor of Computer Science at Florida State University, Tallahassee, Florida. His research interests include computer and network security, cyber-physical system protection, pervasive and ubiquitous systems, trust management and cryptography.

Jonathan Butts, Chair, IFIP Working Group 11.10 on Critical Infrastructure Protection, is an Assistant Professor of Computer Science and the Chief of the Computer Science and Engineering Division at the Air Force Institute of Technology, Wright-Patterson Air Force Base, Ohio. His research interests include critical infrastructure protection and cyber-physical systems security.

Alvaro Cardenas is an Assistant Professor of Computer Science at the University of Texas at Dallas, Dallas, Texas. His research interests include the security and privacy of control systems, SCADA systems, the smart grid and other cyber-physical critical infrastructures.

Richard Chow is a Security Researcher and Privacy Architect at Intel Corporation, Santa Clara, California. His research interests include privacy-enhancing technologies using machine learning and applied cryptography.

Emiliano De Cristofaro is a Research Scientist at PARC (a Xerox company), Palo Alto, California. His research interests include security, privacy and applied cryptography.

Yi Deng is a Research Scientist in the Department of Electrical and Computer Engineering, Arlington Research Center, Virginia Polytechnic Institute and State University, Arlington, Virginia. His research interests include smart grid security, PMU-based wide area measurement, SCADA systems security, software security and software modeling and meta-modeling.

Antonio Di Pietro is a Researcher at ENEA Casaccia Research Centre, Rome, Italy. His research interests include critical infrastructure interdependency modeling and simulation, and SCADA systems security.

Clay Dubendorfer is an M.S. student in Electrical Engineering at the Air Force Institute of Technology, Wright-Patterson Air Force Base, Ohio. His research interests include signals exploitation and critical infrastructure protection.

Chiara Foglietta is a Researcher at the University of Roma Tre, Rome, Italy. Her research interests include industrial control systems, energy management systems, critical infrastructure interdependencies and data fusion techniques.

Rajni Goel is an Associate Professor and Chairman of the Department of Information Systems at Howard University, Washington, DC. Her research interests include railroad security, supply chain networks and applications security.

Dimitris Gritzalis is a Professor of Information and Communications Technology Security and the Director of the Information Security and Critical Infrastructure Protection Laboratory, Department of Informatics, Athens University of Economics and Business, Athens, Greece. His research interests include critical infrastructure protection, privacy in social media, digital forensics and cloud security.

Robert Jaromin is a Developmental Electrical Engineer with the U.S. Air Force. His research interests include critical infrastructure protection and signals exploitation.

Jonathan Jenkins is a Ph.D. student in Computer Science at Florida State University, Tallahassee, Florida. His research interests include computer security and integrity, cyber-physical system security and trust management.

Pranab Kini is a Research Engineer in the School of Engineering and Computer Science at the University of British Columbia, Vancouver, Canada. His research focuses on software engineering solutions for disaster and relief management.

Panayiotis Kotzanikolaou is a Lecturer of Information and Communications Technology Security in the Department of Informatics, University of Piraeus, Piraeus, Greece. His research interests include network security and privacy, critical infrastructure protection and applied cryptography.

Ting Fu Lin is a Research Assistant in the Power Systems Laboratory at the School of Engineering and Computer Science, University of British Columbia, Vancouver, Canada. His research interests include the analysis and design of complex systems.

Thomas Llanso is a member of the Principal Professional Staff at the Johns Hopkins University Applied Physics Laboratory in Laurel, Maryland; and a Ph.D. student in Information Systems at Dakota State University, Madison, South Dakota. His research interests include quantitative risk assessment and cyber investment analysis.

Juan Lopez is a Research Engineer with the Center for Cyberspace Research at the Air Force Institute of Technology, Wright-Patterson Air Force Base, Ohio. His research interests include critical infrastructure protection and radio frequency identification.

Jose Marti is a Professor of Electrical and Computer Engineering at the University of British Columbia, Vancouver, Canada. His research interests include critical infrastructure modeling and the real-time simulation of large-scale systems.

Barry Mullins is an Associate Professor of Computer Engineering at the Air Force Institute of Technology, Wright-Patterson Air Force Base, Ohio. His research interests include cyber operations, software reverse engineering, computer and network security, SCADA systems security and reconfigurable computing systems.

Simone Palmieri is a Ph.D. student in Computer Science and Automation at the University of Roma Tre, Rome, Italy. His research interests include telecommunications networks and SCADA systems, with a special focus on power systems.

Stefano Panzieri is an Associate Professor of Automation and Process Control Engineering at the University of Roma Tre, Rome, Italy. His research interests are in the areas of industrial control systems, robotics and sensor fusion.

Benjamin Ramsey is a Ph.D. student in Computer Science at the Air Force Institute of Technology, Wright-Patterson Air Force Base, Ohio. His research interests include wireless network security and critical infrastructure protection.

Vittal Rao is a Professor of Electrical and Computer Engineering and the Director of the Smart Grid Energy Center at Texas Tech University, Lubbock, Texas. His research interests include cyber security, critical infrastructure protection, smart grid and microgrid systems, wind turbine control and robust control systems.

Aunshul Rege is an Assistant Professor of Criminal Justice at Temple University, Philadelphia, Pennsylvania. Her research interests include cyber crime, organized crime, offender decision-making, and surveillance and regulation.

Sandeep Shukla is a Professor of Electrical and Computer Engineering at the Arlington Research Center, Virginia Polytechnic Institute and State University, Arlington, Virginia. His research interests include formal methods, system-level design languages and frameworks, component-based and platform-based design, smart grid systems, formal verification and its applications to critical infrastructure systems.

Michael Silberglitt is a member of the Principal Professional Staff at the Johns Hopkins University Applied Physics Laboratory in Laurel, Maryland. His research interests include mission-focused risk assessment methodologies, modeling and simulation, and security engineering.

Michael Smith is a Requirements and System Design Manager with the Rail Automation Unit of Siemens, New York, New York. His research interests include software engineering and computer architecture.

Gregg Tally is a member of the Senior Professional Staff at the Johns Hopkins University Applied Physics Laboratory in Laurel, Maryland. His research interests include cyber security engineering methodologies and malware defense.

Michael Temple is a Professor of Electrical Engineering at the Air Force Institute of Technology, Wright-Patterson Air Force Base, Ohio. His research interests include radio frequency systems, wireless networks and critical infrastructure protection.

Marianthi Theoharidou is a Post-Doctoral Researcher in the Information Security and Critical Infrastructure Protection Laboratory, Department of Informatics, Athens University of Economics and Business, Athens, Greece. Her research interests include critical infrastructure protection, risk assessment and cloud security.

Alberto Tofani is a Researcher in the Computing and Technological Infrastructures Laboratory at ENEA Casaccia Research Centre, Rome, Italy. His research interests include critical infrastructure vulnerability assessment and decision support systems for crisis preparedness and mitigation.

Jan Whittington is an Assistant Professor of Urban Design and Planning and an Associate Director of the Center for Information Assurance and Cybersecurity at the University of Washington, Seattle, Washington. Her research interests are in the areas of economics, planning and infrastructure management, including privacy and security issues.

Duminda Wijesekera is a Professor of Computer Science at George Mason University, Fairfax, Virginia. His research includes information security and its application to logical models of security policies, safety and security of wireless-controlled trains, security and privacy of healthcare applications, and financial crime.

Phillip Wood received his M.S. degree in Information Management from the University of Washington, Seattle, Washington. His research interests include technology valuation and the economic impact of political insecurity.

Yanjun Zuo is an Associate Professor of Computer Information Systems at the University of North Dakota, Grand Forks, North Dakota. His research interests include system survivability, trustworthy computing and RFID security and privacy.

Preface

The information infrastructure – comprising computers, embedded devices, networks and software systems – is vital to operations in every sector: information technology, telecommunications, energy, banking and finance, transportation systems, chemicals, agriculture and food, defense industrial base, public health and health care, national monuments and icons, drinking water and water treatment systems, commercial facilities, dams, emergency services, commercial nuclear reactors, materials and waste, postal and shipping, and government facilities. Global business and industry, governments, indeed society itself, cannot function if major components of the critical information infrastructure are degraded, disabled or destroyed.

This book, *Critical Infrastructure Protection VII*, is the seventh volume in the annual series produced by IFIP Working Group 11.10 on Critical Infrastructure Protection, an active international community of scientists, engineers, practitioners and policy makers dedicated to advancing research, development and implementation efforts related to critical infrastructure protection. The book presents original research results and innovative applications in the area of infrastructure protection. Also, it highlights the importance of weaving science, technology and policy in crafting sophisticated, yet practical, solutions that will help secure information, computer and network assets in the various critical infrastructure sectors.

This volume contains fifteen edited papers from the Seventh Annual IFIP Working Group 11.10 International Conference on Critical Infrastructure Protection, held at George Washington University, Washington, DC, March 18–20, 2013. The papers were refereed by members of IFIP Working Group 11.10 and other internationally-recognized experts in critical infrastructure protection.

The chapters are organized into five sections: themes and issues, control systems security, infrastructure security, infrastructure modeling and simulation, and risk assessment. The coverage of topics showcases the richness and vitality of the discipline, and offers promising avenues for future research in critical infrastructure protection.

This book is the result of the combined efforts of several individuals and organizations. In particular, we thank Richard George, Heather Drinan, Nicole Hall Hewett, Lance Hoffman and Firoozeh Rahimian for their tireless work on behalf of IFIP Working Group 11.10. We gratefully acknowledge the Institute for Information Infrastructure Protection (I3P), managed by Dartmouth College, for its sponsorship of IFIP Working Group 11.10. We also thank the Department of Homeland Security and the National Security Agency for their support of IFIP Working Group 11.10 and its activities. Finally, we wish to note that all opinions, findings, conclusions and recommendations in the chapters of this book are those of the authors and do not necessarily reflect the views of their employers or funding agencies.

JONATHAN BUTTS AND SUJEET SHENOI

I

THEMES AND ISSUES

Chapter 1

POLITICAL AND ECONOMIC IMPLICATIONS OF AUTHORITARIAN CONTROL OF THE INTERNET

Daniel Arnaudo, Aaron Alva, Phillip Wood and Jan Whittington

Abstract   During the early days of the 2011 Egyptian Revolution, the Mubarak regime shut down all Egyptian Internet access with the exception of one service provider, Noor ADSL. Analysts have noted that President Mubarak, in attempting to restrict Internet access, suffered from the dictator's digital dilemma, and have speculated that Noor's exceptional treatment was due to its role as a telecommunications provider for the Egyptian Stock Exchange. This paper shows, through an analysis of events, that stock exchange connectivity could not have been the rationale for Noor's continued services and that transaction cost economics, as described by North's theory of the state, provides a more thorough explanation for Mubarak's selective intervention with regard to Internet service. Decisions made during this series of events have implications beyond the Arab Spring. Insights are drawn from the particular case of Noor's role in the Egyptian Revolution and, in the process, a model is developed for future examination of the general case of the potential for loss of critical Internet infrastructure service under authoritarian governments.

Keywords: Authoritarian regimes, Internet governance, Arab Spring, Egypt

1.   Introduction

As defined in the United States and in many countries around the world, the infrastructure is critical to the extent that the economy and society depend on it. This is a public-oriented definition. However, if we use economic theory to interpret the decisions made by authoritarian regimes in the management of critical infrastructures, we may find more self-interested motives in play. Internet access is increasingly valuable to the economy and society; it is itself part of the critical communications infrastructure. National leaders are beginning to

J. Butts and S. Shenoi (Eds.): Critical Infrastructure Protection VII, IFIP AICT 417, pp. 3–19, 2013.
© IFIP International Federation for Information Processing 2013

see the benefits of manipulating the information technology (IT) infrastructure that controls the Internet.

All the regimes that have faced popular uprisings in the Middle East over the last three years have considered the role of the Internet when protesters challenged their legitimacy. Before the events of the Arab Spring, nations around the region, such as Iran, routinely blocked websites or portions of their networks. In recent years, smaller nations such as Myanmar [22] and Libya [9] have shut down the Internet, but they maintained central control of their telecommunications systems through state-run Internet service providers.

The Internet shutdown in Egypt is an interesting case for two reasons. For one, Egypt is a large country compared with the others in the region. It has one of the region's largest economies, built on a growing IT sector that the state had been cultivating since the late 1990s [7]. Egypt had more than 20 million Internet users in 2009, second only to Turkey in the Middle East, using over ten times as much bandwidth in 2005 [5, 26]. Secondly, the Egyptian IT sector fueled the development of a number of independent ISPs that were not subject to direct governmental control and that cultivated a number of powerful clients, including regional and international financial firms as well as government ministries. These conditions present powerful countervailing economic threats to any regime that considers shutting down Internet services.

This paper provides an analysis of the Mubarak regime's shutdown of Internet service during the Arab Spring. Several reasons have been posited. This paper compares the plausibility of the various hypotheses against political, economic and technical data that describe the events related to the Egyptian protests and the government response. The analysis highlights the potential for economic theories that describe self-interested actors in transaction cost contexts to explain the events of the time. Theories that promise to reveal the motives of authoritarian leaders in the management of critical infrastructures provide opportunities to reframe national and international contractual conditions for Internet governance in the interest of critical infrastructure protection for the public good.

2.   Internet Shutdown

Protests in Egypt began on January 25, 2011 and quickly spread throughout the country. After more than three decades in office, President Hosni Mubarak came under significant pressure to step down. The exit of Zine El Abidine Ben Ali, the President of neighboring Tunisia earlier that month did not portend well for Mubarak, yet he refused to relinquish power to an angry opposition. In their desire to grow and sustain their movement, Egyptian protesters benefited from online communications networks that they used to organize, draw support from around the world, and gain attention and exposure to their cause. The protesters also relied heavily on computers and mobile phones to coordinate groups of activists, track government forces and promote pro-democracy sentiments, amongst numerous other informational uses. Mubarak's government and the Egyptian economy also depended on the Internet for communications and to conduct business. If Mubarak decided to shut down the Internet, either by blocking selected websites or by completely blocking access, there would be costs for him as well. Nevertheless, on January 28, 2011, Mubarak made the move to shut down the Internet in Egypt.

After reviewing more than 600 unique incidents involving Internet censorship compiled by researchers at the University of Washington's Communication Department, we discovered that a complete network disconnection had never been attempted on a scale as large as that in Egypt. The precedents were either much smaller, such as Myanmar's decision to cut connections in 2007, or more limited, as in Iran's Internet slowdown during the disputed elections of 2009 [11]. Libya, while immersed in an internal conflict that would end in the downfall of Gaddafi, shut down the Internet in February 2011, but its networks were neither as large as Egypt's nor as important to the nation's economy and infrastructure.

The Mubarak regime had made the decision to cultivate a strong IT sector in the late 1990s. The creation of the Ministry of Information Technology and Communications in 1999 paved the way for the massive growth of Egypt's online population, technology sector and broadband capacity [7]. By the time the Arab Spring erupted, roughly 23 million people – more than one quarter of the Egyptian population – used the Internet on a regular basis [5]. Egypt, a member of the Arab League, set up an Internet exchange in 2004. The country connects to the Internet through three crucial Asia-Europe undersea cables, FLAG, SEA-ME-WE 3 and SEA-ME-WE 4, making the control over these assets an important issue. However, it is also notable that all the Internet exchange point switches (IXPs) were collocated in one facility, allowing the regime to shut them down together by gaining physical control of a central location [23].

In this light, Mubarak's decision to force the country's Internet service providers (ISPs) to stop providing international connections was unprecedented, but it was also incomplete. For a brief period of time, one ISP remained active. This last surviving ISP, Noor ADSL (hereafter referred to as Noor), was responsible for transmitting the country's financial transactions through the Egyptian Stock Exchange, and journalists and technical experts at the time speculated that its persistence lay in this connection [10]. Most have hypothesized that the regime wanted to keep the Egyptian exchange online and, as a result, stopped short of a complete Internet blackout [6]. However, it is not outside the realm of possibility that Noor stayed online to allow the regime to make its own international financial transactions.

3.   Theories of Motivation

Analysts have offered several explanations for the activities in Egypt, most of which suggest that Mubarak faced the "dictator's digital dilemma" [11] – when he weighed the economic opportunity cost of shutting down the Internet against the political consequences of leaving it operating and the protesters using it to further their cause. By this account, Mubarak reacted to the Internet's use for collective action and, by stopping access, acted to preserve his political authority. Perhaps Noor was left operating because, as Howard, *et al.* [11] observe, governmental efforts to organize, even for national security activities, can be crippled when communications networks are compromised.

The dictator's digital dilemma plays off an observation made by former U.S. Secretary of State George Shultz in the 1990s when the Soviet Union grappled with a nascent, but rapidly growing, democracy movement. In a 1985 article in *Foreign Affairs* [28], Shultz noted that the failing Eastern Bloc regimes were facing the same challenges as the Shah of Iran faced when technology fueled the Islamic Revolution in 1979: "Totalitarian societies face a dilemma: either they try to stifle these technologies and thereby fall further behind in the new industrial revolution, or else they permit these technologies and see their totalitarian control inevitably eroded. In fact, they do not have a choice, because they will never be able entirely to block the tide of technological advance."

Building on Shultz's notion, Kedzie [13] coined the term "dictator's dilemma" in the mid-1990s. With each iteration of the theory, the telecommunications networks that form the backbone of each country's command and control, financial and social networking systems (among others) evolve into more robust, strong and dynamic forms that authoritarian regimes find increasingly difficult to control.

While the dictator's digital dilemma may well explain the economic opportunity cost for rulers who, in order to maintain control over an angry public, contemplate shutting down Internet services, transaction cost economics can provide a better lens for viewing the activities in Egypt. When a transaction cost economic approach is taken to discern the motivations of actors, the underlying behavioral assumptions have actors subject to bounded rationality, acting in their self-interest, and doing so strategically, or perhaps even opportunistically and with guile [37]. Actors are not perfect planners and it cannot always be assumed that – when their preferences conflict with others – they will act in the interest of others. Instead, the actors can be assumed to adapt to changing or unfolding situations over time, and to do so to in a self-interested way, presumably for economic gain. Indeed, the economic gain may be personal gain, even when the actor represents an organization such as an authoritarian regime.

These behavioral assumptions are made plain in Williamson's conception of the theory [35, 37] and, given applicability to the question of authoritarian action through a theory of the state, an exercise in the logic of self-interested ruling parties as described by North [20]. In North's theory, specialization and division of labor bring about economic growth as well as transaction costs. The costs of information, which play a significant role in holding back the economic growth of nations, are one form of transaction cost. As conceived by Williamson and furthered by North, all economic activity – even exchange between the state and the public – can be conceived to be contractual, economic exchange. Within their "contractual" arrangements, authoritarian rulers have a choice between acting in the public interest and acting in their personal interest. To act in the public interest brings economic growth. However, economic growth also increases the incentive that rulers have to expropriate funds for their personal interest. Indeed, these two interests can be acted upon concurrently.

North hypothesized that technological change, even when it brings about economic growth, can cause economic instability and have a destabilizing effect on a country. Autocratic rulers find themselves in a conflict between their desire to build a system that seeks rent from their population versus one that maximizes economic output and efficiency through technological advances such as the Internet [20]. An important corollary to this hypothesis is that a reduction in the costs of information will lead to an alteration in an individual's ideology, because he can more easily discern that different, more personally beneficial systems – potential "contractual" relations – of exchange exist elsewhere. As North says, "the cost of maintaining ideological consensus is inversely related to the costs of information and directly related to the stability of relative prices" [20]. In this theory of the state, ideological consensus reduces the transaction cost of maintaining the state. The Internet lowers the cost of information and, thus, transaction costs for the public. Prices shift, economies are disrupted and more growth is made possible, but so is a diverse and dynamic pace of ideological change. When ideological consensus erodes, the transaction costs for the ruler to maintain the existing "contract" with the public rise, perhaps to extremes, as the perception of injustice or the illegitimacy of the ruling party threatens to become the core message in a new ideological consensus.

In this transaction cost conception of authoritarian rule, it is in the interest of the ruler to attempt to selectively intervene, in a calculated way, in the governance of the Internet. The perspective of the ruler may begin with a dilemma, but what results in the case of the critical infrastructure may be more reasonably described as a calculated act of selective intervention. The dictator's digital dilemma expresses the concern that a ruler may have for the impact that may result from the initial choice of whether or not to invest in the Internet, or whether or not to intervene in the provision of Internet services. When public services are shut down, the transaction costs shift abruptly from the ruler to the public. However, the calculated act occurs when Internet services that can serve the personal interests of the ruler are allowed to remain viable, while the services of value to the greater public are eliminated.

The next section examines events in Egypt during the Arab Spring for evidence to support or refute these positions.

4. Data Sources

We analyzed events using political, economic and technical data from several sources. We define a reputable source for political data as a news organization that has an established record for reporting; these sources include *The Guardian*, *The New York Times*, Al Jazeera, CNN, Reuters and Associated Press. Accuracy in reporting news is paramount in these organizations. Given that some of the sources are blogs published by news organizations, it is important to note that the Associated Press suggests that blogs may also be used as valid news sources [8].

Detailed economic data has been difficult to obtain, although we located sources that provide data about the Egyptian economy as a whole. The stock market is traditionally used as a measure of reactions to events – sometimes in business, sometimes in politics. It is common knowledge that stock markets are economic indicators for nations and regions. Resources such as Bloomberg and Google Finance were used to track the EGX 30 stock index, which offers a snapshot of Egypt's market economy. By monitoring the rise and fall of financial measures, we were able to discern trends related to the interaction between the events of 2011 and the Egyptian economy. Stock market closures also provided insights into the government's critical actions during moments of crisis.

However, after the Egyptian Stock Exchange was closed, the primary economic indicator for the country was no longer available. This made it necessary to assess economic trends in Egypt using data from outside Egypt. We concluded that our analysis would have to move a degree or two away from Egypt's central economy (or the CASE 30 index that measures it). Therefore, we used data sources that were invested in Egypt's economy without actually being a part of Egypt's economy.

We examined two sources. One source was the value of major currencies in relation to the Egyptian pound. Egypt may have been able to close its domestic banks, but it could not silence how other nations reacted to its political upheaval. Tracking the Egyptian pound to monetary heavy-hitters (such as the dollar, euro and British pound) provided insights into how these nations reacted to the crisis in Egypt – and, in fact, a glimpse into the world's perception at a macroeconomic scale. Bloomberg and Google Finance permit the mapping of multiple currencies on one graph using a predetermined time frame, allowing narrow currency comparisons that revealed reactions to individual events in the Egyptian crisis timeline.

Data pertaining to the fluctuating stock prices of multinational corporations based in Egypt was also used. In particular, we examined NYSE Arca: EGPT, which comprises companies that derive at least 50% of their revenues from Egyptian sources; this was deemed to be a worthwhile second-degree data source because it is traded on the NYSE. The EGPT companies trade in markets independent of Egypt's EGX 30, and their activities provide economic data during the period that the Mubarak regime shut down the stock market. This data provides a glimpse into the market decisions and motivations of Egyptian stock holders in America, which may be a more direct and independent indicator than the U.S. dollar to Egyptian pound exchange rate.

Our main source of technical data was Renesys, a company that tracks Internet usage around the world in real time. Renesys posts information in the public domain about the number of networks that each Egyptian ISP administers, when they went down and when they returned to operation. Renesys also provides trace-route information from computers within Egypt that allows measurements of the speed, route and availability of connections with U.S.-based systems.

We also secured an account with Renesys Market Intelligence that enabled us to understand how Noor and other Egyptian ISPs connected financial markets to the Internet. We confirmed the data with other information provided in blogs as well as data drawn directly from regional Internet registries, primarily Reseaux IP Europeens Network Coordination Center (RIPE NCC), which coordinates routing tables for Europe and the Middle East. We also reviewed the number of Internet users within the country based on figures from the International Telecommunications Union [12]; this helped quantify the scale of the Internet shutdown in relation to the size of the protests and other political events.

5.   Stakeholders

We selected several stakeholders to follow during the events of Egypt's Arab Spring based on their perceived political, economic and technical power or influence.

- **Hosni Mubarak:** Hosni Mubarak was Egypt's President for almost thirty years. The revolution began as a protest against Mubarak's repressive and corrupt regime, and the desire to change decades of one-party rule in Egypt [30]. At the time, Mubarak's financial holdings were estimated to be between $1 billion and $70 billion, largely amassed through illegal means [15].

- **Protesters:** The Egyptian protesters were tired of the intense repression and rampant corruption during Mubarak's one-party rule [30]. The protesters, not all of whom were members of political organizations, demanded regime change and imposed unrelenting pressure during the eighteen days of the revolution. The protesters organized massive rallies throughout the country, with Cairo's Tahrir Square as the focal point.

- **Noor:** Noor is a mid-sized ISP that serves a number of clients who are dependent or "critically dependent" on it for access to the Internet (critically dependent means that Noor provides a client its sole connection to the Internet). ISPs provide software, hardware and services, but they use fiber optic cables and other transmission resources owned and managed by telecommunications firms. Noor connects with international networks through two providers, Telecom Italia and Reliance Globalcom, an Indian telecommunications firm. Noor's clients include the Commercial International Bank of Egypt, the largest privately-held bank in Egypt; Allianz Financial, a German insurance company; AT Holding Corporation, a subsidiary of the Saudi conglomerate Dalla Al-Baraka; and a number of smaller financial and IT firms. A large portion of Noor's traffic also comes from a subsidiary provider, The Wayout Internet Solutions. At the time, this company provided Internet connections for about one hundred networks.

- **Other ISPs:** The largest provider and the flagship government carrier is Telecom Egypt, which is also responsible for the country's telephone infrastructure [38]. Telecom Egypt provided Internet services to roughly 800 sub-networks at the time it was taken down. Other providers with access to the international Internet included two Egyptian IT companies, Link Egypt (roughly 740 networks), and Internet Egypt (100); Raya Holding Corporation (150), which is controlled by Vodafone; and Etisalat Misr (640), the Egyptian subsidary of Etisalat, an Abu Dhabi based multinational corporation [6].

- **Egyptian Stock Exchange:** The Egyptian Stock Exchange is based in Cairo and Alexandria. Its EGX 30 index is the primary indicator of Egypt's economic performance. EGX 30 comprises 30 large Egyptian companies that have a free float (publicly-traded shares) of 15% or more. The Egyptian Stock Exchange is open Sunday through Thursday. When data from EGX 30 was unavailable, the Market Vectors Egypt Index (EGPT) served as an economic indicator. EGPT is an Egyptian exchange-traded fund that tracks publicly-traded companies listed on an Egyptian stock exchange. EGPT firms that are not traded on an Egyptian exchange must generate at least 50% of their revenues in Egypt. It is worth noting that the EGPT does not permit losses of more than 10% during a trading day [27].

- **Mubarak Family:** Gamal is the youngest son of Mubarak and the younger brother of Alaa. Gamal was one of the most powerful people in Egypt before the revolution. He was Deputy Secretary General of the then ruling National Democratic Party (NDP) and also led NDP's Policies Committee, which was largely responsible for setting the course of the government. He has a background in finance; he received an MBA degree from the University of Cairo and worked in investment banking for many years, notably with the Bank of America. Later, he founded Medinvest, a private equity firm based in London (from which he has been forced to disinvest). Gamal is thought to have millions of dollars of assets worldwide; the Egyptian newspaper *Al Ahram* uncovered evidence that he controlled bank accounts at the National Bank of Egypt valued at more than $275 million.

  Gamal's older brother Alaa is also very wealthy. They reportedly had an argument about whether their father should give his resignation speech. During the argument, Alaa accused Gamal of dragging the nation into corruption [2]. Gamal and Alaa, along with their wives, are now under investigation for money laundering and stock market manipulation.

- **Egyptian Army:** The Egyptian Army has for many decades commanded the respect and reverence of the Egyptian people [17]. At the time of the revolution, the Army had considerable independent political power, including key government posts [17]. During the revolution, the Army made the decision to allow the protests. This decision was cheered by the protesters and gave standing to their cause. The Army gained complete control of the country after Mubarak stepped down.

- **Egyptian Financial Firms:** Four financial firms, Commercial International Bank, AT Holding Corporation, Beltone Financial and Allianz Financial, represent some of the largest businesses in Egypt. The Mubarak family is suspected of having substantial investments in these firms [1]. Some of these firms trade on the EGX 30 while others are traded externally. Noor provides Internet services to these firms and enabled them to continue their business activities after the Mubarak regime shut down the other Egyptian ISPs [38].

6.   Principal Events

The events are described in chronological order as they occurred in 2011. When specific times are listed, they refer to the Eastern European Time Zone, which is observed by Egypt.

Event 1 (Tuesday, January 25): Protests Start

On January 25, 2011, massive numbers of Egyptians took to the streets to protest against decades of repression and corruption perpetrated by Mubarak's regime. The protests were called "A Day of Rage" and coincided with Police Day, an Egyptian holiday [21]. The Day of Rage was apparently inspired by the successful protests in Tunisia. An invitation to protest on January 25 was widely circulated on Facebook, where it received more than 95,000 positive responses [21]. The Twitter hashtag #Jan25 was used for social media communications and helped protesters coordinate their activities.

Economic data was particularly difficult to obtain during the downward spiral that followed. An Associated Press headline claimed that the Egyptian Stock Exchange closed immediately after falling 6% in fifteen minutes, but it was not possible to verify the headline with a full report.

The government appeared to start blocking Twitter almost immediately. Numerous sources, including Twitter itself, reported that it was no longer accessible from Egyptian IP addresses. The next day, Facebook also appeared to be blocked from inside Egypt, according to local reports and data from HerdictWeb, a project of Harvard University's Berkman Center for Internet and Society that tracks web blockages worldwide [4].

Event 2 (Thursday, January 27, 2:30 PM): Stock Market Closes

EGX 30 suffered significant losses. The day after the protests began, EGX 30 lost 4.6%. At the end of the trading week (Thursday, January 27) and just three days after the protests started, EGX 30 had fallen 15% (from 6,723 to 5,646 points). The Egyptian Stock Market closes on Thursday and reopens on Sunday, but after closing on Thursday, January 27, amid escalating protests, the

stock market did not reopen the following Sunday. The government announced
that the market would remain closed [31]. In fact, the market did not open
again until Wednesday, March 23, 2011.

Nations that held a significant amount of Egyptian debt saw their currency
exchange rates slide after the protests began. In the week ending January 28,
2011, the Egyptian pound lost 0.9% against the U.S. dollar and euro. The
following week, the Egyptian pound lost 1.4% against the British pound. The
British pound and euro would continue to fall, reaching their lowest exchange
rates in three years in April 2011, shortly after the Egyptian Stock Market
resumed trading.

Event 3 (Friday, January 28, 12:30 AM): Internet is Shut Down
Just after midnight on January 28, three days after the protests began and on
a Friday, a holy day in Islam and the beginning of the weekend in Egypt, the
Egyptian ISPs, Telecom Egypt, Raya Holding Company, Etisalat Misr, Internet
Egypt and Link, shut down all their connections to international networks [38].
By 12:35 AM, Noor was the only Egyptian ISP that provided access to the
global Internet. Later that day, Vodafone Egypt, which also controls Raya,
announced that it had been ordered by the government to take down its mobile
services, saying that, under Egyptian law, it was obliged to comply with the
order [32]. Vodafone was likely referring to Egypt's Telecommunication Regulation Law of 2003 [19] that requires every telecommunications service provider
to have a plan it would implement in cases involving general mobilization and
national security. Since the start of the protests, Egypt's Market Vector Index had lost more than 20% of its value and the Egyptian pound had fallen
markedly against the dollar.

The day leading up to the overnight shutdown of the Internet saw continued
protests. A call was made to have the largest protest yet on the following day
(Friday, January 28); this was billed as "The Friday of Anger and Freedom."
Given the potential scale of the Friday protest, the Internet shutdown was
described by some media sources as an apparent attempt to keep the protesters
from organizing demonstrations [6].

Event 4 (Saturday, January 29, 12:18 AM): Mubarak Announces the
Government Will Resign and a New Government Will be Formed
Mubarak spoke on Egyptian state television at 12:18 AM on Saturday, January
29 [33]. This was the first time he addressed the nation since the protests began.
Mubarak announced that he would force the government to resign and appoint
a new government the following day. Mubarak stated that he would continue
to protect the security of the nation and the people, and he made it clear that
he would not step down. Mubarak also criticized the protestors for creating
chaos and added that he would "not let this happen."

On the day of Mubarak's speech, the American-traded EGPT fund pulled
out of its free-fall; it rose 10% within a week of the speech. The protesters did
not response positively to Mubarak's speech [33]. Vigorous protests calling for
him to step down continued.

Event 5 (Monday, January 31, 12:46 AM): Noor Shuts Down Internet Services

At about 12:46 AM in the early hours of January 31, Noor lost its connection to the Internet. The company had been administering roughly one hundred networks and none of them were reachable [38]. With the exception of a few phones with satellite connections [11], the entire country of Egypt was effectively offline.

The previous day of protests had brought more violence to the streets of Egypt. Protesters refused to leave Cairo's Tahrir Square in defiance of a curfew imposed by the Egyptian Army.

Event 6 (Tuesday, February 1, 10:57 PM): Mubarak Announces He Will Not Run for Re-Election But Will Not Step Down

Following intense pressure from the protesters, Mubarak announced on state-run television that he would not run for re-election. Despite this concession, he refused to step down. He appointed a new Vice President, Omar Suleman, who was tasked with conducting a dialogue with "all the political forces and factions" regarding democratic reform [29]. The protesters in Tahrir Square renewed their chants of "Leave, Leave" during Mubarak's live speech. It is worthwhile to note that Mubarak did not promise that his son, Gamal, would not run for election – one of the protesters' major demands [14].

Reports indicate that pressure from the Egyptian Army may have been a factor in this announcement by Mubarak. The Egyptian Army, as a major stakeholder, had increasingly condoned the efforts of the protesters, announcing support for the people's legitimate demands and that it would not use force against peaceful demonstrators.

Event 7 (Wednesday, February 2, 11:29 AM): Internet is Turned Back On

On February 2 at 11:29 AM, all the Egyptian ISPs except for Noor returned to service. Al Jazeera reported at the time that Internet services were at least partially restored in Cairo after a five-day blackout aimed at stymieing the protests. At 12:52 PM, Noor returned to service as well. The total number of networks was slightly smaller than before due to a process called re-aggregation, in which ISPs clear redundant routes that clients are no longer using. On the day the Internet was turned back on, the euro traded for 0.126 Egyptian pounds, a 0.7% increase from the day before. Exchange rates with other major currencies also improved, but more modestly.

Event 8 (Saturday, February 5, 5:36 PM): Ruling Party Leadership Resigns

The leadership of Egypt's ruling party, including Mubarak's son Gamal, resigned. One of the protesters' principal demands was that Gamal would not succeed his father [2]; this demand was finally met. With the Egyptian Stock Market closed indefinitely and American and European markets closed on the weekend, it was not possible to gauge the economic significance of this event.

Event 9 (Sunday, February 6, 10:00 AM): Banks Officially Reopen for 3.5 Hours
After a week of protests, Egyptian banks reopened for a shortened work day, allowing Egyptians their first access to cash since the protests began. From 10:00 AM to 1:30 PM, banks saw long lines of citizens who wanted to withdraw as much cash as possible, sometimes up to a full pension in one transaction [34].

Event 10 (Friday, February 11, 6:03 PM): Mubarak Resigns
Following eighteen days of intense protests, Mubarak's reign finally ended. The Vice President announced on state-run television: "My fellow citizens, in the difficult circumstances our country is experiencing, President Muhammad Hosni Mubarak has decided to give up the Office of the President of the Republic and instructed the Supreme Council of the Armed Forces to manage the affairs of the country" [18]. Protesters in Tahrir Square celebrated, chanting "We have brought down the regime! We have brought down the regime!" [18]. There was jubilation all over Egypt.

The previous day, Mubarak had announced the delegation of authority to the Vice President, but the protesters, as well as the Army, were deeply disappointed that Mubarak had refused to resign. The resulting protests were the most intense to date and precipitated Mubarak's resignation. The week following the resignation, the EGPT fund closed at 18.73, its highest closing price since the protests began in January 2011 and a price that has not been exceeded at the time of this writing.

Event 11 (Wednesday, March 23, 10:30 AM): Stock Market Reopens and Continued Effects
When trading resumed on March 23, 2011, EGX 30 fell 8.9%, losing 504 points to close at 5,142. During the eight weeks of closure, the EGPT fund lost 4.7%, dropping from 16.22 to 15.45. EGX 30 continued to tumble, reaching its lowest value of 3,632 in December 2011, around the time that Egypt held preliminary democratic elections. This low water mark was duplicated by the EGPT fund, which closed under 10 points in late December 2011 before making a minor turnaround. As of this writing, EGX 30 has not matched its closing market value on January 24, 2011, the last day before its temporary closure and the beginning of the Egyptian Revolution. The Organization for Economic Cooperation and Development (OECD) [25] has estimated that the Egyptian telecommunications and Internet services sector alone lost $90 million during the revolution. The losses in the other dependent sectors were also significant.

7.   Analysis

At its most basic level, a revolution is a transaction between a populace and its political authorities. Events in Tunisia, coupled with the lower transaction cost of collective action brought about by widespread communications via the Internet and mobile services, allowed the rapid and effective formation of protests in Egypt. Yet, revolution must be motivated by more than just low transaction costs. In transaction cost terms, it is reasonable to view the seeds of public discontent as *ex ante* misalignment between the Egyptian people and Mubarak, blossoming into *ex post* mal-adaptation over his nearly thirty-year reign. If the transaction cost of obtaining a better bargain with ruling authorities is lowered by communication technologies, then the populace may begin to perceive the potential benefits of revolution, and to organize in an attempt to obtain the better bargain.

The idea that authoritarian rulers face a choice when such events unfold is captured in the idea of the dictator's dilemma and, specific to the decision to shut down Internet service, the choice suggested by the dictator's digital dilemma. The dictator's dilemma is founded on the idea that dictators desire to stay in power. Economic theories spell out a more direct personal motive for action. This idea is described in North's theory of the state [20], in which rulers of the state are analogous to monopolists who are tempted to and may actually sequester quasi-rents for their personal use regardless of the public interest.

At the time of the revolution, observers suggested that Noor remained online in order to keep the Egyptian Stock Exchange connected to the world. However, the stock exchange was closed before the Internet shutdown and remained closed during the time that Noor was the sole operating ISP in Egypt. In addition to the connectivity provided to the stock exchange, Noor connected Egypt with major European and Middle Eastern financial firms such as Allianz and Dalla Al-Baraka. The Mubarak family controlled a large portion of the economy and had millions of dollars in domestic bank accounts and in firms that relied on Noor's network. The Mubarak family may have intended to use Noor's network to transfer their monies out of the country.

When compared with the dictator's digital dilemma, this idea is more closely in tune with North's conception of inefficiencies of the state. It also supports the notion that Mubarak may have perceived that the duration of his transaction with the Egyptian people was at risk and could soon end. On June 4, 2012, Gamal and his brother Alaa were charged with money laundering and insider trading on the stock market. Egypt's Illicit Gains Authority, which is investigating the financial crimes perpetrated by the Mubarak regime, estimates that the Mubarak family controls more than $500 million in assets worldwide.

We posit that Noor's continued operation during the protests was because it advanced the Mubarak regime's personal financial interests. If indeed Mubarak faced – in the *ex ante* moments of the decision to shut down Internet access – the dictator's digital dilemma, then the opportunity costs of doing so may have been strategically lessened by his ability to gain control of ISPs in a calculated and selective way. Noor served the Commercial International Bank of Egypt (a joint venture of the National Bank of Egypt and Chase Manhattan Bank), and several other financial interests that were useful to the Mubarak regime. The Commercial International Bank was, according to Renesys, critically dependent on Noor for Internet service, meaning that Noor provided the firm's only access to the Internet. In contrast, the majority of the Egyptian populace used Telecom Egypt for Internet access.

Although investigations of the financial irregularities of the Mubarak regime are ongoing and the forensic analysis necessary to confirm our claim is beyond the scope of this paper, the fact that Noor, with its potential to serve Mubarak's personal interests, remained online while the services of most importance to the general public were taken offline, lends support to a transaction cost economic interpretation of events. Transaction cost economists call this selective intervention. It did not last *ex post*, because the transaction did indeed reach an end with both the complete shutdown of the Internet and the resignation of Mubarak. The temporary selection of Noor for exceptional treatment, however, provides insights into the critical importance of determining the motives in play during the high-stakes game of political bargaining that occurred during the Egyptian Revolution of 2011.

8.   Conclusions

Conflicts between stakeholders intensify as the fight over control of the Internet moves from domestic to international forums. The 2012 World Conference on International Telecommunications (WCIT) held in Dubai became the latest battleground in the debate over the control of Internet infrastructure as governments confronted the challenges under the auspices of the International Telecommunications Union (ITU). The ITU is a UN-supported organization that has traditionally mandated the rules of the road for long distance telephony, but has more recently begun to examine its role with regard to regulating the Internet. At the Dubai conference, a number of mostly Middle Eastern authoritarian states led by China pushed a proposal to mandate greater government controls over domestic ISPs. Interestingly, Egypt was named as an author of some of the earlier drafts that were leaked; although Egypt later denied that it was involved in the process [16]. Language from these drafts was integrated into the final Acts of the WCIT [12], which eventually gained the support of the majority of nations present, including Egypt, but was opposed by the U.S. and European Union.

Repressive governments are well aware of the power that the Internet provides citizens and have attempted to maintain control through censorship. The events of Egypt point to more turmoil in repressive countries and authoritarian countries recognize this trend. During the Egyptian Revolution, China blocked the word "Egypt" from the country's popular Twitter-like services in an attempt to restrict coverage of the events in Egypt [24].

Future work should extend this research on the effects of the Egyptian Revolution of 2011 to other authoritarian regimes, and seek out cases with the potential to validate or refute the hypotheses presented in this paper. The work could employ a similar transaction cost analysis to determine the economic effects – to the public and the personal leadership of nations – of Internet outages in countries such as Iran and Libya. The research could also project the costs and benefits of partial or complete shutdowns in the case of ongoing conflicts as in Syria. Research could also comparatively examine the contractual arrangements between ruling parties and ISPs from nation to nation, along with evidence of or opportunity for rent-seeking behavior on the part of ruling parties. If the theory holds, rent-seeking behavior on the part of ruling parties could become a rationale for contractual hazards in the governance of the critical Internet infrastructure.

References

[1] Ahram Online, Gamal Mubarak's friendship becomes kiss of death for banking heads, Cairo, Egypt, February 22, 2011.

[2] Al Arabiya, Egypt ruling party executive committee resigns, Cairo, Egypt, February 5, 2011.

[3] A. Al-Youm, Mubaraks have 40 villas and LE1 bln in Egyptian banks, illicit gains authority reveals, *Egypt Independent*, June 4, 2012.

[4] Berkman Center for Internet and Society, Herdict: Twitter Inaccessibility Report (01/23/2011 – 03/31/2011), Technical Report, Harvard University, Cambridge, Massachusetts, 2011.

[5] Central Intelligence Agency, Egypt, The World Factbook, Langley, Virginia (www.cia.gov/library/publications/the-world-factbook/geos/eg.html).

[6] J. Cowie, Egypt leaves the Internet, Renesys Blog, Renesys, Manchester, New Hampshire (www.renesys.com/blog/2011/01/egypt-leaves-the-internet.shtml), January 27, 2011.

[7] Economic and Social Commission for Western Asia, National Profile of the Information Society in the Arab Republic of Egypt, United Nations, Geneva, Switzerland (www.escwa.un.org/wsis/reports/docs/Egypt-07-E.pdf), 2007.

[8] L. Fisher, AP begins crediting bloggers as news sources, *The Next Web*, September 7, 2010.

[9] M. Fisher, Web monitor: 100 percent of Syria's Internet just shut down, *Washington Post*, November 29, 2012.

[10] L. Greenemeier, How was Egypt's Internet access shut off? *Scientific American*, January 28, 2011.

[11] P. Howard, S. Agarwal and M. Hussain, When do states disconnect their digital networks? Regime responses to the political uses of social media, *The Communication Review*, vol. 14(3), pp. 216–232, 2011.

[12] International Telecommunications Union, WCIT-12 – Signatories of the Final Acts: 89, Geneva, Switzerland (www.itu.int/osg/wcit-12/highlights/signatories.html), 2012.

[13] C. Kedzie, Communication and Democracy: Coincident Revolutions and the Emergent Dictators, RAND Corporation, Santa Monica, California, 1997.

[14] M. Landler, H. Cooper and D. Kirkpatrick, Mubarak of Egypt agrees not to run again, *The New York Times*, February 1, 2011.

[15] K. Laub and T. El-Tablawy, Probe of Mubarak family finances sought, *msnbc.com*, February 17, 2011.

[16] T. Lee, Authoritarian regimes push for larger ITU role in DNS system, *Ars Technica*, December 8, 2012.

[17] N. Macfarquhar, Egypt's military is seen as pivotal in next step, *The New York Times*, January 28, 2011.

[18] C. McGreal and J. Shenker, Hosni Mubarak resigns – and Egypt celebrates a new dawn, *The Guardian*, February 11, 2011.

[19] National Telecommunication Regulatory Authority, Telecommunication Regulation Law No. 10 of 2003, Arab Republic of Egypt, Cairo, Egypt (`www.tra.gov.eg/uploads/law/law_en.pdf`), 2003.

[20] D. North, *Structure and Change in Economic History*, Norton, New York, 1981.

[21] A. Nowaira, Egypt's day of rage goes on. Is the world watching? *The Guardian*, January 27, 2011.

[22] OpenNet Initiative, Burma (Myanmar), OpenNet Initiative University of Toronto, Toronto, Canada (`opennet.net/research/profiles/myanmar-burma`), 2012.

[23] Organization for Economic Cooperation and Development, The Relationship between Local Content, Internet Development and Access Prices, OECD Digital Economy Papers, Organization for Economic Cooperation and Development, Paris, France (`www.oecd-ilibrary.org/content/workingpaper/5k4c1rq2bqvk-en`), 2013.

[24] J. Page, Beijing blocks protest reports, *Wall Street Journal*, January 31, 2011.

[25] T. Reynolds and A. Mickoleit, The economic impact of shutting down Internet and mobile phone services in Egypt, Organization for Economic Cooperation and Development, Paris, France (`www.oecd.org/countries/egypt/theeconomicimpactofshuttingdowninternetandmobilephoneservicesinegypt.htm`), 2011.

[26] N. Saleh, Egypt's digital activism and the dictator's dilemma: An evaluation, *Telecommunications Policy*, vol. 36(6), pp. 476–483, 2012.

[27] A. Shahine, A. Namatalla and Z. Hankir, Egypt stock trading to resume with loss limits as GDRs fall, *BusinessWeek*, March 23, 2011.

[28] G. Shultz, New realities and new ways of thinking, *Foreign Affairs*, vol. 63(4), pp. 705–721, 1985.

[29] The Guardian, Hosni Mubarak's speech: Full text, London, United Kingdom, February 1, 2011.

[30] The New York Times, Times Topics: Hosni Mubarak, New York (`topics.nytimes.com/top/reference/timestopics/people/m/hosni_mubarak/index.html`), January 2, 2012.

[31] The Telegraph, Egypt's limited reserves raise fears of financial crisis, London, United Kingdom, January 31, 2011.

[32] Vodafone, Statements – Vodafone Egypt, Newbury, United Kingdom (`www.vodafone.com/content/index/media/ press_statements/statement_on_egypt.html`), January 28, 2011.

[33] M. Weaver, H. Siddique, R. Adams and T. Hill, Protests in Egypt – as they happened, *The Guardian*, January 28, 2011.

[34] P. Werr and S. El Madany, Customers queue at Egypt banks after protests, *Reuters*, February 6, 2011.

[35] O. Williamson, *Markets and Hierarchies: Analysis and Antrtrust Implications*, The Free Press, New York, 1975.

[36] O. Williamson, The economics of organization: The transaction cost approach, *American Journal of Sociology*, vol. 87(3), pp. 548–577, 1981.

[37] O. Williamson, *The Economic Institutions of Capitalism*, The Free Press, New York, 1985.

[38] E. Zmijewski, Egypt's net on life support, Renesys Blog, Renesys, Manchester, New Hampshire (`www.renesys.com/blog/2011/01/egypts-net-on-life-support.shtml`), January 31, 2011.

Chapter 2

DATA HANDLING IN THE SMART GRID: DO WE KNOW ENOUGH?

Richard Chow, Alvaro Cardenas and Emiliano De Cristofaro

Abstract   Data privacy in the smart grid is an important requirement for consumers. Central to the data privacy issue is the handling of energy-usage data, in particular, data retention, aggregation and anonymization. Government and industry groups have formulated various policies in this area, mostly based on fair information practice principles. This paper argues that the current policy-level work is insufficient – scientific work is needed to fully develop and implement privacy policies. A research agenda is proposed that balances the advantages of fine-grained energy-usage data with the associated privacy risks. For comparison purposes, the paper describes analogous policies and implementations related to telecommunications, web search and medical data.

Keywords: Smart grid, data handling, privacy

1.   Introduction

The smart grid is being designed to enable utilities, customers and third-party providers to monitor and control energy use. Data collected by the smart grid will provide several advantages to all parties, including better decisions regarding energy-usage, enhanced understanding of consumer demands and increased energy distribution efficiency.

The smart grid also raises the issue of data privacy – especially for consumers – because smart meters will allow large-scale data collection, making individual household data available at unprecedented levels of granularity. Monitoring energy consumption at low levels of granularity can facilitate the inference of detailed information about consumer behavior. The behavioral information is highly valuable to advertising companies, law enforcement and criminals. The potential for egregious invasions of personal privacy makes it imperative to ensure that proper controls are in place.

Responding to these concerns, governments and standards organizations are developing privacy standards and policies to guide smart grid deployments.

J. Butts and S. Shenoi (Eds.): Critical Infrastructure Protection VII, IFIP AICT 417, pp. 21–32, 2013.

Recommendations for privacy controls in smart grid deployments have been provided by the North American Energy Standards Board (NAESB) [35], National Institute of Standards and Technology (NIST) [29], U.S. Department of Energy (DOE) [34], Texas Legislature and Public Utility Commission [25] and California Public Utilities Commission (CPUC) [4], among others. The Smart Grid Policy Framework [22] released in 2011 by the Executive Office of the President specifically recommends that, as a starting point, state and federal regulators must consider methods to ensure that detailed energy-usage data is protected in a manner consistent with the fair information practice principles drafted by the Federal Trade Commission (FTC) [8].

Recent work in the area of smart grid privacy has been necessarily broad in its coverage of systems and use cases. This paper concentrates on the handling of energy-usage data. Data handling issues cut across multiple privacy use cases and include data retention, aggregation and anonymization. Gaps in existing work are highlighted and a roadmap is proposed for areas that require exhaustive research. In particular, this paper describes technical issues that must be addressed in order to implement government and industry policies.

Data handling in the smart grid is a relatively immature issue. Consequently, this paper considers precedents with regard to handling potentially sensitive telecommunications, web search and medical data. The analysis of privacy strategies in these domains provides useful lessons that can guide research efforts for securing smart grid data.

2.   Related Work

This section describes data handling issues covered in existing standards, guidelines and regulations. Much of the relevant prior work focuses on policy-level issues. Although there appears to be general agreement on data handling principles and goals, little work has been done on concrete approaches to achieve the data handling objectives.

2.1   Standards Bodies and Industry Guidelines

NIST's NISTIR 7628 document [29] provides general, policy-level guidance on data handling. For instance, the guidance on data collection recommends:

> *"Limit the collection of data to only that necessary for smart grid operations, including planning and management, improving energy use and efficiency, account management, and billing."*

The guidance on retention recommends:

> *"Limit information retention. Data, and subsequently created information that reveals personal information or activities from and about a specific consumer location, should be retained only for as long as necessary to fulfill the purposes that have been communicated to the energy consumers."*

The guidance on aggregation recommends:

> *"Energy data and any resulting information, such as monthly charges for service, collected as a result of smart grid operations should be aggregated and anonymized by removing personal information elements wherever possible to ensure that energy data from specific consumer locations is limited appropriately."*

The guidance on deletion recommends:

> *"When no longer necessary, consistent with data retention and destruction requirements, the data and information, in all forms, should be irreversibly destroyed."*

The general guidance is similar to the computer security principle of least privilege [27]. In practice, however, it may not be clear what privileges are actually required. Indeed, utilities are unable to turn policy to practice. For example, utilities are advised to collect "only ... necessary [data] for smart grid operations, including planning and management." More efficient planning and management are possible with more data. Similarly, utilities are advised to retain data "only for as long as necessary." However, more data maintained for a longer period of time typically supports better trend analysis and forecasting.

The NAESB provides business practices to follow with respect to third-party access and disclosure of energy-usage data [35]. The guidelines apply to data access directly from utilities but, like NISTIR 7638 [29], the guidelines are at a high level.

The U.S. Department of Energy's Advanced Security Acceleration Project for the Smart Grid (ASAP-SG) has produced two formal documents that outline the security requirements that a third party should meet in order to access electricity-usage data: (i) Security Profile for Advanced Metering Infrastructure [1]; and (ii) Security Profile for Third Party Data Access [2]. However, these documents primarily focus on general security principles rather than privacy concerns.

The document from the National Regulatory Research Institute entitled, Must There Be Conflict Between Energy Management and Consumer Privacy? [18], notes that categorizing usage data can reduce the potential for privacy compromise associated with personal information, billing data, operational data and event data. The document also mentions that aggregating data can make it safe to share; however, the method for aggregating data is not provided. Similarly, an early policy paper from the Office of the Information and Privacy Commissioner of Ontario [5] discusses the privacy implications of data mining and, in particular, fair information practices, but again, the guidance is at a high level. Privacy organizations such as the Electronic Privacy Information Center, Center for Democracy and Technology, and Electronic Frontier Foundation have also weighed in on data handling policies for the smart grid.

2.2 State and Utility Commission Regulations

The CPUC Rulemaking 08-12-009 document [4] contains general rules for utilities, contractors and other third parties that are modeled on the FTC's fair information practice principles [8]. Like the work produced by the standards bodies, the guidance is policy-oriented rather than implementation-oriented.

Another example is the Colorado Public Utilities Commission's Decision No. R11-0922 [26], which describes the so-called "15/15 Rule:"

> *"In aggregating customer data to create an aggregated data report, a utility must take steps to ensure the report is sufficiently anonymous in its aggregated form so that any individual customer data or reasonable approximation thereof cannot be determined from the aggregated amount. At a minimum, a particular aggregation must contain: (i) at least fifteen customers or premises; and (ii) within any customer class, no single customer's customer data or premise associated with a single customer's customer data may comprise 15 percent or more of the total customer data aggregated per customer class to generate the aggregated data report (the "15/15 Rule"). Notwithstanding, the 15/15 Rule, the utility shall not be required to disclose aggregated data if such disclosure would compromise the individual customer's privacy or the security of the utility's system."*

This is one of a few guidelines that define the meaning of safe aggregation. However, the reasoning and privacy guarantees underlying the 15/15 Rule are not clear. Other examples of high-level guidance are provided in Oklahoma HB 1079 [23], the Illinois Statewide Smart Grid Collaborative: Collaborative Report [6], and the National Association of Regulatory Utility Commissioners Resolution on Smart Grid Principles [21].

Regulations have also considered other issues such as data ownership and third-party data access. While utility companies are responsible for protecting electricity consumption records from unauthorized use, the data may be shared with third parties by consumers who are most likely unaware of the privacy risks. While some regulations give consumers "ownership" of their electricity consumption data, others (e.g., Oklahoma HB 1079 [23]) stipulate that the utility company owns the smart meter data and that the utility company is "authorized to share customer data without customer consent with third parties who assist the utility in its business and services, as required by law, in emergency situations, or in a business transaction such as a merger" [23].

2.3   Research Literature

The research literature focuses on technical approaches that can improve privacy – examples include cryptographic mechanisms for facilitating data aggregation [28], differential privacy for sharing aggregated smart grid data with third parties (while preventing the identification of patterns about a single consumer) [30], and the use of batteries to mask electricity consumption [17]. While these mechanisms are promising, they do not answer the questions about data handling and data governance posed in this paper. In addition, most of these approaches are not yet ready for deployment. For example, the "zero-knowledge proofs of knowledge" that are required by the work on cryptographic commitments are computationally impractical. Similarly, using batteries to mask electricity consumption will pose challenges due to the additional costs and the operational requirements involved in managing battery lifetime.

The research literature related to data handling primarily focuses on the information that can be inferred from very fine-grained electricity consumption data in the scale of seconds. However, most advanced metering infrastructures will collect data at fifteen-minute intervals or longer. There is a need to understand the trade-offs existing between data collection intervals and the associated privacy risks.

3. Comparison with Other Domains

This section discusses the approaches used to implement similar privacy policies in other domains. The focus is on the treatment, disclosure and retention of user data in the context of: (i) telephone logs; (ii) web search data; and (iii) health data.

3.1 Telephone Logs

In the United States, privacy policies for telecommunications-related data (e.g., data about customer usage stored by carriers) have mainly been the responsibility of the Federal Communications Commission (FCC). In 1996, the FCC was granted the authority to regulate how customer proprietary network information (CPNI) is treated. In 2007, the FCC began to regulate how data collected by telecommunications companies about customer telephone calls may be used [7]. The key points of the regulation are: (i) limiting information that carriers may provide to third parties without customer consent; (ii) defining how customer service representatives may share call details; and (iii) requiring notification obligations on the part of carriers. Like energy-usage data, telecommunications data has value beyond telecommunications companies (e.g., law enforcement and intelligence). This complicates the formulation and implementation of privacy policies.

At this time, there are no strict regulations governing the length of time that carriers may retain telephone logs. This has contributed to the variety of data retention policies that are implemented across the telecommunications industry [15]. Some U.S. carriers store call activity logs for days, some for months, some even retain call and text message content. Data retention policies are supposed to be opaque; information about these policies is available to the public because of a recent leak from the U.S. Department of Justice.

3.2 Web Search Data

Most Internet providers maintain logs of user search queries. This practice has raised serious privacy concerns because search data contains potentially sensitive information about the interests and web behavior of Internet users. Anonymization is a natural solution, but historical examples highlight the pitfalls. For instance, when AOL released anonymized user search queries, researchers were able to reconstruct the identities of some users [13]. Most Internet search engine providers have independently created the data retention policies they implement. According to a 2011 *New York Times* article [14], Google maintains search records for nine months, Microsoft implements a six-month retention policy and Yahoo! has extended its retention time for detailed user records from three month to eighteen months. The privacy measures implemented by search engine providers are unclear because details about their anonymization techniques have not been released.

Another reason for implementing a data retention policy is to address liability issues. Because security breaches often result in the loss of user information, it is prudent for companies to minimize the financial risk they incur when handling sensitive data.

No U.S. legislation specifically addresses the control that users have over personal information related to their online activities, although guidelines are being developed. The FTC has encouraged the protection of online user privacy through several initiatives, such as through its report entitled, Protecting Consumer Privacy in an Era of Rapid Change [9]. Additionally, the FTC's fair information practice principles [8] help control personal information in the electronic marketplace by introducing notice, awareness, consent, access and security principles. The U.S. Department of Commerce's Internet Policy Task Force has released a report entitled, Commercial Data Privacy and Innovation in the Internet Economy: A Dynamic Policy Framework [33], which describes policy guidelines and regulations regarding commercial data privacy. Another effort named Do Not Track Us [19], which is spearheaded by academia, enables Internet users to opt out of website tracking.

3.3   Health Data

The sensitivity of health-related data has prompted privacy concerns that have been the focus of regulation as well as research efforts. In 1996, the U.S. Government enacted the Health Insurance Portability and Accountability Act (HIPAA) [31], which establishes national standards for electronic health care transactions and addresses the security and privacy of health data. In 2003, the Privacy Rule was added, which requires companies and providers to notify individuals about the use of protected health information and to keep track of disclosures. HIPAA also grants an individual the right to file complaints with the Office for Civil Rights of the Department of Health and Human Services.

The extreme sensitivity of genetic information has also been recognized. Protection is provided by the Genetic Information Nondiscrimination Act (GINA) of 2008 [32]. Among other points, GINA strictly regulates the retention, disclosure and treatment of data collected by genetic testing companies.

Privacy laws such as HIPAA and GINA provide much greater protection than laws and regulations associated with telephone calls and web search data. Indeed, the need to enforce health-related regulations is now almost universally recognized [12].

3.4   Outlook for the Smart Grid

Based on the treatment, disclosure and retention of telephone logs, web search data and health data, we make some projections regarding energy-usage data. First, privacy regulations and policies for most electronic user data are specified at a high level, if at all. As a result, it is likely that implementation practices for handling smart grid data will be left to utilities and their meter data management partners and vendors. The concern is, of course, that data handling issues are subtle. For example, the implications of employing even seemingly simple anonymization and aggregation techniques need to be considered carefully.

Second, companies often self-regulate their data handling even in the absence of regulations. However, as seen with telephone logs and web search data, each company generally has different policies and procedures for data handling, most of which are opaque to the consumer. The same trend will likely be seen in the smart grid where utilities will implement their own policies and procedures for energy-usage data. Indeed, without proper guidance, privacy analysis would require case-by-case evaluation.

4.   Open Issues Related to Data Handling

This section discusses important issues related to the handling of energy-usage data in the context of the smart grid. These issues are excellent candidates for research in the area of smart grid privacy.

4.1   Safe Data Intervals

A key fair information practice is data minimization, which stipulates that data should not be collected unless it is needed and should not be kept longer than necessary. Many smart grid applications such as demand-response analysis will require the collection and storage of fine-grained data. However, any fine-grained data that is collected could be coarsened after it is no longer needed. This coarse data could be preserved in long-term storage or it could be released in various contexts after first checking the privacy implications.

Releasing even "coarse" monthly energy-usage data can result in an invasion of privacy, as demonstrated by the controversy surrounding the public disclosure of Al Gore's utility bills for his 10,000-square-foot Nashville mansion [36]. Perhaps more interesting is whether a two-hour collection interval or a four-hour interval would be considered safe. Clearly, this question depends on the perspectives of the end-users and the information that can be inferred from the collected data. Two-hour or four-hour data would not be safe if it reveals that the resident is on vacation. However, usage data at this level of granularity may not reveal specific appliance usage or other fine-grained usage patterns and could, therefore, be stored by utilities for the long term.

One of the key factors when considering safe data collection and retention policies is the ability to identify electricity appliances via non-intrusive load

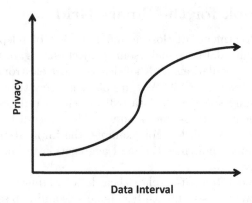

Figure 1. Conceptual plot of privacy versus data interval size.

monitoring (NILM) [3, 11]. Most of the research in this field has considered residential electricity consumption monitors, such as The Energy Detective (TED) and Current Cost, instead of residential smart meters provided by electric utilities. The residential electricity consumption monitors collect and analyze consumption data at sub-second intervals. However, current smart meter deployments do not have these levels of granularity. The vast majority of smart meter deployments collect data in intervals of fifteen minutes or more.

In general, there is a notable lack of research on the types of inferences that can be made with different levels of data granularity. Figure 1 shows the perceived relationship between privacy and data interval size. Clearly, privacy increases as the size of the data interval increases, but very little is known about the precise nature of this tradeoff. Prudenzi [24] is one of a few researchers who has examined energy-usage data in intervals ranging from a few minutes to a few hours.

In order to implement the data minimization principle, it is important to understand exactly what can be inferred from smart meter data as a function of various data intervals. Further research is needed to explore the trade-off between data collection intervals and the associated levels of privacy that are attained.

4.2 Data Aggregation Across People

Aggregation of energy-usage date across people – instead of over time – must also be considered. The privacy risks associated with fine-grained electricity-usage data can be reduced by computing aggregates across people (e.g., neighborhoods) and deleting individual usage data. However, the release of such aggregated data may still have some privacy implications. It is, therefore, important to conduct scientific studies on the conditions under which aggregations of energy-usage data could leak information about individual users and to devise appropriate strategies for mitigating the privacy risks.

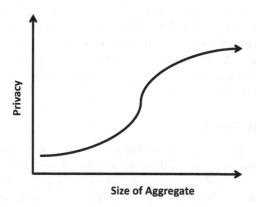

Figure 2. Conceptual plot of privacy versus aggregation size.

Figure 2 shows a conceptual plot of privacy versus aggregation size. In the representation, privacy increases as the size of the aggregate increases. However, the precise nature of the relationship has not been studied by the research community. Providing a scientific backing for Colorado's "15-15 Rule" [26], which intuitively postulates a safe aggregation principle, would be highly desirable. More research is needed to identify sound aggregation rules instead of simply specifying rules based on intuition.

Another issue is that aggregation does not protect an individual when all the individuals whose data is aggregated are similar in some way. For example, usage metrics associated with high-income communities are likely to be different from low-income communities. While this particular example may not raise privacy concerns, there may be situations where aggregated data compromises the privacy of the individuals who are part of the aggregate. In-depth studies are needed that focus on the privacy properties of aggregated smart grid data.

4.3 Consequences of Latency for Data Access

One concern about real-time electricity consumption data is that it could facilitate burglaries – prospective burglars could tell whether or not residents are home. Latency can help mitigate this privacy threat. For example, consumption data could be released one week or one month later. While some data might be required in real-time, algorithms such as those used for energy disaggregation to identify faulty or inefficient devices or appliances can be performed days, weeks or months later instead of in real time or near real time.

4.4 Safe Anonymized Data

Simply removing identifying information, such as a name or address, is insufficient to anonymize many kinds of personal data. For example, location traces can easily reveal home and work locations from which the identities of individuals can be deduced [10, 16]. As in the case of the AOL incident, user identities can be discerned from web search data [13]. A linkage attack may also be used to de-anonymize data. For example, electricity-usage patterns could be de-anonymized by linking them to electricity-usage patterns of users in another database. An instantiation of this idea is discussed by Narayanan, *et al.* [20], where anonymized Netflix users were identified by matching their data to the IMDb database.

5. Conclusions

The vast majority of the work on handling energy-usage data has been at the policy level and is based primarily on fair information practices. Very little research has focused on strategies for implementing these policies and identifying the vulnerabilities that remain. Based on a comparison with other industries, it appears that implementation strategies for smart grid privacy will not be regulated in the near term. Thus, each utility will be forced to develop its own data handling strategy and architecture. Therefore, significant technical research is required in order to provide concrete guidance to designers. This guidance would bridge the gap between policy and implementation.

An important research agenda item is to understand the tradeoff between privacy and data interval size. Another is the development of safe anonymization, sanitization and aggregation strategies. Yet another is the examination of the privacy effects of data latency.

Clearly, all these issues are intertwined. A working system may very well involve the combination of a particular data interval, aggregation and latency strategy. Acquiring a sophisticated understanding of these concepts will be difficult as it will cover technical, legal and human factors issues; however, it is an important first step to enhancing privacy in the smart grid.

References

[1] Advanced Security Acceleration Project for the Smart Grid (ASAP-SG), Security Profile for Advanced Metering Infrastructure, EnerNex Corporation, Knoxville, Tennessee, 2009.

[2] Advanced Security Acceleration Project for the Smart Grid (ASAP-SG), Security Profile for Third Party Data Access, EnerNex Corporation, Knoxville, Tennessee, 2011.

[3] D. Bergman, D. Jin, J. Juen, N. Tanaka, C. Gunter and A. Wright, Distributed non-intrusive load monitoring, *Proceedings of the IEEE Power Engineering Society Conference on Innovative Smart Grid Technologies*, 2011.

[4] California Public Utilities Commission, Decision Adopting Rules to Protect the Privacy and Security of the Electricity Usage Data of the Customers of Pacific Gas and Electric Company, Southern California Edison Company and San Diego Gas and Electric Company, Rulemaking 08-12-009, Sacramento, California, 2011.

[5] A. Cavoukian, Data Mining: Staking a Claim on Your Privacy, Office of the Information and Privacy Commissioner of Ontario, Ontario, Canada, 1998.

[6] EnerNex Corporation, Illinois Statewide Smart Grid Collaborative: Collaborative Report, Knoxville, Tennessee (`www.ilgridplan.org/Shared%20Documents/ISSGC%20Collaborative%20Report.pdf`), 2010.

[7] Federal Communications Commission, Report and Order and Further Notice of Proposed Rulemaking, FCC 07-22, Washington, DC, 2007.

[8] Federal Trade Commission, Fair Information Practice Principles, Washington, DC, 2012.

[9] Federal Trade Commission, Protecting Consumer Privacy in an Era of Rapid Change, FTC Report, Washington, DC, 2012.

[10] P. Golle and K. Partridge, On the anonymity of home/work location pairs, *Proceedings of the Seventh International Conference on Pervasive Computing*, pp. 390–397, 2009.

[11] G. Hart, Nonintrusive appliance load monitoring, *Proceedings of the IEEE*, vol. 80(12), pp. 1870–1891, 1992.

[12] Hewlett-Packard, HIPAA goes hitech, Palo Alto, California (`h20195.www2.hp.com/v2/GetPDF.aspx/4AA1-4056ENW.pdf`), 2010.

[13] D. Kawamoto and E. Mills, AOL apologizes for release of user search data, *CNET*, August 7, 2006.

[14] V. Kopytoff, Yahoo! will keep search queries for 18 months, *New York Times*, April 18, 2011.

[15] D. Kravets, Which telecoms store your data the longest? Secret memo tells all, *Wired*, September 28, 2011.

[16] J. Krumm, Inference attacks on location tracks, *Proceedings of the Fifth International Conference on Pervasive Computing*, pp. 127–143, 2007.

[17] F. Li, B. Luo and P. Liu, Secure information aggregation for smart grids using homomorphic encryption, *Proceedings of the First IEEE International Conference on Smart Grid Communications*, pp. 327–332, 2010.

[18] S. Lichtenberg, Smart Grid Data: Must There Be Conflict Between Energy Management and Consumer Privacy? National Regulatory Research Institute, Silver Spring, Maryland, 2010.

[19] J. Mayer and A. Narayanan, Do Not Track, Universal Web Tracking Opt Out, Center for Internet and Society, Stanford Law School, Stanford, California (`donnottrack.us`).

[20] A. Narayanan and V. Shmatikov, Robust de-anonymization of large sparse datasets, *Proceedings of the IEEE Symposium on Security and Privacy*, pp. 111–125, 2008.

[21] National Association of Regulatory Utility Commissioners, Resolution on Smart Grid Principles, Washington, DC (`www.naruc.org/smartgrid`), 2011.

[22] National Science and Technology Council, A Policy Framework for the 21st Century Grid: Enabling Our Secure Energy Future, Executive Office of the President, Washington, DC, 2011.

[23] Oklahoma State Legislature, House Bill 1079, Oklahoma City, Oklahoma, 2011.

[24] A. Prudenzi, A neuron nets based procedure for identifying domestic appliances pattern-of-use from energy recordings at meter panel, *Proceedings of the IEEE Power Engineering Society Winter Meeting*, vol. 2, pp. 941–946, 2002.

[25] Public Utility Commission of Texas, Electric Substantive Rules – Chapter 25, Austin, Texas 2007.

[26] Public Utility Commission of the State of Colorado, Proposed Rules Relating to Smart Grid Data Privacy for Electric Utilities, Decision No. R11-0922, Denver, Colorado, 2011.

[27] J. Saltzer and M. Schroeder, The protection of information computer systems, *Proceedings of the IEEE*, vol. 63(9), pp. 1278–1308, 1975.

[28] E. Shi, T. Chan, E. Rieffel, R. Chow and D. Song, Privacy-preserving aggregation of time-series data, *Proceedings of the Network and Distributed System Security Symposium*, 2011.

[29] Smart Grid Interoperability Panel – Cyber Security Working Group, Guidelines for Smart Grid Cyber Security: Vol. 2, Privacy and the Smart Grid, NISTIR 7628, National Institute of Standards and Technology, Gaithersburg, Maryland, 2010.

[30] G. Taban and V. Gligor, Privacy-preserving integrity-assured data aggregation in sensor networks, *Proceedings of the International Conference on Computational Science and Engineering*, vol. 3, pp. 168–175, 2009.

[31] United States Congress, Health Insurance Portability and Accountability Act of 1996, Public Law 104-191, 104th Congress, Washington, DC, 1996.

[32] United States Congress, Genetic Information Nondiscrimination Act of 2008, H.R. 493, 110th Congress, Washington, DC, 2008.

[33] U.S. Department of Commerce, Commercial Data Privacy and Innovation in the Internet Economy: A Dynamic Policy Framework, Internet Policy Task Force Green Paper, Washington, DC, 2010.

[34] U.S. Department of Energy, Data Access and Privacy Issues Related to Smart Grid Technologies, Washington, DC, 2010.

[35] R. Varela, NAESB is developing smart grid data privacy standards, American Public Power Association, Washington, DC, March 2, 2011.

[36] T. Zeller, An inconveniently easy headline: Gore's electric bills spark debate, *New York Times*, February 28, 2007.

II

CONTROL SYSTEMS SECURITY

Chapter 3

DESIGN AND IMPLEMENTATION OF INDUSTRIAL CONTROL SYSTEM EMULATORS*

Robert Jaromin, Barry Mullins, Jonathan Butts and Juan Lopez

Abstract   The first step to grappling with the security problems that face modern supervisory control and data acquisition (SCADA) systems and industrial control networks is investing in research and education. However, because of the specialized nature of industrial control systems and networks, the cost of even a modest testbed for research or education can quickly get out of hand. Hardware-based testbeds are often not practical due to budgetary constraints, and they do not readily scale to meet educational demands. Software simulations are a cost-effective alternative, but current solutions focus primarily on network aspects, not the implementation of field device and application functionality. This paper describes the design and implementation of a programmable logic controller emulator using VMware. The emulator solution is both cost-effective and scalable. Moreover, it can accurately replicate real-world field device functionality to meet research and educational requirements.

Keywords: Industrial control systems, programmable logic controllers, emulation

1.   Introduction

Understanding and mitigating attacks on industrial control systems requires researchers and operators who have extensive theoretical and practical knowledge of industrial processes and control systems. However, the cost of even a modest industrial control system can exceed $100,000, making the investment in security research and education prohibitive for most organizations. Clearly, cost-effective solutions are required to build human capital in industrial con-

---

J. Butts and S. Shenoi (Eds.): Critical Infrastructure Protection VII, IFIP AICT 417, pp. 35–46, 2013.
© IFIP International Federation for Information Processing 2013 (outside the US)

trol systems security and to analyze, detect and mitigate attacks on industrial control systems that are widely used in the critical infrastructure.

Current solutions for industrial control systems research and education are inadequate in terms of cost and scalability. Full-scale, hardware-based SCADA testbeds are limited to research applications because of their capital, operational and maintenance costs, while smaller educational testbeds often lack the scalability to tackle real-world problems. Meanwhile, computer-based simulations are cost effective and useful for conducting research on certain types of large-scale, network-based systems, but they are inadequate for education and training.

This paper discusses the research and educational requirements associated with industrial control emulators. Also, it presents a novel emulation solution that is attractive in terms of its ability to accurately replicate real-world field device functionality as well as its cost and scalability.

## 2.	Background

Public and private sector entities have made significant investments in experimental industrial control facilities for researching threats and vulnerabilities. Recognizing the need to develop security solutions for industrial control systems, the U.S. Department of Energy spearheaded the creation of the $114 million National SCADA Testbed at Idaho National Laboratory [5]. As America's premier SCADA research facility, the testbed supports the identification and mitigation of vulnerabilities and the development of advanced system architectures for secure and robust SCADA systems. The testbed provides an exceptional environment for investigating real-world SCADA security threats, but similar testbeds are not feasible at academic and research institutions [7]. Mississippi State University, for example, has implemented an educational SCADA network [12], but it is limited to five control devices and two master stations. The environment is practical for educational purposes, but it does not scale up to large industrial applications.

Pure software-based simulations of SCADA networks and hybrid software-hardware configurations have been implemented as alternatives to SCADA equipment. Examples include the Cyber Security Testbed at the University of Illinois [2] and the SCADA Security Testbed at the Royal Melbourne Institute of Technology [14]. These testbeds leverage network simulation frameworks such as the Real-Time Immersive Network Simulation Environment for Network Security Exercises (RINSE) and Emulab [4]. Although they are useful for network-level evaluations, the testbeds do not provide the ability to make fine adjustments to simulate SCADA device features such as firmware uploads and malware propagation

Unlike most simulation efforts, which focus on network-level and/or device-level functionality to replicate real-world industrial control systems, this paper focuses on emulating programmable logic controllers (PLCs) that control the underlying physical processes. PLCs are specialized embedded computers with three core characteristics: (i) the ability to complete electronic circuits and measure electronic signals; (ii) the ability to be programmable to respond to inputs according to a predefined algorithm or protocol; and (iii) the ability to be networked with other devices.

Emulated industrial control systems combine the advantages of dedicated hardware and cost-effective, scalable software simulations. Emulators achieve these properties by implementing algorithms, protocols and services associated with industrial control systems using flexible programming platforms such as Linux. However, significant technical challenges are associated with emulating PLCs. A single product family, or even a single device, could involve multiple architectures and platforms. To further complicate the task, firmware can be packed or cryptographically encoded so that it can only be decoded by special hardware [9]. Additionally, errors or failures in the operating firmware should, by extension, be replicated in the emulator.

3. Industrial Control System Emulators

This section discusses the applications of industrial control system emulators in research and education, and presents the advantages of emulators over hardware testbeds, software simulations and hybrid hardware-software systems.

3.1 Research Environments

Industrial control emulators provide many of the same advantages as real hardware in a research environment. Accurate emulators not only implement the responses to user queries in the same manner as their hardware counterparts, but they also emulate the operational profile. When protocol responses are emulated accurately, the devices can be used in the same manner as real hardware for research experiments with less cost and reduced setup and maintenance times.

Accurate emulators have several advantages over real hardware devices. In addition to reduced cost, emulators can be more robust because error conditions such as buffer overflows and erroneous firmware uploads do not affect the underlying physical system. While a real PLC might be permanently damaged by such actions, it is a trivial matter to reset an emulated device and continue with the experiments.

3.2 Educational Environments

Currently, the only way to gain hands-on experience with industrial control networks is to implement an actual system, but this can be prohibitively expensive. The same is true for features that are specific to physical devices such as uploading and downloading ladder logic programs. Although simulators are available for developing and testing ladder logic programs, it is difficult, if not impossible, to adequately test network communications and functionality without using actual industrial control devices [16, 17].

In an academic setting, emulators can be used to provide a deep understanding of the tools and techniques used to conduct attacks on industrial control networks. Indeed, an emulator can be used to extend the application of tools

such as Nmap [8] and Metasploit [15] to industrial control networks. In particular, attacks on a PLC emulator can help demonstrate traditional information
technology attacks as well as their effects on an industrial control system. An
emulator that responds to scans and attacks from tools such as Nmap and
Metasploit in the same manner as a real PLC can provide hands-on attack
experience without putting the industrial control system at risk. Also, an emulator can be remotely setup by instructors to model any number of device
configurations and vulnerabilities and record the techniques used by students
to exploit the device.

A PLC emulator must have high fidelity; for example, it should accurately
mimic the responses of a real PLC to fingerprinting and port scanning tools.
However, even a lower-accuracy emulator has value in a training environment
– students could learn to identify control system devices by employing network
scanning and protocol dissection techniques.

3.3   Advantages of Emulation

Industrial control devices are notoriously sensitive due their lack of input
sanitization and use of non-robust communications protocols. Even seemingly
benign network mapping tools can cause serious problems. A 2005 Sandia
report [3] describes several instances where network scans of SCADA networks
disrupted industrial control systems. The reported behavior included erratic
movements of a nine-foot robotic arm in an area shared with human operators,
a malfunction of a microchip manufacturing process that resulted in $50,000
damage to electrical components, and a large natural gas delivery failure due
to unresponsive SCADA equipment.

A significant advantage of an emulator is that it retains the robustness of
the underlying system architecture. Even if the emulator locks up – i.e., it
becomes "bricked" – there is no flash bootloader to accidentally overwrite or
electronically-erasable programmable read-only memory (EEPROM) to accidentally erase because it is implemented purely in software. A simple reset of
the software returns the emulator to its normal operating state, unlike a real
PLC, which would require the use of a hardware debugging device or even the
replacement of PLC components.

An industrial control emulator is cost effective compared with control system
hardware, especially when a single PLC can easily cost more than $10,000.
Power constraints are also a factor – incorporating large numbers of PLCs
in an educational or training environment may not be possible due to power
requirements.

An emulator is scalable and is easily ported to different platforms. Multiple
emulators can be chained together without serious interoperability problems.
Also, emulators can be configured to model different vendor platforms (e.g.,
Siemens, Allen-Bradley and Koyo) and myriad network parameters (e.g., MAC
address, IP address, host name and ID).

4.   Emulator Design Considerations

Despite the fact that industrial control systems are fragile, quickly anti-quated from a technology standpoint and often designed without security considerations, they are expensive, complex and invariably networked with other devices. Most modern PLCs provide application-level services such as web configuration interfaces, file transfer services, remote programming services and remote monitoring services through a network interface. All these services have to be replicated in an emulator.

The accuracy of an emulator can be assessed using observable characteristics that a user would leverage to establish device authenticity. These attributes may be derived from the standard process that an attacker would use to discover, interrogate, fingerprint and exploit a networked device [11]. In general, four accuracy considerations exist for an emulator:

- **Superficial Accuracy:** This is established when a user believes that a device is authentic based on what is visually observed, such as the appearance of the web interface.

- **Packet-Level Accuracy:** This is established when a user believes that a device is authentic based on the packets that are sent to and received from the device.

- **Scanning Tool Accuracy:** This is established when a user believes that a device is authentic based on the results produced by an automated scanning tool.

- **Attack Tool Accuracy:** This is established when a user believes that a device is authentic based on the success achieved by an exploitation tool.

Like a network emulation, a control system emulation must accurately reflect the operational environment. Accuracy is a measure of the realism of the emulation compared with the actual device. For example, an emulation of a web interface in a modern PLC is accurate if the webpage has the same appearance (e.g., banner, form elements and graphics) and provides the same functionality. Additionally, the packets transmitted during query and response interactions must match the packets transmitted to and received from the actual PLC.

5.   Emulator Implementation

This section provides implementation details regarding the emulator along with an evaluation of the accuracy of the emulator.

5.1   Implementation Details

The emulator runs on a Dell Latitude D630 with 2 GB RAM, Intel Core2 Duo CPU 2.00 GHz processor running VMware with Linux Ubuntu 2.6.35. The Linux kernel was built with `iptables` and Netfilter NFQUEUE modules to provide the necessary Linux firewall and user-space network packet functionality.

The emulated PLC comprised the Koyo DirectLogic 405 CPU with a D4-08ND3S digital input module, D4-08TR digital relay module and H4-ECOM-100 Ethernet communications module. This PLC was selected because it demonstrated certain security vulnerabilities, including the vulnerability to an automated method that cracks device passwords [13, 18]. The emulated firmware used in our work was version H4-ECOM 4.0.1735, which contains a known vulnerability and an associated Metasploit module koyo_login [18].

The emulator is written in C and includes several interpreted Python modules. The emulator incorporates seven simultaneously running user-space processes in addition to the iptables firewall kernel module. It offers three network services to users: (i) a web server on TCP port 80 providing a configuration interface; (ii) a Modbus TCP service on TCP port 502; and (iii) a Host Automation Products (HAP) service on UDP port 28784. The Modbus TCP service is indicative of the Koyo PLC implementation of the common industrial protocol service. The HAP service enables remote management and configuration of the Koyo PLC.

For purposes of this research, the Modbus service was replicated strictly for device fingerprinting associated with the Koyo PLC. Because the research focus was on the Koyo PLC application and not messaging protocol standards, the Modbus functionality was not evaluated. Note, however, that Modbus functionality is readily incorporated as demonstrated by Berman, *et al.* [1].

5.2   Emulator Accuracy

The emulated PLC was evaluated for consistency with the Koyo PLC in terms of superficial accuracy, packet-level accuracy, scanning tool accuracy and attack tool accuracy. Each of the two emulated services, web and HAP, had standard and non-standard types of interactions, yielding a total of four types of queries. These queries were selected for the evaluation because they are representative of the interactions associated with an attacker targeting an Internet-connected PLC.

- **Standard Web Queries:** These queries are associated with interactions with a web server listening on TCP port 80. The queries represent normal, within-bounds requests from an Internet Explorer web browser.

- **Non-Standard Web Queries:** These queries are associated with OS fingerprinting scans using Nmap that attempt to identify a device based on the responses to non-standard TCP, IP and ICMP packets sent to the device. By default, Nmap chooses the lowest open TCP port on a device to perform its tests. Therefore, Nmap selects TCP port 80 unless it is directed otherwise.

- **Standard HAP Queries:** These queries are associated with interactions with the HAP industrial protocol server listening on UDP port 28784. These queries represent normal, within-bounds requests from NetEdit3 [6], a free vendor tool.

No.	Dest Addr	Src Addr	Protocol	Length	Info
2	10.1.0.147	10.1.0.79	TCP	60	http > 5000 [SYN, ACK] Seq=2374868006 Ack=1606421648 Win=2048 Len=0 MSS=512
5	10.1.0.147	10.1.0.79	TCP	60	http > 5000 [ACK] Seq=2374868007 Ack=1606421904 Win=2048 Len=0
6	10.1.0.147	10.1.0.79	HTTP	566	HTTP/1.1 200 OK (text/html)
8	10.1.0.147	10.1.0.79	HTTP	566	Continuation or non-HTTP traffic
10	10.1.0.147	10.1.0.79	HTTP	566	Continuation or non-HTTP traffic
12	10.1.0.147	10.1.0.79	HTTP	494	Continuation or non-HTTP traffic
14	10.1.0.147	10.1.0.79	TCP	60	http > 5000 [FIN, ACK] Seq=2374869983 Ack=1606421904 Win=2048 Len=0
16	10.1.0.147	10.1.0.79	TCP	60	http > 5000 [ACK] Seq=2374869984 Ack=1606421905 Win=2048 Len=0

Emulator response.

No.	Dest Addr	Src Addr	Protocol	Length	Info
2	10.1.0.147	10.1.0.93	TCP	60	http > 5000 [SYN, ACK] Seq=540754409 Ack=3851000542 Win=2048 Len=0 MSS=512
5	10.1.0.147	10.1.0.93	TCP	60	http > 5000 [ACK] Seq=540754410 Ack=3851000798 Win=2048 Len=0
6	10.1.0.147	10.1.0.93	HTTP	566	HTTP/1.1 200 OK (text/html)
8	10.1.0.147	10.1.0.93	HTTP	566	Continuation or non-HTTP traffic
10	10.1.0.147	10.1.0.93	HTTP	566	Continuation or non-HTTP traffic
12	10.1.0.147	10.1.0.93	HTTP	494	Continuation or non-HTTP traffic
14	10.1.0.147	10.1.0.93	TCP	60	http > 5000 [FIN, ACK] Seq=540756386 Ack=3851000798 Win=2048 Len=0
16	10.1.0.147	10.1.0.93	TCP	60	http > 5000 [ACK] Seq=540756387 Ack=3851000799 Win=2047 Len=0

Koyo PLC response.

Figure 1. Web server responses showing differences in TCP congestion window sizes.

- **Non-Standard HAP Queries:** These queries are associated with attacks on HAP protocol security measures using the koyo_login Metasploit module to exploit vulnerabilities.

The accuracy of the responses to the four types of queries are discussed below. The results are useful in educational environments where students learn scanning techniques and attack strategies that target industrial control systems. Additionally, the results showcase the applicability of the emulator in control system research efforts.

- **Standard Web Responses:** To analyze the superficial accuracy, the Koyo website HTML source was used to duplicate the original content and visual representation. Although it appears to be trivial, the notion of superficial accuracy should not be underestimated. For example, in a honeypot application, even a slight visual difference can alert a potential attacker that the device is not authentic.

  Web pages were transmitted byte-for-byte from the PLC to the user's browser. As such, packet-level accuracy is an important consideration in PLC emulation. A single web query to index.html of the Koyo PLC generates 2,432 bytes. Excluding the non-deterministic header fields (e.g., TCP sequence and acknowledgement numbers), there are 2,330 bytes that are expected to be identical. The emulator differs by only five bytes of the 2,330 total bytes, demonstrating a consistency of 99.8%.

  Four of the five differences occur in the TCP response header as a result of the Koyo PLC TCP/IP stack implementation handling procedures for the TCP push flag and TCP congestion window. Figure 1 shows the web server responses from the emulator and the Koyo PLC for different TCP congestion window sizes. Correcting these differences requires the modification and recompilation of the Linux kernel.

The fifth difference is the result of an implementation error in the emulator that appears in the `index.html` web page. The emulator value is `0x3a` (ASCII ":" character) while the Koyo PLC value is `0x0a` (ASCII line feed character). Because this difference occurs with a whitespace character, it is likely the result of a copy-and-paste error. Whatever the cause, the difference is readily fixed by changing the `index.html` source code of the emulator.

■ **Non-Standard Web Responses:** An Nmap operating system scan uses TCP/IP stack fingerprinting to identify the operating system of a target device [10]. From the point of view of scanning accuracy, the emulator must respond to an Nmap operating system scan in a manner that is consistent with the Koyo PLC. Indeed, the scan should provide no indications that the emulator is running a Linux operating system within a virtual environment.

Figure 2 shows the results obtained for non-standard web queries to the emulator and Koyo PLC. The Nmap scan results differ only in the TCP sequence number prediction fields (SP and ISR) and in the unused ICMP port unreachable field non-zero field (UN). The corresponding scanning tool accuracy is 97.25%. Note that an Nmap scan on a similar VMware configuration with no installed emulator correctly identified the Linux operating system. The results indicate that the emulator sufficiently conforms to the Koyo PLC with regard to the operating system characteristics gleaned using external communications.

■ **Standard HAP Responses:** Standard HAP requests were sent using the UDP transmission protocol. In the experiment, 305 of the 309 total bytes in the HAP response from the Koyo PLC were deterministic, and the emulator was 100% accurate for the deterministic bytes. Figure 3 shows the response bytes for HAP protocol queries to the emulator and Koyo PLC. Note that the non-deterministic fields are highlighted and include the Ethernet address, IP header checksum, IP source address and UDP header checksum.

The accurate responses produced for standard HAP requests indicate the emulator is capable of interacting with any tool in a manner that conforms with the HAP protocol standard. As such, engineering modifications and device configuration updates are appropriately handled by the emulator, consistent with the expected operations of the Koyo PLC.

■ **Non-Standard HAP Responses:** The attack tool accuracy for the Metasploit module was determined based on successful attack execution and device exploitation. Figure 4 demonstrates an execution of the `koyo_login` Metasploit module to brute-force the emulator password. The exploit works in the same manner as the Koyo PLC and discovers the correct emulator password ("A0000322"). Thus, the emulator can be

```
Not shown: 131067 closed ports
PORT        STATE         SERVICE
80/tcp      open          http
502/tcp     open          asa-appl-proto
28784/udp open|filtered unknown
MAC Address: 00:E0:62:60:46:24 (Host Engineering)
Device type: specialized
Running: Koyo embedded
OS details: Koyo DirectLogic PLC
TCP/IP fingerprint:
OS:SCAN(V=5.21%D=12/13%OT=80%CT=1%CU=1%PV=Y%DS=1%DC=D%G=Y%M=00E062%TM=50CA4
OS:A87%P=x86_64-unknown-linux-gnu)SEQ(SP=5D%GCD=1%ISR=C5%TI=Z%CI=Z%II=RI%TS
OS:=U)OPS(O1=M200%O2=M200%O3=M200%O4=M200%O5=M200%O6=M109)WIN(W1=800%W2=800
OS:%W3=800%W4=800%W5=800%W6=800)ECN(R=Y%DF=Y%T=FF%W=800%O=M200%CC=N%Q=)T1(R
OS:=Y%DF=Y%T=FF%S=O%A=S+%F=AS%RD=0%Q=)T2(R=N)T3(R=Y%DF=Y%T=FF%W=800%S=O%A=S
OS:+%F=AS%O=M109%RD=0%Q=)T4(R=Y%DF=Y%T=FF%W=800%S=A+%A=S%F=AR%O=%RD=0%Q=)T5
OS:(R=Y%DF=Y%T=FF%W=800%S=A%A=S+%F=AR%O=%RD=0%Q=)T6(R=Y%DF=Y%T=FF%W=800%S=A
OS:%A=S%F=AR%O=%RD=0%Q=)T7(R=Y%DF=Y%T=FF%W=800%S=A%A=S+%F=AR%O=%RD=0%Q=)U1(
OS:R=Y%DF=Y%T=FF%IPL=38%UN=B390%RIPL=G%RID=G%RIPCK=G%RUCK=G%RUD=G)IE(R=Y%DF
OS:I=S%T=FF%CD=S)
Network Distance: 1 hop
TCP Sequence Prediction: Difficulty=93 (Good luck!)
IP ID Sequence Generation: All zeros
Read data files from: /usr/share/nmap
OS detection performed. Please report any incorrect results at http://
Nmap done: 1 IP address (1 host up) scanned in 3657.08 seconds
           Raw packets sent: 159858 (5.634MB) | Rcvd: 131086 (6.293MB)
```

Nmap OS scan result.

```
Not shown: 131067 closed ports
PORT        STATE         SERVICE
80/tcp      open          http
502/tcp     open          asa-appl-proto
28784/udp open|filtered unknown
MAC Address: 00:E0:62:60:46:23 (Host Engineering)
Device type: specialized
Running: Koyo embedded
OS details: Koyo DirectLogic PLC
TCP/IP fingerprint:
OS:SCAN(V=5.21%D=12/15%OT=80%CT=1%CU=1%PV=Y%DS=1%DC=D%G=Y%M=00E062%TM=50CCF
OS:062%P=x86_64-unknown-linux-gnu)SEQ(SP=2F%GCD=1%ISR=9A%TI=Z%CI=Z%II=RI%TS
OS:=U)OPS(O1=M200%O2=M200%O3=M200%O4=M200%O5=M200%O6=M109)WIN(W1=800%W2=800
OS:%W3=800%W4=800%W5=800%W6=800)ECN(R=Y%DF=Y%T=FF%W=800%O=M200%CC=N%Q=)T1(R
OS:=Y%DF=Y%T=FF%S=O%A=S+%F=AS%RD=0%Q=)T2(R=N)T3(R=Y%DF=Y%T=FF%W=800%S=O%A=S
OS:+%F=AS%O=M109%RD=0%Q=)T4(R=Y%DF=Y%T=FF%W=800%S=A+%A=S%F=AR%O=%RD=0%Q=)T5
OS:(R=Y%DF=Y%T=FF%W=800%S=A%A=S+%F=AR%O=%RD=0%Q=)T6(R=Y%DF=Y%T=FF%W=800%S=A
OS:%A=S%F=AR%O=%RD=0%Q=)T7(R=Y%DF=Y%T=FF%W=800%S=A%A=S+%F=AR%O=%RD=0%Q=)U1(
OS:R=Y%DF=Y%T=FF%IPL=38%UN=D046%RIPL=G%RID=G%RIPCK=G%RUCK=G%RUD=G)IE(R=Y%DF
OS:I=S%T=FF%CD=S)
Network Distance: 1 hop
TCP Sequence Prediction: Difficulty=47 (Good luck!)
IP ID Sequence Generation: All zeros
Read data files from: /usr/share/nmap
OS detection performed. Please report any incorrect results at http://
Nmap done: 1 IP address (1 host up) scanned in 125.85 seconds
           Raw packets sent: 131091 (4.721MB) | Rcvd: 131085 (6.292MB)
```

Koyo PLC scan result.

Figure 2. Nmap operating system scan results.

```
0000   00 1c 23 1a 37 21 00 e0   62 60 46 25 08 00 45 00   ..#.7!..b`F%..E.
0010   01 27 00 00 40 00 ff 11   65 e2 0a 01 00 4f 0a 01   .'..@...e....O..
0020   00 93 70 70 13 88 01 13   e5 80 48 41 50 25 00 bc   ..pp......HAP%..
0030   c3 02 01 00 00 48 34 2d   45 43 4f 4d 31 30 30 20   .....H4-ECOM100
0040   45 74 68 65 72 6e 65 74   20 43 6f 6d 6d 75 6e 69   Ethernet Communi
0050   63 61 74 69 6f 6e 73 20   4d 6f 64 75 6c 65 2e 00   cations Module..
0060   00 00 00 00 00 00 00 00   00 00 00 00 00 00 00 00   ................
0070   00 00 00 00 00 00 00 00   00 00 00 00 00 00 00 00   ................
```

Emulator response.

```
0000   00 1c 23 1a 37 21 00 e0   62 60 46 23 08 00 45 00   ..#.7!..b`F#..E.
0010   01 27 00 00 40 00 ff 11   65 dd 0a 01 00 54 0a 01   .'..@...e....T..
0020   00 93 70 70 13 88 01 13   e5 7b 48 41 50 25 00 bc   ..pp.....{HAP%..
0030   c3 02 01 00 00 48 34 2d   45 43 4f 4d 31 30 30 20   .....H4-ECOM100
0040   45 74 68 65 72 6e 65 74   20 43 6f 6d 6d 75 6e 69   Ethernet Communi
0050   63 61 74 69 6f 6e 73 20   4d 6f 64 75 6c 65 2e 00   cations Module..
0060   00 00 00 00 00 00 00 00   00 00 00 00 00 00 00 00   ................
0070   00 00 00 00 00 00 00 00   00 00 00 00 00 00 00 00   ................
```

Koyo PLC response.

Figure 3.   Standard HAP packet responses.

```
Module options (auxiliary/scanner/scada/koyo_login):

   Name            Current Setting    Required    Description
   ----            ---------------    --------    -----------
   PREFIX          A                  yes         The prefix to use for the password (default: A)
   RECV_TIMEOUT    3                  no          Time (in seconds) to wait between packets
   RHOSTS          10.1.0.79          yes         The target address range or CIDR identifier
   RPORT           28784              yes         The target port
   THREADS         1                  yes         The number of concurrent threads

msf auxiliary(koyo_login) > exploit

[*] 10.1.0.79:28784 - KOYO - Checking the controller for locked memory...
[*] 10.1.0.79:28784 - KOYO - Controller locked; commencing bruteforce...
[+] 10.1.0.79:28784 - KOYO - Found passcode: A0000322...
[*] Scanned 1 of 1 hosts (100% complete)
[*] Auxiliary module execution completed
msf auxiliary(koyo_login) >
```

Figure 4.   Metasploit module `koyo_login` executing successfully on the emulator.

used quite effectively in research and educational settings to demonstrate PLC exploitation techniques.

Obviously, it is important that the emulator behave in a manner that is consistent with the Koyo PLC. Table 1 shows the emulator results for the various types of accuracy associated with the two emulated services. When emulating the standard web and standard HAP services, the emulator is accurate at the superficial and packet levels. The non-standard web service is accurate at the scanning level – when a user scans the emulator using Nmap, the scanning results confirm the authenticity of the device. Finally, the non-standard HAP service is accurate at the attack tool level because the emulator is vulnerable to a Metasploit attack consistent with the Koyo PLC.

Table 1. Emulator services and accuracy considerations.

Service	Query Type	Superficial	Packet	Scan	Attack
Web	Standard (Browser)	X	X		
	Non-Standard (Nmap)			X	
HAP	Standard (NetEdit3)	X	X		
	Non-Standard (Metasploit)				X

6.   Conclusions

The PLC emulator implemented in the VMware virtual environment provides a cost-effective and scalable emulation solution. Experimental evaluations
demonstrate that the emulator accurately replicates a real PLC with respect
to standard and non-standard web and HAP services.

We hope that this work stimulates renewed efforts at developing sophisticated industrial control system emulators for research and educational environments. Industrial control system emulators provide significant advantages
over hardware-based testbeds and simulation environments. Their robustness,
versatility and configurability are attractive for understanding, developing and
analyzing defensive and offensive techniques, more so because these efforts can
be conducted without concern for damaging costly equipment.

Note that the views expressed in this paper are those of the authors and do
not reflect the official policy or position of the U.S. Air Force, U.S. Department
of Defense or the U.S. Government.

References

[1] D. Berman and J. Butts, Towards a characterization of cyber attacks on
industrial control systems: Emulating field devices using Gumstix technology, *Proceedings of the Fifth International Symposium on Resilient Control
Systems*, pp. 63–68, 2012.

[2] C. Davis, J. Tate, H. Okhravi, C. Grier, T. Overbye and D. Nicol,
SCADA cyber security testbed development, *Proceedings of the Thirty-
Eighth North American Power Symposium*, pp. 483–488, 2006.

[3] D. Duggan, Penetration Testing of Industrial Control Systems, Sandia Report SAND2005-2846P, Sandia National Laboratories, Albuquerque, New
Mexico, 2005.

[4] Flux Research Group, Network Emulation Testbed, School of Computing,
University of Utah, Salt Lake City, Utah (www.emulab.net).

[5] K. Gatens, INEEL establishes National SCADA Test Bed, Feature Story,
Idaho National Laboratory, Idaho Falls, Idaho (www.inl.gov/feature
stories/2003-03-25.shtml), 2003.

[6] Host Engineering, NetEdit v3, Jonesborough, Tennessee (www.hosteng.
com/SW-Products/NetEdit3.htm).

[7] Idaho National Engineering and Environmental Laboratory, INEEL establishes National SCADA Testbed, *Need to Know*, vol. 3(2), pp. 1–3, 2003.

[8] Insecure.com, Nmap Security Scanner, Sunnyvale, California (`nmap.org`).

[9] N. Kisserli, D. Schellekens and B. Preneel, Self-encrypting code to protect against analysis and tampering, *Proceedings of the First Benelux Workshop on Information and System Security*, 2006.

[10] G. Lyon, Nmap Network Scanning, The Official Nmap Project Guide to Network Discovery and Security Scanning, Insecure.com, Sunnyvale, California, 2008.

[11] S. McClure, J. Scambray and G Kurtz, *Hacking Exposed 7: Network Security Secrets and Solutions*, McGraw-Hill, Emeryville, California, 2012.

[12] T. Morris, R. Vaughn and Y. Dandass, A testbed for SCADA control system cyber security research and pedagogy, *Proceedings of the Seventh Annual Workshop on Cyber Security and Information Intelligence Research*, article no. 27, 2011.

[13] D. Peck and D. Peterson, Leveraging Ethernet card vulnerabilities in field devices, *Proceedings of the SCADA Security Scientific Symposium*, 2009.

[14] C. Queiroz, A. Mahmood, J. Hu, Z. Tari and X. Yu, Building a SCADA security testbed, *Proceedings of the Third International Conference on Network and System Security*, pp. 357–364, 2009.

[15] Rapid7, Metasploit Framework, Boston, Massachusetts (`www.metasploit.org`).

[16] Rockwell Automation, GuardPLC Safety Control Programming Software, Milwaukee, Wisconsin.

[17] Siemens, LOGO! Software, Munich, Germany.

[18] R. Wightman, Koyo/Automation direct vulnerabilities, Digital Bond, Sunrise, Florida (`www.digitalbond.com/blog/2012/02/08/koyoautomation-direct-vulnerabilities`), 2012.

Chapter 4

ZIGBEE DEVICE VERIFICATION FOR SECURING INDUSTRIAL CONTROL AND BUILDING AUTOMATION SYSTEMS*

Clay Dubendorfer, Benjamin Ramsey and Michael Temple

Abstract Improved wireless ZigBee network security provides a means to mitigate malicious network activity due to unauthorized devices. Security enhancement using RF-based features can augment conventional bit-level security approaches that are solely based on the MAC addresses of ZigBee devices. This paper presents a device identity verification process using RF fingerprints from like-model CC2420 2.4 GHz ZigBee device transmissions in operational indoor scenarios involving line-of-sight and through-wall propagation channels, as well as an anechoic chamber representing near-ideal conditions. A trained multiple discriminant analysis model was generated using normalized multivariate Gaussian test statistics from authorized network devices. Authorized device classification and ID verification were assessed using pre-classification Kolmogorov-Smirnov (KS) feature ranking and post-classification generalized relevance learning vector quantization improved (GRLVQI) relevance ranking. A true verification rate greater than 90% and a false verification rate less than 10% were obtained when assessing authorized device IDs. When additional rogue devices were introduced that attempted to gain unauthorized network access by spoofing the bit-level credentials of authorized devices, the KS-test feature set achieved a true verification rate greater than 90% and a rogue reject rate greater than 90% in 29 of 36 rogue scenarios while the GRLVQI feature set was successful in 28 of 36 scenarios.

Keywords: ZigBee devices, RF fingerprinting, ID verification, rogue rejection

*This is a work of the US Government and is not subject to copyright protection in the United States. Foreign copyrights may apply.

J. Butts and S. Shenoi (Eds.): Critical Infrastructure Protection VII, IFIP AICT 417, pp. 47–62, 2013.
© IFIP International Federation for Information Processing 2013 (outside the US)

1. Introduction

The deployment of wireless personal area networks in industrial control and monitoring applications is increasing due to their energy efficiency, low complexity and low cost. Standards-based protocols such as ZigBee and IEEE 802.15.4 commonly provide connectivity in wireless sensor network applications that support energy management and industrial control automation. ZigBee solutions are also implemented with radio frequency identification tags in hospital environments to track expensive medical equipment and patient stay, and to continuously monitor patient vital signs. High levels of security are essential in ZigBee networks used in critical infrastructure applications, including public health and the smart grid, where sensitive personal information is handled or physical systems are controlled.

Improved security and authentication measures must be developed to counter open source hacking tools such as KillerBee [11] that can undermine ZigBee networks. Rogue devices can spoof bit-level credentials such as MAC addresses and network encryption keys. This has motivated research in physical layer (PHY) features that can uniquely identify network nodes. PHY features are inherently difficult to replicate, especially when derived from unintentional waveform modulation effects. Recent work has shown that, once they are identified and extracted, PHY-based features (e.g., RF fingerprints) can achieve human-like device discrimination even when using a relatively simple multiple discriminate analysis (MDA), maximum likelihood (ML) classification technique [4, 5, 8, 10].

This paper expands the use of radio frequency distinct native attribute (RF-DNA) fingerprints for device classification and verification using 2.4 GHz ZigBee devices in a typical indoor office environment. Line-of-sight and through-wall propagation channels are considered with dynamic multi-path and signal attenuation factors such as interior walls and human foot traffic. Time-domain exploitation of the entire 40-bit IEEE 802.15.4 synchronization header response (SHR), a mandatory element of every ZigBee transmission, is considered. The experimental results demonstrate the feasibility of ZigBee device ID verification using collected responses in operational and near-ideal environments.

Device ID verification is characterized using a test statistic based on normalized multivariate Gaussian distributions of MDA-projected fingerprints and receiver operating characteristics (ROC) curve analysis. The MDA-based device ID verification process is demonstrated using RF fingerprints comprising dimensionally-reduced feature sets – minimal features translate to minimal computational complexity. Dimensional reduction analysis (DRA) is used to select reduced feature sets based on pre-classification Kolmogorov-Smirnov (KS) feature ranking and post-classification generalized relevance learning vector quantization-improved (GRLVQI) relevance ranking. A classification performance benchmark of $\%C = 90\%$ is used for comparative assessment and for verification assessment. The device ID verification process is assessed based on the true verification rate (TVR) for authorized devices and the rogue reject rate (RRR) for unauthorized rogue devices.

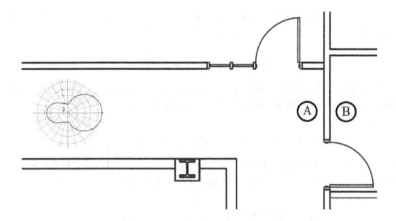

Figure 1. Operational indoor collection geometry.

2. Experimental Methodology

An Agilent E3238S receiver (Rx) was used to collect emissions from ten CC2420 2.4 GHz IEEE 802.15.4 ZigBee devices (denoted as Dev1, Dev2, ..., Dev10). For each transmitting (Tx) device, a total of $N_{SHR} = 1,000$ SHRs were collected under three operating conditions: (i) Tx and Rx inside a Ramsey STE3000 RF shielded anechoic chamber (CAGE); (ii) Tx and Rx with a clear line-of-sight (LOS) along a hallway – Location A in Figure 1; and (iii) Tx and Rx on opposite sides of a wall (WALL) – Location B in Figure 1. A 6 dB gain Ramsey LPY2 log periodic antenna was placed in the hallway with the main beam directed at the collection devices.

The collected signals were down-converted, digitized using a 12-bit analog-to-digital converter and stored as complex in-phase and quadrature components for subsequent post-collection processing. Amplitude-based burst detection and baseband processing were performed as described in [1, 6] using a sample frequency $f_s = 11.875$ Msps and an eighth-order Butterworth filter with bandwidth $W_{BB} = 1$ MHz.

2.1 RF Fingerprint Generation

RF fingerprints were extracted from SHR emissions using instantaneous amplitude (a), phase (ϕ) and frequency (f) responses. Characteristics sequences ($a[n]$, $\phi[n]$ and $f[n]$) were generated using collected complex in-phase and quadrature signal samples from the SHR region, centered (i.e., mean removal) and then normalized (i.e., division by maximum value) [5, 9]. Statistical RF fingerprint features of variance (σ^2), skewness (γ) and kurtosis (κ) were calculated to create regional fingerprint markers generated by: (i) dividing each selected characteristic sequence $\{a[n]\}, \{\phi[n]\}$ and $\{f[n]\}$ into N_R contiguous equal-length subsequences; (ii) calculating N_S metrics for each subsequence, plus the entire fingerprinted region as a whole ($N_R + 1$ total regions); and (iii) arranging the metrics in vector form as:

$$F_{R_i} = [\sigma^2_{R_i} \; \gamma_{R_i} \; \kappa_{R_i}]_{1 \times N_S} \tag{1}$$

where $i = 1, 2, \ldots, N_R + 1$. Marker vectors from Equation (1) are concatenated to form the composite characteristic vector given by:

$$\mathbf{F} = [F_{R_1} \vdots F_{R_2} \vdots F_{R_3} \ldots F_{R_{N_R+1}}]_{1 \times [N_S \times (N_R+1)]}. \tag{2}$$

When all $N_C = 3$ signal characteristics are used, the final RF fingerprint is generated by concatenating vectors from Equation (2) according to:

$$\mathbf{F} = [\mathbf{F}^a \vdots \mathbf{F}^\phi \vdots \mathbf{F}^f]_{1 \times [N_S \times (N_R+1) \times N_C]}. \tag{3}$$

Full-dimensional RF-DNA fingerprints are based on a total of $N_R = 80$ SHR subsequences using $N_C = 3$ signal characteristics (a, ϕ, f) and $N_S = 3$ statistics (σ^2, γ, κ), for a total of $N_{Full} = N_S \times (N_R + 1) \times N_C = 729$ features per RF fingerprint.

2.2   Device Discrimination

Statistical RF fingerprints for ZigBee SHR responses were generated according to Equation (3) and input to a device discrimination process shown in Figure 2. The device discrimination process supports both classification and verification using selected measures of similarity and test statistics. The process involves separating collected RF-DNA fingerprints into training and testing sets for $N_D = 4$ ZigBee devices (Dev1, Dev2, Dev3 and Dev4). The training emissions were used for device-specific model development for both device classification and device ID verification. Device classification and verification assessments were accomplished by projecting the testing RF fingerprints into a mapped feature space derived through MDA model development and generating measures of similarity using probability-based test statistics.

Multiple Discriminate Analysis Model Development. MDA is an extension of the Fisher linear discriminant process for discriminating more than two device classes ($N_D > 2$). MDA reduces feature dimensionality by projecting RF fingerprints into an $N_D - 1$ dimensional subspace. The MDA projection matrix $\mathbf{W}$ was developed using an iterative K-fold training process with the goal of projecting higher-dimensional input fingerprint $\mathbf{F}$ data into a lower dimensional mapped feature space such that the out-of-class separation is maximized and the within-class spread is minimized [2]. The best performing projection matrix $\mathbf{W}_B$ in the K-fold training process was retained and used to project training fingerprints into the mapped feature space, where projected means and covariances were measured for each of the N_D devices. The means and covariances were used to develop an assumed multivariate Gaussian distributed device specific model. The developed model shown as $\mathbf{M}$ in

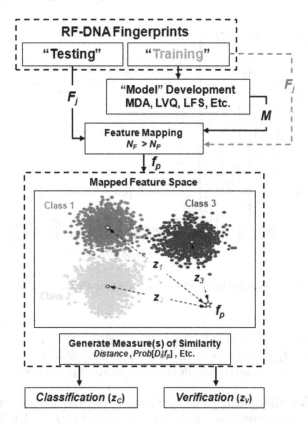

Figure 2. Block diagram of device discrimination.

Figure 2 comprises a projection matrix $\mathbf{W}_B(SNR)$, device projected means $\mu_i(SNR)$, and a pooled covariance matrix $\Sigma_P(SNR)$ where the parenthetical signal-to-noise ratio (SNR) denotes that the model generally varies with SNR and $i = 1, 2, \ldots, N_D$.

Maximum Likelihood Classification. Device classification was performed using an ML classifier derived from Bayesian decision theory with the testing RF fingerprints classified as affiliated with one of the N_D possible devices. For ML classification, the prior probabilities were assumed to be equal, the costs uniform and the device likelihoods to have a multivariate Gaussian distribution generated during MDA model development. The ML classification process involved: (i) inputting a testing RF fingerprint $\mathbf{F}_j$ generated according to Equation (3) for a collected emission from an unknown device D_j; (ii) projecting $\mathbf{F}_j$ into the mapped feature space using $\mathbf{f}_j = \mathbf{F}_j \mathbf{W}_B$; and (iii) associating $\mathbf{f}_j$ with the device yielding the maximum conditional likelihood probability:

$$D_i \; : \; \arg\max_i \Big[\, p(\mathbf{f}_j | D_i) \,\Big] \tag{4}$$

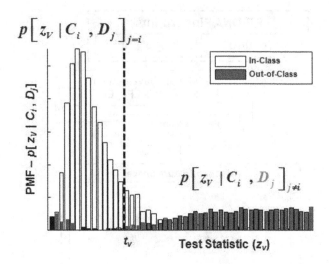

Figure 3.   Representative in-class and out-of-class probability mass functions.

where $i = 1, 2, \ldots, N_D$ and $p(\mathbf{f}_j | D_i)$ is the conditional likelihood probability that fingerprint $\mathbf{f}_j$ belongs to device D_i. This was done for all testing RF fingerprints in order to assess the device classification performance.

Device ID Verification.   The RF fingerprinting methodology used for device ID verification is consistent with the process used in [1, 7]. RF fingerprints can authenticate the claimed bit-level identity of a device (e.g., the device wants to access a network and has presented a MAC address, SIM number or IMEI number to gain access). Since bit-level credentials can be replicated by rogue devices, RF fingerprint verification provides a means to mitigate unauthorized access attempts. Device ID verification was accomplished using a one-to-one comparison of current versus claimed RF signatures. The similarity measure or verification test statistic z_V reflects how well the current and claimed RF fingerprint identities match and is compared with a threshold t_V to verify the ID claimed by the device and grant or deny network access to the device.

Figure 3 shows representative in-class (unfilled) and out-of-class (filled) probability mass functions (PMFs) generated from test statistic z_V and a fixed threshold t_V. The in-class probability is defined as $p[z_V | C_i, D_j]$ where $j = i$, C_i is the claimed device ID and D_j is the actual device. The out-of-class distribution was generated using z_V for the case when an unknown device falsely claims to be an authorized device, where the unknown device is: (i) a rogue device ($j \neq 1, 2, \ldots, N_D$); or (ii) an authorized device claiming the identity of a different authorized device ($j = 1, 2, \ldots, N_D$). The out-of-class probability is denoted as $p[z_V | C_i, D_j]$ where $i \neq j$ and $i = 1, 2, \ldots, N_D$.

Device ID verification was assessed using conventional ROC curve analysis [3]. Varying the threshold t_V and measuring the area under the curve for

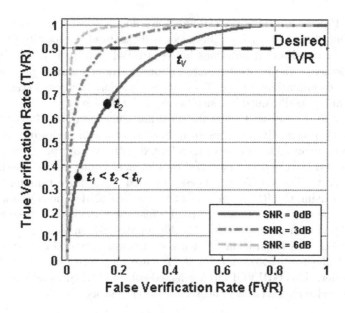

Figure 4. Device ID verification ROC curves.

each PMF enabled the determination of the true and false device ID verification rates. The TVR is a measure of how well current RF fingerprints match the true claimed ID and is the area under the in-class PMF when $z_V < t_V$. The corresponding false verification rate (FVR) provides a measure of how well current RF fingerprints match a false claimed ID and is the area under the out-of-class PMF when $z_V < t_V$.

The threshold t_V was varied and the corresponding device TVRs and FVRs were used to generate ROC performance curves for 6 dB > 3 dB > 0 dB. Figure 4 shows the variation in ROC curve performance as a function of three arbitrarily selected SNR values. Representative performance points for various thresholds ($t_1 < t_2 < t_V$) are shown to emphasize that the verification threshold value dictates TVR and FVR performance.

2.3   Dimensional Reduction Analysis

The Fisher-based MDA process inherently masks the feature contribution to the resulting discrimination performance, inhibiting the ability to determine the features that have the greatest impact. The goal of DRA is to minimize the number of RF fingerprint features while achieving the desired classification accuracy. Identifying the features that provide the most significant contribution to classification while removing less relevant features may be accomplished using two techniques: (i) a pre-classification KS goodness-of-fit test [6]; and (ii) a feature relevance ranking provided by GRLVQI processing [7].

The quantitative pre-classification feature reduction process was used to identify and select the l most relevant features from the full-dimensional RF feature set $\mathbf{F}$ prior to MDA/ML classification. The KS-test is a suitable option for analyzing statistical feature differences and was used to quantify differences in cumulative distribution functions between full-dimensional RF feature sets from two devices. The KS-test results are presented as summed p-values from all pairwise combinations of the N_D devices considered, where lower p-values indicate a more significant difference between the data sets.

The second alternative to feature selection considered was GRLVQI processing, which inherently provides an indication of feature relevance following model development. The process was adopted entirely from previous research that shows that GRLVQI is a powerful tool for performing device classification and DRA [7, 8]. The GRLVQI process provided a relevance ranking for each feature comprising the RF fingerprint at a specified SNR. The relevance ranking value is the contribution of a particular feature to device separation within the GRLVQI classification process. The higher the relevance value, the greater the impact on class separation. Feature dimensional reduction was achieved by selecting the top l features from the feature relevance ranking of the GR-LVQI classifier. This GRLVQI DRA selected subset of features was used in the MDA/ML device classification and ID verification processes.

3.   Experimental Results

MDA training was accomplished using $N_{SHR} = 500$ independent ZigBee SHR responses collected from each location (CAGE, LOS and WALL) for each device (Dev1, Dev2, Dev3 and Dev4). In addition, $N_z = 5$ independent, like-filtered Monte Carlo noise realizations were added to the SHR responses for each analysis SNR considered. Thus, for MDA training with $N_D = 4$ devices, K-fold generation of the best $\mathbf{W}_B(SNR)$, $\mu_i(SNR)$, $\Sigma_P(SNR)$ and multivariate Gaussian statistics of projected training fingerprints involved a total of $N_{TNG} = 500$ (SHR) $\times$ 3 (locations) $\times$ 5 (N_z) = 7,500 independent realizations per device. The classification and verification results were likewise based on $N_{SHR} = 500$ testing fingerprints per location for each device and $N_z = 5$ noise realizations per SNR, resulting in $N_{TST} = 7,500$ test realizations.

3.1   Device Classification (Full-Dimensional)

Full-dimensional RF fingerprints included features based on $N_C = 3$ signal characteristics (a, ϕ and f), $N_S = 3$ statistical fingerprint features (σ^2, γ and κ), and $N_R + 1 = 81$ regions, for a total fingerprint $\mathbf{F}$ comprising $N_F = 729$ features as specified by Equation (3). Figure 5 shows the full-dimensional testing classification performance for the hybrid location scenario (i.e., responses from CAGE, LOS and WALL) at SNRs ranging from 0 to 24 dB. Note that a performance benchmark of $\%C = 90\%$ is achieved at SNR $\approx$ 10 dB, with all the devices achieving $\%C = 80\%$ or better classification.

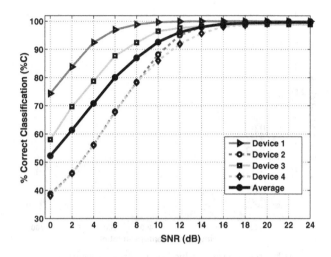

Figure 5. MDA/ML device classification performance.

3.2 DRA Feature Selection

Feature dimensional reduction analysis was subsequently performed to determine the minimum number of features required to achieve the $\%C = 90\%$ benchmark. Feature relevance was determined by fixing the RF fingerprints at SNR = 10 dB and performing a quantitative assessment on the $N_F = 729$ full-dimensional features using the pre-classification KS-test feature selection and the feature relevance ranking from the GRLVQI classifier.

Quantitative feature assessment enabled the identification and selection of the most relevant subset of full-dimensional features. Figure 6 shows the $N_F = 729$ full-dimensional feature indices and relevance indicators for SNR = 10 dB based on the pre-classification KS-test and the GRLVQI feature relevance ranking. Note that lower KS-test p-values and higher GRLVQI λ-values indicate greater relevance. The results at SNR = 10 dB correspond to the cross-device average $\%C \approx 90\%$ shown in Figure 5.

3.3 Device Classification (DRA Performance)

Figure 7 shows the results of reducing the RF fingerprint features using the pre-classification KS-test feature selection and the feature relevance ranking from the GRLVQI classifier. For the KS-test, the top $N_F = 243$ features to the top $N_F = 50$ features require SNR $\approx$ 10 to 17 dB to achieve the $\%C = 90\%$ classification benchmark. Note that the top $N_F = 25$ features never reach the $\%C = 90\%$ benchmark. For the GRLVQI classifier, a range of SNR $\approx$ 10 to 29 dB is necessary to achieve 90% classification accuracy for the top $N_F = 243$ features to the top $N_F = 25$ features.

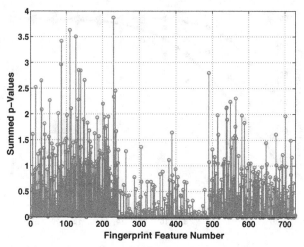

(a) KS-test (lower p-value implies greater relevance).

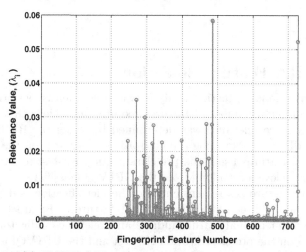

(b) GRLVQI (higher λ-value implies greater relevance).

Figure 6.   DRA feature relevance indicators at SNR = 10 dB.

3.4   Device ID Verification (Authorized Devices)

Device ID verification was performed using a one-to-one comparison of the current RF fingerprint versus claimed ID RF fingerprints. The current RF fingerprint was compared with the stored reference fingerprint template associated with the claimed bit-level identity. The stored reference fingerprint template was created in the MDA training process using $N_{TNG} = 7,500$ independent realizations for the $N_D = 4$ authorized devices. The projected training fingerprints were used to generate the in-class PMF constructed from the verification

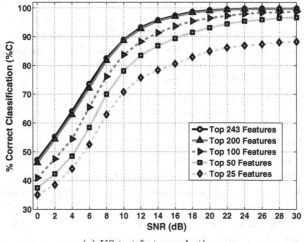

(a) KS-test feature selection.

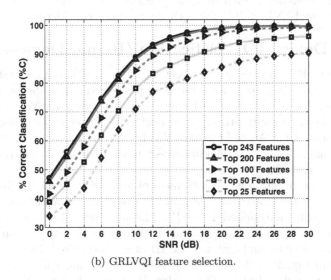

(b) GRLVQI feature selection.

Figure 7. MDA/ML device classification using DRA subsets.

test statistic z_V. This test statistic z_V was derived from the inherent MATLAB classify function, which outputs a normalized conditional multivariate Gaussian posterior probability given by:

$$z_V = \frac{p(\mathbf{f}_j|D_i)}{\sum\limits_{k=1}^{N_D} p(\mathbf{f}_j|D_k)} \qquad (5)$$

where $i = 1, 2, \ldots, N_D$ and $\mathbf{f}_j$ is the current projected RF fingerprint claiming to have an ID from device D_i. The test statistic z_V from Equation (5) was stored when the projected fingerprint $\mathbf{f}_j$ was actually from the claimed ID device.

Each designated authorized device has a stored RF signature template to use when a testing input RF fingerprint is received and claims the ID of an authorized device. In authorized device ID verification, the current testing RF fingerprints were selected from a pool of N_D authorized devices and claimed IDs of authorized devices. The test statistic from Equation (5) for current testing fingerprints was used to create the out-of-class PMF. The resulting in-class and out-of-class PMFs were used to produce device ID verification ROC curves.

Figure 8 shows the device ID verification performance for each of the $N_D = 4$ authorized devices using a reduced feature set ($N_F = 50$) selected with pre-classification KS values and post-classification GRLVQI relevance rankings. The resulting ID verification ROC curves were evaluated at SNR =18 dB based on the classification performance benchmark ($\%C = 90\%$) for the reduced feature set ($N_F = 50$). As seen in each plot, there is a device-dependent verification threshold t_V such that all authorized device IDs can be verified at TVR > 90% and FVR < 10% for both the methods considered.

3.5   Device ID Verification (Rogue Devices)

The use of RF fingerprints to reject rogue devices is demonstrated using the same device ID verification process implemented for authorized devices. In this case, the out-of-class PMFs were constructed from $N_U = 6$ (Dev5, Dev6, ..., Dev10) unauthorized rogue device RF fingerprints collected from the three locations (CAGE, LOS and WALL). A total of N_{TST}= 1,000 (SHR) × 1 (location) × 5 (N_z) = 5,000 previously unseen RF fingerprint realizations were used for each N_U device.

Rogue device rejection is an assessment of how well current RF fingerprints selected from a pool of rogue (previously unseen and unauthorized) devices match the claimed authorized device ID. The authorized device reference template created in MDA training was used when a rogue testing input RF fingerprint was received and claimed the ID of an authorized device. The test statistic from Equation (5) for current rogue testing fingerprints was used to create the out-of-class PMFs. The in-class PMF of each of the $N_D = 4$ authorized device stored templates was compared with the newly-generated rogue scenario out-of-class PMF, producing four ROC curves (one for each claimed authorized device ID). $N_U = 6$ rogue devices were used in nine different rogue device placements (three each located at CAGE, LOS and WALL) where each rogue device claimed the identity of each of the $N_D = 4$ authorized devices, producing a total of 36 rogue scenarios.

Figure 9 presents the rogue rejection results for the device ID verification process. Specifically, the figure shows the rogue device rejection for $N_U = 6$ unauthorized devices spoofing the bit-level IDs of the $N_D = 4$ authorized devices (36 total scenarios). The assessment is based on the top ranked $N_F = 50$ features with the KS-test and GRLVQI selected features. The grey ROC

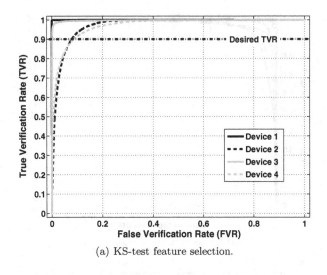

(a) KS-test feature selection.

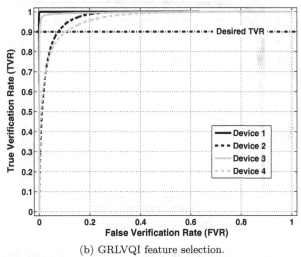

(b) GRLVQI feature selection.

Figure 8. Authorized device ID verification for $N_D = 4$ authorized devices.

curves correspond to scenarios where RAR < 10% is not achieved. Each case includes 36 rogue scenarios corresponding to the feature dimensional reduction method where the top $N_F = 50$ feature sets selected were evaluated at SNR = 18 dB. The results are plotted as the rogue accept rate (RAR) versus TVR, where the rogue reject rate (RRR) is defined as RRR = 1 − RAR (higher RAR reflects poorer security performance). As shown in Figure 9, KS-test selected features perform similar to GRLVQI selected features in the case of rogue rejection. When selecting a threshold such that TVR > 90%, the KS-test feature set achieves an RRR > 90% in 29 of 36 rogue scenarios considered

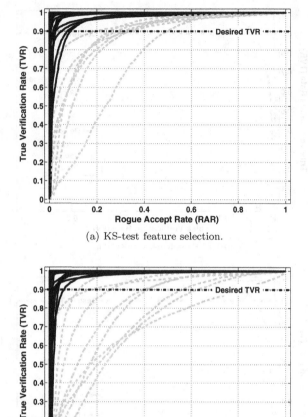

(a) KS-test feature selection.

(b) GRLVQI feature selection.

Figure 9.   Rogue device rejection for $N_U = 6$ unauthorized devices.

while the GRLVQI selected features are successful in 28 of 36 scenarios (shown as solid black ROC curves).

4.   Conclusions

Unauthorized ZigBee network access is a serious concern in industrial control and building automation systems. RF fingerprinting techniques have the potential to identify rogue devices that spoof the bit-level credentials of authorized devices. The experimental results demonstrate that ID verification with dimensionally-efficient RF fingerprints can detect and reject unauthorized rogue devices very effectively. The RF fingerprints were obtained using a dimensional reduction analysis process with relevant features identified by a pre-classification KS-test process and a post-classification GRLVQI process.

The MDA-based device ID verification process was demonstrated using $N_D = 4$ authorized devices. Using RF fingerprints comprising DRA $\approx 93\%$ of the feature subset, the classification performance benchmark of $\%C = 90\%$ was achieved at SNR ≈ 18 dB for the KS-test and GRLVQI selected features, and each method yielded a TVR greater than 90% and an FVR less than 10% for all authorized devices. The KS-test feature set achieved a rogue reject rate exceeding 90% in 29 of 36 rogue scenarios considered while the GRLVQI selected features were successful in 28 of 36 scenarios.

Note that the views expressed in this paper are those of the authors and do not reflect the official policy or position of the U.S. Air Force, U.S. Department of Defense or the U.S. Government.

References

[1] C. Dubendorfer, B. Ramsey and M. Temple, An RF-DNA verification process for ZigBee networks, *Proceedings of the Military Communications Conference*, pp. 1–6, 2012.

[2] R. Duda, P. Hart and D. Stork, *Pattern Classification*, Wiley, New York, 2001.

[3] T. Fawcett, *ROC Graphs: Notes and Practical Considerations for Researchers*, Kluwer Academic, Dordrecht, The Netherlands, 2004.

[4] R. Klein, M. Temple and M. Mendenhall, Application of wavelet-based RF fingerprinting to enhance wireless network security, *Journal of Communications and Networks*, vol. 11(6), pp. 544–555, 2009.

[5] R. Klein, M. Temple, M. Mendenhall and D. Reising, Sensitivity analysis of burst detection and RF fingerprinting classification performance, *Proceedings of the IEEE International Conference on Communications*, 2009.

[6] B. Ramsey, M. Temple and B. Mullins, PHY foundation for multi-factor ZigBee node authentication, *Proceedings of the IEEE Global Telecommunications Conference*, pp. 795–800, 2012.

[7] D. Reising, Exploitation of RF-DNA for Device Classification and Verification Using GRLVQI Processing, Ph.D. Dissertation, Department of Electrical and Computer Engineering, Air Force Institute of Technology, Wright-Patterson Air Force Base, Ohio, 2012.

[8] D. Reising, M. Temple and M. Oxley, Gabor-based RF-DNA fingerprinting for classifying 802.16e WiMAX mobile subscribers, *Proceedings of the International Conference on Computing, Networking and Communications*, pp. 7–13, 2012.

[9] W. Suski, M. Temple, M. Mendenhall and R. Mills, Using spectral fingerprints to improve wireless network security, *Proceedings of the IEEE Global Telecommunications Conference*, 2008.

[10] M. Williams, M. Temple and D. Reising, Augmenting bit-level network security using physical layer RF-DNA fingerprinting, *Proceedings of the IEEE Global Telecommunications Conference*, 2010.

[11] J. Wright, KillerBee: Framework and tools for exploiting ZigBee and IEEE 802.15.4 networks, version 1.0 (`code.google.com/p/killerbee`).

Chapter 5

DEFENSIVE REKEYING STRATEGIES FOR PHYSICAL-LAYER-MONITORED LOW-RATE WIRELESS PERSONAL AREA NETWORKS*

Benjamin Ramsey and Barry Mullins

Abstract   ZigBee networks are integrating rapidly into critical infrastructures such as the smart grid and public health centers. Numerous ZigBee-based smart meters have been installed in metropolitan areas and hospitals commonly employ ZigBee technology for patient and equipment monitoring. The associated ZigBee networks transport sensitive information and must be secured against exfiltration and denial-of-service attacks. Indeed, novel tools that exploit and disrupt ZigBee networks are already under development. Security monitors that can uniquely identify nodes by their radio frequency characteristics can be a valuable countermeasure if implemented in a practical manner. This paper investigates rekeying in response to suspected malicious devices that may be internal or external to a ZigBee network. It extends prior discussions of practical physical layer monitor implementation, and introduces a novel backward-compatible ZigBee message obfuscation technique based on preamble modifications. Experimental results demonstrate that common wireless ZigBee sniffers can be thwarted with 100% effectiveness without reducing packet reception to specific transceiver models.

Keywords: ZigBee networks, security, RF fingerprinting, cyber-physical systems

1.   Introduction

ZigBee networks provide low-rate, low-power and low-cost wireless connectivity through standards that build upon the IEEE 802.15.4 low-rate wireless personal area network (LR-WPAN) physical (PHY) and medium access con-

J. Butts and S. Shenoi (Eds.): Critical Infrastructure Protection VII, IFIP AICT 417, pp. 63–79, 2013.
© IFIP International Federation for Information Processing 2013 (outside the US)

trol (MAC) specifications [13]. ZigBee Smart Energy, Building Automation and Health Care standards have enabled ZigBee networks to become significant components in critical infrastructures around the world, including tens of millions of utility meters with bidirectional communications incorporated in advanced metering infrastructures [23]. Critical ZigBee networks form cyber-physical systems, where malicious activity on the networks affects the physical behavior of appliances and electrical systems. Public health networks employing ZigBee technology are also common in civilian and military hospitals. Disruptions of these networks can impact medical equipment and patient monitoring, possibly endangering lives.

The ZigBee security architecture relies on the safekeeping of symmetric keys to implement message confidentiality, message integrity, and device authentication. While the small size and low complexity of ZigBee devices make them effective to deploy in large numbers, these traits also result in tight constraints on device memory and computations. A single network key (NK) is shared by every device in a ZigBee network, although device-to-device confidentiality is also possible using link keys (LK) at the application layer. Small, inexpensive wireless sensors are unlikely to have robust defenses against theft and tampering, resulting in physical vulnerabilities to key confidentiality [20]. Key extraction from first- and second-generation ZigBee chips has been shown to be relatively straightforward [9], and inexpensive tools have been developed for locating ZigBee devices [15, 18]. Keys may also be compromised through social engineering or keys may intercepted (if transmitted to end devices without encryption) by open source tools such as KillerBee [24] and Api-do [21].

The ZigBee specification is dependent on symmetric cryptography, which precludes key distribution without a central authority called the trust center (TC). The computational complexity of symmetric cryptography is lower than that of public key cryptography. The tradeoff, however, is a significantly more challenging key management process.

Previous research has investigated the application of public key cryptography to ZigBee devices and networks [2, 10–12, 17]; this research has contributed to a provision in the ZigBee Smart Energy Profile for secure LK establishment through certificates signed by a certificate authority [25]. The alternative key establishment procedure is based on a shared master key (MK) used to derive the LK. If the MK is not preloaded on the end device, the TC broadcasts it without encryption, potentially compromising the subsequent LK establishment.

Methods for detecting rogue devices in ZigBee-type networks are an active area of research, including anomalous-behavior-based fingerprinting [14] and radio frequency (RF) device fingerprinting [6, 8, 19]. Given the threats to ZigBee symmetric keys, an efficient and secure redistribution of keys must occur to thwart a known eavesdropper or active rogue device on the network.

This paper examines rekeying strategies for a compromised ZigBee network. In particular, it investigates how PHY-based monitoring systems proposed in [6, 8, 19] can be integrated in ZigBee networks. Also, the paper describes a novel method for protecting sensitive ZigBee traffic from eavesdroppers using modified PHY preambles.

2. Key Distribution

Key distribution mechanisms in wireless sensor and control networks have four general requirements [3]:

- **Scalability:** The key distribution mechanism must remain practical for a large increase in the number of network devices.

- **Efficiency:** The key distribution mechanism must involve limited memory usage, computational complexity and communications complexity.

- **Probability of Key Sharing:** Key sharing among devices must be limited to what is necessary to implement the desired network functionality.

- **Resilience:** The key distribution mechanism must be resistant to node tampering and theft. In particular, security credentials that are extracted from a device or eavesdropped should not reveal security information of other devices in the network.

Note that these four requirements are generally mutually exclusive. Thus, every key distribution solution must make trade-offs as appropriate.

2.1 ZigBee Nodes and Topologies

The IEEE 802.15.4 standard for wireless MAC and PHY specifications defines two primary device types: (i) full function devices (FFDs); and (ii) reduced function devices (RFDs) [13]. Mains-powered FFDs are always actively listening on the network, whereas RFDs are battery powered and primarily operate in the sleep mode, waking up only to check for pending messages or periodic updates.

ZigBee specifies three node classes within the IEEE 802.15.4 construct: (i) ZigBee coordinator (ZC); (ii) ZigBee router (ZR); and (iii) ZigBee end device (ZED). The ZCs and ZRs must be FFDs, while ZEDs can be either FFDs or RFDs. There can only be one ZC per WPAN, and it is responsible for establishing the network, allocating network layer addresses and routing traffic. The network fails without the ZC. ZRs extend the wireless range by routing messages between their child RFD ZEDs using multi-hop configurations, such as the cluster tree and mesh topologies is shown in Figure 1. Note that the star topology is shown for completeness; however, it does not support multi-hop communications. In a cluster tree topology, ZEDs have no children and can only communicate with the ZC and other ZEDs through their parent ZR. The ZigBee stack profile 0x01 limits the number of children for each ZR to $N_c = 20$, six of which can be ZRs. The ZigBee PRO specification (stack profile 0x02) increases this limit to $N_c = 254$ children per ZR. Mesh topologies are only allowed under ZigBee PRO, and permit FFD ZEDs to communicate directly with each another to form a self-healing network.

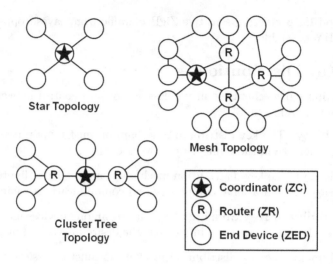

Figure 1. ZigBee LR-WPAN topologies.

2.2　Stationary Networks

The term "stationary network" refers to a network in which the logical and physical topologies are both fixed. It includes the star and cluster tree topologies. ZigBee networks for building and home automation, utility meter reading, industrial control and environmental sensing typically utilize stationary networks. Unlike mobile nodes, stationary nodes can be mains powered and always active.

The ZigBee Smart Energy Profile describes standard practices suitable for securing stationary networks [26]. In order to join a network, every new device must pass an administrator-directed commissioning process. The commissioning process is not typically automated because neighboring systems have no way to identify the devices that should be associated with one another without administrator guidance [4]. At no point should any cryptographic keys be transmitted in the clear, a recommendation that is mirrored in [16]. At a high level of abstraction, a typical device commissioning process involves the following steps [26]:

- The ZC is informed via out-of-band means (e.g., remote login, handheld controller or phone call to a service center) that a new device must be added to the network.

- The network enters into a permit joining ON state for a short period of time (e.g., 10 seconds).

- The installer, with physical access to the new device, presses a button or navigates a menu that instructs the new device to attempt to join the network through a join procedure.

- The new device attempts to join the network. After the new device is verified as being authentic by its MAC address and/or secret key, it receives new cryptographic keys and successfully joins the network.

- The installer receives visual feedback from the new device that the network join was successful.

- The new device may now operate in the network.

The short window of the commissioning process protects against rogue devices from joining the network. This process is also robust against tools like KillerBee's `zbassocflood` that transmit numerous association requests from spoofed MAC addresses to exhaust the network address pool in a denial-of-service attack.

Smart Energy Profile standards identify three types of keys: (i) NK; (ii) application layer LKs shared by pairs of devices; and (iii) trust center link keys (TCLKs), which are LKs that are shared by a device and the TC. The NK is common to all devices in a network and protects management and control communications [26]. LKs provide end-to-end confidentiality. The TC periodically refreshes the NK to protect the network from cryptographic attacks from outside the network (e.g., key cracking). The NK must also be refreshed in response to a suspected rogue device within the network. Rekeying is thus performed point-to-point from the TC to every trusted device on the network using TCLKs for confidentiality. The complexity of this action amounts to $O(n)$, where n is the number of devices in the network. After every trusted device receives the new NK, the broadcasted `Switch Key` command instructs all devices to simultaneously switch to the new NK. The TC also revokes any LKs that were previously established to a rogue device.

2.3 Mobile Networks

The term "mobile network" refers to a network in which the logical and physical topologies change unpredictably. Examples include medical patient monitoring and inventory tracking systems. Mobile devices may drift out of communication range of other network nodes long enough to require a network rejoin, which cannot be performed manually as with stationary networks. Physical security is also significantly more difficult to maintain for mobile devices.

The ZigBee Health Care Profile [27] provides key distribution recommendations for mobile networks. As with stationary networks, key delivery in the clear is prohibited. Instead, NK and LK distribution proceeds via mandatory TCLKs. Mobile nodes are also much more likely than stationary nodes to be battery powered; therefore, the nodes spend significant time in the sleep mode. If a network layer rekey occurs while a medical device is asleep, it will experience a delay in reporting its sensing data because it must first receive the new NK. To minimize such delays, devices should check periodically if they have the current NK [27]. Rekeying requires all end devices to expend more of their finite energy supply than is functionally necessary, so the rate of periodic rekeying must be set based on battery longevity requirements. Nevertheless, rekeying in response to a suspected rogue device is essential.

2.4   Alternative Key Distribution Methods

Numerous key distribution mechanisms exist for ZigBee-like wireless sensor networks and *ad hoc* networks [3]. Each key distribution mechanism results in different computational, energy and memory burdens being placed on network nodes. The ZigBee protocol stack requires that the NK be shared by all the devices in a network. This fundamental requirement necessitates that NK rekeying be performed on every network device if the NK is suspected to be compromised.

The TC must revoke all point-to-point LKs established between a benign device and the suspected rogue device. In this case, techniques that reduce the number of required LKs also reduce the number of required LK revocations. For example, the upper limit for a ZigBee network is $2^{16} \approx 65{,}000$ nodes, requiring $n(n-1)/2 \approx 2$ billion LKs for full connectivity. In a hierarchical keying system [22], the number of required LKs reduces to $log_2(n) + 2 = 18$ LKs. However, full connectivity is rare in practice, and LKs are frequently limited to communications between end devices and their associated data aggregation nodes. Note that spatial clustering methods, including the Hubenko Architecture [1], are not relevant to ZigBee LK rekeying because LKs secure unicast traffic rather than multicast traffic. Indeed, a compromised node reveals nothing about the LKs in use by any two other nodes, so TC-directed LK revocation is sufficient for threat mitigation.

3.   ZigBee Air Monitor Integration

Recent research [8, 19] has proposed a ZigBee air monitor (ZAM) system to secure networks by observing wireless transmission characteristics to augment bit-layer security mechanisms. Dubendorfer, *et al.* [8] have demonstrated the feasibility of unique device-level identification under realistic indoor office conditions. The next three sections explore how ZAMs can integrate into and defend critical ZigBee networks organized in star, cluster tree and mesh topologies.

3.1   Star Topology

The star topology is the least complex ZigBee network topology. In this topology, end devices communicate solely with the ZC. ZigBee PRO allows a ZR or ZC to have up to $N_c = 254$ child nodes, but such a dense network can experience significant transmission congestion. A best practice is to limit the number of devices in an area to utilize spatial reuse [5]. The utilization ratio U is given by:

$$U = \frac{4 < Density < 16}{Total\ Devices} \tag{1}$$

where the density (i.e., number of devices per unit area where the unit used is the square of their reliable range) is between four and sixteen. A star network should, therefore, be limited to approximately fourteen end devices (15 devices − 1 coordinator).

The ZAM is co-located with the ZC and observes every transmission, sending a packet reject notice to the ZC through a wired channel if the RF fingerprint of the packet does not closely match the fingerprint stored in the ZAM for the claimed origin device [19]. The ZigBee application support (APS) layer permits up to two retries for each packet. False rejections of packets from trusted devices follow a binomial distribution with the probability p of successful packet delivery given by:

$$p = 1 - (\rho + PER)^{1+r} \qquad (2)$$

where ρ is the probability of false rejection, PER is the packet error rate for the network and r is the number of total retries by the APS layer. For $\rho = 0.2$, $r = 2$ and $PER = 0.1$, the probability of benign packet delivery exceeds 99%. Dubendorfer, *et al.* [8] report rejection rates of $\rho \leq 0.2$ for seven like-model devices at $SNR = 10$ dB. For star topology networks with mains-powered devices, the energy spent on retransmission due to false packet rejections is negligible, particularly in a neighborhood advanced metering infrastructure where utility usage and pricing updates occur a few times per hour. A low utilization ratio as mentioned above mitigates network congestion introduced by frequent packet retransmissions.

The ZAM must make verification decisions within a short time, constrained by the transmission timeout settings at the APS layer. A typical value for the unicast timeout is $t = 1.6$ seconds per try, for a total of $t_{total} = 4.8$ seconds [7]. Computational and memory usage requirements increase for the ZAM as the number of nodes increases, but the unicast timeout places a strict upper limit on the total packet accept/reject response time.

3.2 Cluster Tree Topology

The cluster tree topology extends the scale of a stationary ZigBee network beyond that of the star topology by leveraging spatial reuse and a data aggregation backbone of ZRs. The utilization ratio defined in Equation (1) still applies, limiting the practical number of child nodes per ZR, while the total number of nodes can increase substantially.

ZAMs co-located with every ZR provide oversight of all network traffic and provide the same per-packet rejection feedback for child nodes in their cluster as described in the star topology. The device fingerprint database in each ZAM remains at the approximate scale of the star topology scenario. No sharing of fingerprint information between ZAMs is necessary because the network nodes do not stray from their ZRs.

3.3   Mesh Topology

The mesh topology poses the greatest security challenge among the three topologies. ZAMs distributed throughout the mesh network physical topology observe all network traffic, including point-to-point traffic between ZEDs. ZAMs co-located with the core ZRs may be sufficient for full network observation, otherwise additional ZAMs must be co-located with sufficient FFD ZEDs to cover the outermost traffic. FFDs are mains powered, so power is also available for the co-located ZAMs.

FFD ZRs and ZEDs, with co-located ZAMs, receive wired per-packet feedback as in the star and cluster tree topologies. However, the logical network topology is variable and an FFD ZED unattached to a ZAM can receive a packet from a neighboring ZED. In this case, the receiving ZED requests a packet accept/reject feedback from the observing ZAM using the ZigBee network. An alternative solution is to require all packets to traverse FFDs with co-located ZAMs while still allowing the logical topology to change over time. The variable mesh topology increases the number of fingerprints that each ZAM must store to verify true packet origin, with an upper bound of n representing a fingerprint profile for every network node.

4.   PHY-Based Sensitive Message Obfuscation

Although they are functionally consistent, transceiver implementations vary between manufacturers due to their design, components used and other unique attributes. These variations provide an opportunity to develop unique signatures for fingerprinting devices based on their implementation characteristics. This section describes a method for preventing common wireless sniffers from detecting ZigBee packets, while retaining their compatibility with available hardware. The method involves varying the length of the IEEE 802.15.4 preamble and measuring response differences that result from manufacturer implementations.

4.1   Methodology

The IEEE 802.15.4 beacon request is a standard command used by a device to locate all coordinators within transmission range. Replies by the coordinators are compulsory (i.e., unicast frames with the acknowledgment flag set garner replies from individually addressed devices).

A Tektronix TDS6124C digital storage oscilloscope was used to receive and store a single beacon request using a Ramsey LPY2 log periodic antenna with 6 dBi gain. The sampling rate R_s was 1.25 GS/s and the collection length l_c was 1 ms, which was long enough to capture the entire $l = 512$ μs beacon request. The collection yielded a vector of 1.25 million data points. All ZigBee transmissions at $f_c = 2.4$ GHz begin with a $l = 128$ μs preamble of $l_p = 32$ bits represented by eight O-QPSK symbols. As shown in Figure 2, when the

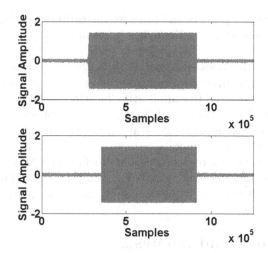

Figure 2. Beacon requests with standard (top) and shortened preambles (bottom).

first half of the preamble (four O-QPSK symbols) is absent, the entire beacon request transmission shortens by 12.5%.

A Tektronix AWG7102 arbitrary waveform generator was used to replay the original and modified beacon requests through the same Ramsey LPY2 log periodic antenna used for signal collection. The center frequency remained constant at $f_c = 2480$ MHz to mitigate interference from neighboring IEEE 802.11 networks during the experiments. The received signal strength was approximately −79 dBm at the target devices and the response behavior remained constant through differing distances and signal strengths. All the hardware devices correctly replied to the original beacon request, but not all the devices replied to modified beacon requests. This indicates that some transceiver types cannot synchronize to the shortened preambles and are unable to interpret the message contents.

Figure 3. Atmel RZUSBStick (left) and Microchip ZENA wireless adapter (right).

4.2   ZigBee Sniffer Hardware

Two widely available hardware platforms for wireless ZigBee sniffing are the Atmel RZUSBStick and the Microchip ZENA wireless adapter (Figure 3). Both platforms are inexpensive, contain a USB connector, include support for real-time viewing of ZigBee packets and can save the captured traffic to a local file. A limiting factor common to both devices is the lack of support for an external antenna.

The RZUSBStick includes an Atmel AT86RF230 transceiver with -101 dBm receiver sensitivity and maximum transmit power of $P_t = 3$ dBm. Atmel Wireless Studio is the associated free application for wireless sniffing. Alternatively, open source KillerBee software and firmware fully support the RZUSBStick, enabling arbitrary ZigBee packet generation, key sniffing, denial-of-service attacks and transmitter positioning.

The ZENA wireless adapter includes a Microchip MRF24J40MA transceiver module with -94 dBm receiver sensitivity. The Microchip Wireless Development Studio, which controls wireless sniffing on the adapter, may be downloaded free of charge.

4.3   Results and Analysis

The six device types considered in this research included the two sniffers (Atmel AT86RF230, Microchip MRF24J40MA) and four other transceivers configured as coordinators (XBee XBP24CZ7PIS, Freescale MC13213, Texas Instruments (TI) CC2420 and Jennic JN5148). Beacon requests with shortened preambles emanated from the arbitrary waveform generator toward the six device types simultaneously. Beacon replies occured within milliseconds and were staggered to avoid collisions using the PHY Carrier Sensing Multiple Access Collision Avoidance Algorithm. In the case of the two sniffers, correctly interpreted packets appeared in the display windows of the sniffing control software. The four transceiver models configured as ZigBee coordinators replied to the correctly-interpreted beacon requests, and the two sniffers recorded all the replies for post-experiment analysis. Each preamble modification was transmitted a total of 100 times – five repetitions of 20 transmissions each.

The mean packet reception exceeded 98% for all device types when the beacon requests were transmitted with standard preambles. When the standard eight O-QPSK symbol preamble was shortened to five symbols, two of the six transceiver models began experiencing difficulty interpreting the packets. Figure 4 shows the mean ZigBee packet reception rates at a 95% confidence interval when only 5/8 of the preamble was present. The Atmel transceiver received a mean of 40% of the beacons, while the XBee transceiver received a mean of 87% of the beacons. No significant loss in packet reception occured for the Microchip, Freescale, TI and Jennic transceivers.

Figure 5 shows the mean ZigBee packet reception rates at a 95% confidence interval when only 4/8 of the preamble was present. In both cases, the sniffers were unable to interpret any of the packets. The XBee transceiver was thwarted, while the Freescale, TI and Jennic transceivers experienced no significant difficulty receiving packets. The Freescale MC13213 could not interpret packets with preambles shorter than four O-QPSK symbols, while the TI CC2420 and Jennic JN5148 still received all the packets.

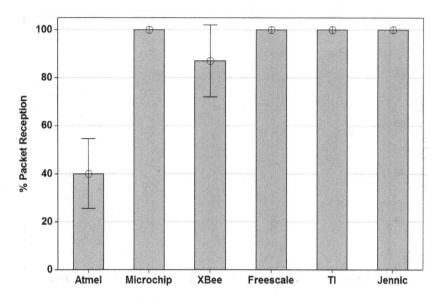

Figure 4. Packet reception rate per device type (5/8 preamble).

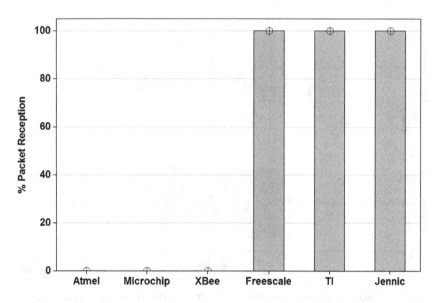

Figure 5. Packet reception rate per device type (4/8 or 12/8 preamble).

Figure 6 shows the mean ZigBee packet reception rates at a 95% confidence interval when only 2/8 of the preamble was present. Consistent with the experimental trend, only the TI and Jennic hardware correctly interpreted packets. The Jennic JN5148 continued to interpret packets without difficulty, while the TI CC2420 failed to interpret approximately half of the packets.

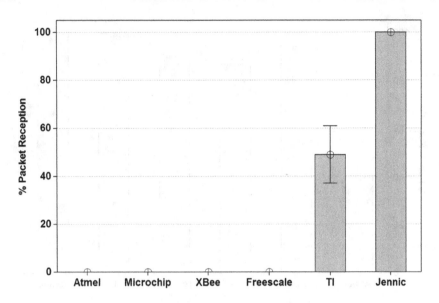

Figure 6.   Packet reception rate per device type (2/8 preamble).

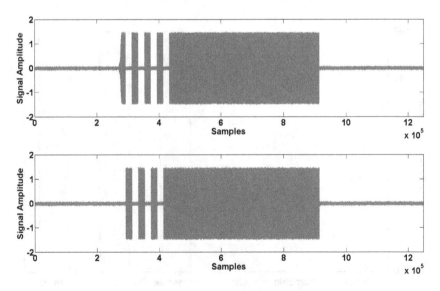

Figure 7.   Beacon requests – odd (top) and even (bottom) preamble symbols.

Hundreds of O-QPSK symbol-wise modifications to the standard preamble are possible, providing a sizable search space for future research. The two modifications investigated in this paper are perforated preambles with only odd numbered symbols and only even numbered symbols present (Figure 7). Packet reception rates for the two perforated preamble modifications are shown in Figures 8 and 9. When only odd-numbered symbols were present (symbols

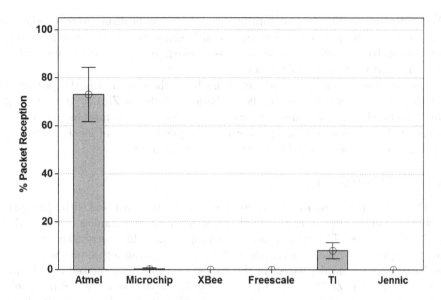

Figure 8. Packet reception rate per device type (odd preamble symbols).

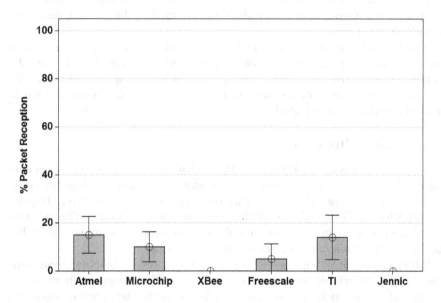

Figure 9. Packet reception rate per device type (even preamble symbols).

1, 3, 5 and 7), the Atmel AT86RF230 interpreted approximately 75% of the packets, the TI CC2420 interpreted less than 10% and all the other devices were effectively thwarted. In the case of the second perforated preamble where only even-numbered symbols were present, all six device types found it difficult to interpret packets – the mean packet reception rates fell below 20% for all the transceivers. The two perforated preamble modifications were similar in composition, but they resulted in significantly different packet reception rates. The transceiver-specific responses to non-standard preambles reveal underlying differences in hardware implementations.

A promising research avenue stemming from these results is the potential for the remote identification of the make and model of ZigBee transceivers. Remote classification of transceiver models is essential for comprehensive cyber situational awareness, including identifying rogue devices and locating devices that are vulnerable to specific key extraction techniques.

5. Discussion

The packet reception rates suggest that interrogation packets with appropriately modified preambles can uniquely identify transceiver models based on the packet reply rates. This fingerprinting technique somewhat mirrors the network and transport layer based operating system fingerprinting techniques pioneered by Nmap. For example, based on the six device types investigated in this paper, an unknown ZigBee device that responds to packets with 4/8 preamble but not to packets with 2/8 preamble is most likely to be a Freescale MC13213 transceiver. Our future research will leverage these preliminary results to develop a remote ZigBee transceiver identification methodology to enhance cyber situational awareness.

An alternative strategy for identifying rogue devices and active eavesdroppers is to broadcast acknowledgement requests with preambles that are invisible to trusted hardware. An observed reply could only have originated from a device that is not a part of the trusted network. Such a device could then be tracked down and investigated.

6. Conclusions

ZigBee networks are widely used in the critical infrastructure, but an increasing number of tools are being developed to exploit and disrupt these networks. Under these circumstances, a rekeying technique that can effectively respond to suspected malicious ZigBee devices has considerable value. The rekeying technique proposed in this paper employs novel backward-compatible ZigBee message obfuscation based on preamble modifications.

Experiments involving the rekeying technique reveal that common wireless ZigBee sniffers can be thwarted with 100% effectiveness without reducing packet reception by transceiver models. In particular, specially-modified ZigBee messages sent to Freescale MC13213, TI CC2420 and Jennic JN5148 transceivers can be protected from interception by two popular sniffers and the XBee XBP24CZ7PIS, simply by shortening the IEEE 802.15.4 preamble by 50%. Packets with preambles reduced to 25% of the IEEE 802.15.4 specification completely thwart the Freescale MC13213. Alternatively, covert communications to Atmel AT86RF230 transceivers is possible using perforated preambles where only the odd-numbered O-QPSK symbols are present. When combined

with effective rekeying strategies, message obfuscation can effectively complement network defense. An important advantage is that the message obfuscation
is backward compatible with tens of millions of existing ZigBee devices and can
be leveraged to defend key exchanges or any other sensitive message traffic in
wireless networks.

Note that the views expressed in this paper are those of the authors and do
not reflect the official policy or position of the U.S. Air Force, U.S. Department
of Defense or the U.S. Government.

Acknowledgements

The authors wish to thank John M. Greenwell for his invaluable support
with the test equipment.

References

[1] C. Antosh, B. Mullins, R. Baldwin and R. Raines, A comparison of keying methods in the Hubenko Architecture as applied to wireless sensor
networks, *International Journal of Autonomous and Adaptive Communication Systems*, vol. 3(3), pp. 350–368, 2010.

[2] M. Blaser, Industrial-strength security for ZigBee: The case for public-key
cryptography, *Embedded Computing Design*, May 13, 2005.

[3] S. Camtepe and B. Yener, Key Distribution Mechanisms for Wireless Sensor Networks: A Survey, Technical Report TR-05-07, Department of Computer Science, Rensselaer Polytechnic Institute, Troy, New York, 2005.

[4] Daintree Networks, Understanding ZigBee Commissioning, Mountain
View, California, 2007.

[5] Daintree Networks, Building and Operating Robust and Reliable ZigBee
Networks, Mountain View, California, 2008.

[6] B. Danev and S. Capkun, Transient-based identification of wireless sensor
nodes, *Proceedings of the International Conference on Information Processing in Sensor Networks*, pp. 25–36, 2009.

[7] Digi International, XBee/XBee-PRO ZB SMT Modules, Minnetonka,
Minnesota (ftp1.digi.com/support/documentation/90002002_C.pdf),
2012.

[8] C. Dubendorfer, B. Ramsey and M. Temple, An RF-DNA verification
process for ZigBee networks, *Proceedings of the Military Communications
Conference*, 2012.

[9] T. Goodspeed, Extracting keys from second generation ZigBee chips, Presented at the *Black Hat USA Conference*, 2009.

[10] J. Heo and C. Hong, Efficient and authenticated key agreement mechanism
in low-rate WPAN environment, *Proceedings of the First International
Symposium on Wireless Pervasive Computing*, 2006.

[11] Q. Huang, J. Cukier, H. Kobayashi, B. Liu and J. Zhang, Fast authenticated key establishment protocols for self-organizing sensor networks, *Proceedings of the Second ACM International Conference on Wireless Sensor Networks and Applications*, pp. 141–150, 2003.

[12] Q. Huang, H. Kobayashi and B. Liu, Energy/security scalable mobile cryptosystem, *Proceedings of the Fourteenth IEEE International Symposium on Personal, Indoor and Mobile Radio Communications*, vol. 3, pp. 2755–2759, 2003.

[13] Institute of Electrical and Electronics Engineers, Wireless Medium Access Control (MAC) and Physical Layer (PHY) Specifications for Low-Rate Wireless Personal Area Networks (WPANs), Part 15.4, IEEE Standard 802.15.4a-2007, New York, 2007.

[14] P. Jokar, H. Nicanfar and V. Leung, Specification-based intrusion detection for home area networks in smart grids, *Proceedings of the IEEE International Conference on Smart Grid Communications*, pp. 208–213, 2011.

[15] C. Kiraly and G. Picco, Where's the mote? Ask the MoteHunter! *Proceedings of the Thirty-Seventh IEEE Conference on Local Computer Networks (Workshop on Practical Issues in Building Sensor Network Applications)*, pp. 982–990, 2012.

[16] K. Masica, Recommended Practices Guide for Securing ZigBee Wireless Networks in Process Control System Environments, Draft, U.S. CERT, Department of Homeland Security, Washington, DC, 2007.

[17] S. Nguyen and C. Rong, ZigBee security using identity-based cryptography, *Proceedings of the Fourth International Conference on Autonomic and Trusted Computing*, pp. 3–12, 2007.

[18] B. Ramsey, B. Mullins and E. White, Improved tools for indoor ZigBee warwalking, *Proceedings of the Thirty-Seventh IEEE Conference on Local Computer Networks (Workshop on Practical Issues in Building Sensor Network Applications)*, pp. 925–928, 2012.

[19] B. Ramsey, M. Temple and B. Mullins, PHY foundation for multi-factor ZigBee node authentication, *Proceedings of the IEEE Global Telecommunications Conference*, pp. 813–818, 2012.

[20] E. Shi and A. Perrig, Designing secure sensor networks, *IEEE Wireless Communications*, vol. 11(6), pp. 38–43, 2004.

[21] R. Speers and R. Melgares, Api-do: Tools for ZigBee and 802.15.4 Security Auditing, Department of Computer Science, Dartmouth College, Hanover, New Hampshire (`code.google.com/p/zigbee-security`), 2012.

[22] Y. Sun and K. Liu, Hierarchical group access control for secure multicast communications, *IEEE/ACM Transactions on Networking*, vol. 15(6), pp. 1514–1526, 2007.

[23] T. Whittaker, Final word, *Control and Automation*, vol. 18(3), p. 48, 2007.

[24] J. Wright, KillerBee: Framework and Tools for Exploiting Zigbee and IEEE 802.15.4 Networks, Version 1.0, InGuardians, Washington, DC (`code.google.com/p/killerbee`), 2011.

[25] E. Yuksel, H. Nielson and F. Nielson, ZigBee-2007 security essentials, *Proceedings of the Thirteenth Nordic Workshop on Secure IT Systems*, pp. 65–82, 2008.

[26] ZigBee Alliance, ZigBee Smart Energy Profile Specification, ZigBee Document 075356r15, San Ramon, California, 2008.

[27] ZigBee Alliance, ZigBee Health Care Profile Specification, ZigBee Document 075360r15, San Ramon, California, 2010.

Chapter 6

A DISTRIBUTED REAL-TIME EVENT CORRELATION ARCHITECTURE FOR SCADA SECURITY

Yi Deng and Sandeep Shukla

Abstract   Supervisory control and data acquisition (SCADA) systems require real-time threat monitoring and early warning systems to identify cyber attacks. Organizations typically employ intrusion detection systems to identify attack events and to provide situational awareness. However, as cyber attacks become more sophisticated, intrusion detection signatures of single events are no longer adequate. Indeed, effective intrusion detection solutions require the correlation of multiple events that are temporally and/or spatially separated. This paper proposes an innovative event correlation mechanism for cyber threat detection, which engages a semantic event hierarchy. Cyber attacks are specified via low-level events detected in the communications and computing infrastructure and correlated to identify attacks of a broader scope. The paper also describes a distributed architecture for real-time event capture, correlation and dissemination. The architecture employs a publish/subscribe mechanism, which decentralizes limited computing resources to distributed field agents in order to enhance real-time attack detection while limiting unnecessary communications overhead.

Keywords: SCADA systems, event correlation, temporal-spatial correlation

1.   Introduction

Supervisory control and data acquisition (SCADA) systems are essential to the control and management of operations in the critical infrastructure (e.g., electrical power systems, water and wastewater treatment facilities, oil and gas pipelines, transportation assets and industrial process environments) [12]. A SCADA system uses sensors to monitor various physical quantities of the system under control and report them in real-time to a SCADA master (or control center). The execution of a state estimation algorithm, followed by

J. Butts and S. Shenoi (Eds.): Critical Infrastructure Protection VII, IFIP AICT 417, pp. 81–93, 2013.

the application of control laws, generate control inputs that are sent to field devices to manipulate the control settings of actuators. In the case of an emergency (e.g., abnormal behavior is detected), the SCADA system must execute contingency responses to restore the system. Advanced communications techniques are widely adopted in SCADA systems to ensure the accurate and timely transmission of sensor data and control inputs [16].

In most SCADA systems, administrators are able to monitor and manipulate the data generated by field devices remotely – even from their homes. Often, field devices installed in remote areas are connected to an integrated network, which eliminates manual surveillance and maintenance of the devices. The use of networking technologies provides convenience for system operators, increased productivity for maintenance personnel and greater efficiency for critical infrastructure asset owners.

However, the adoption of advanced communications and computing technologies increases the susceptibility to cyber attacks. Consider the notorious Stuxnet malware that targeted a nuclear processing plant in Iran. Stuxnet was designed with four zero-day attacks and highly complicated intrusion functionality. It spread indiscriminately through flash drives and targeted Siemens industrial control equipment running a specific version of Microsoft Windows [6, 10]. Stuxnet significantly increased concerns about SCADA security. Meanwhile, several industry consortia (e.g., ISAC), standards agencies (e.g., NIST and NERC) and government agencies (e.g., DHS) have developed publications that outline regulations, best practices and guidelines for securing SCADA systems from cyber attacks.

In traditional information technology (IT) systems, intrusion detection systems (IDSs) are deployed to detect network-borne attacks. However, intrusion detection associated with SCADA networks must augment or revamp traditional IDSs because events often occur in the physical system. In traditional IT systems, signature-based and anomaly-based IDSs are typically used to detect intrusions and malicious behavior based on predefined attack patterns and deviations from normal behavior, respectively [4, 11, 13]. Although IDSs have seen much success in traditional IT systems, there are some inherent disadvantages when they are employed in SCADA systems. First, most IDSs are not specifically designed for SCADA systems so they are incapable of analyzing SCADA-specific communications protocols. Second, depending on the application scenario, the number of reported events generated by an IDS can vary considerably. For example, under normal operating conditions, IDS events are reported at regular, specified intervals; however, during potential malicious events, the reporting rate may increase significantly. In the case of a SCADA system, an overwhelming number of events could potentially paralyze the system. Third, legacy SCADA systems have limited computing and communications resources; as a result, IDSs are unable to satisfy the real-time constraints imposed on SCADA systems. Consequently, it is important to design and develop SCADA-specific IDSs that meet the requirements of the operating environment.

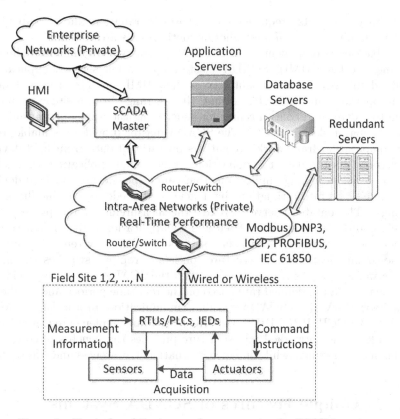

Figure 1. Typical architecture and components of a SCADA system.

2. SCADA System Architecture and Features

This section describes the architecture of a typical SCADA system and its principal features.

2.1 Distributed Architecture

A SCADA system is a mission-critical system that integrates advanced networking, computing and control technologies [19]. Although the scale of a SCADA system varies according to its application environment, it generally comprises three components: field site components, back-end platform components and a communications infrastructure (Figure 1).

The field site components generally include remote terminal units (RTUs), programmable logic controllers (PLCs), intelligent electronic devices (IEDs), remote sensors and actuators. RTUs are terminal devices that receive measurements from remote sensors and send instructions to actuators. PLCs are microprocessor-based controllers that can handle multiple inputs and outputs. IEDs are application-specific devices. In the electric power industry, IEDs measure voltages, currents, frequencies and phasor information, and are capable of tripping circuit breakers if anomalies or contingencies are detected.

The back-end components of a SCADA system typically include a human machine interface (HMI), SCADA master, application servers, application-specific databases and redundant servers. The HMI presents process data to human operators in a readable format. It can range from a single computer screen to a dedicated control center for supervising thousands of transmission lines at a major electric utility. The SCADA master provides a scalable, real-time computation framework. It gathers operational data from field devices and retransmits the data to application servers. The application servers implement decision-making applications that cannot be executed by field devices (e.g., wide-area state estimation, intelligent load shedding and intelligent islanding). The database servers archive the measurements and process data as well as provide data retrieval services for applications. Redundant servers provide backup services to other data servers to enhance system reliability.

The communications infrastructure consists of routers, switches and intra-area networks. Data is transmitted between the SCADA master and field site components at a pre-defined rate based on the real-time performance of the internal network. Various SCADA-specific communications protocols (e.g., Modbus, DNP3, ICCP, PROFIBUS and IEC 61850) are implemented in SCADA systems [8]. The networked infrastructure provides the benefits of cost, time and manpower savings, while enhancing situational awareness and control flexibility.

2.2   Unique Features of SCADA Systems

Unlike traditional enterprise IT systems, SCADA systems require enhanced reliability and availability, real-time performance, determinism, concurrency and security.

- **Reliability and Availability:** The requirements of system reliability and availability for process control systems are much higher than those for IT systems. Traditional IT systems can tolerate service outages (e.g., a webpage becoming slow or unresponsive) due to unstable hardware or an overwhelming number of access requests. In the case of control systems, system availability is critical. Furthermore, the designed mean time between failures (MTBF) for a SCADA system is much higher than that for IT systems. For example, the MTBF requirement for RTU modules is recommended to be greater than 720,000 hours [1, 5, 15].

- **Real-Time Performance:** SCADA systems must meet real-time requirements. When a contingency occurs, a SCADA system must detect and respond with the appropriate actions before events cascade to produce a large-scale physical impact. Compared with the real-time requirements of multimedia systems and virtual-reality systems [3], a SCADA system is required to meet strict, deterministic deadlines to ensure proper operation.

- **Determinism:** To safely manage a control system, SCADA systems require strict determinism to prevent random, uncertain or unknown states. A SCADA system requires that the monitoring system correctly reflect the underlying status of the control system. However, the increasing complexity and scale make the determinism difficult to achieve. Additionally, network communications present a challenge with regard to determinism. In the past, the network topology of a SCADA system was regular and relatively static [19]. An experienced system operator was familiar with the topology and the logical relationships between field devices. When a fault event occurred, the operator could infer the fault location by manually analyzing event types. Current SCADA network topologies, however, change dynamically based on the applications and operating requirements.

- **Concurrency:** The number of sensors varies according to the scale of a SCADA system. As such, SCADA systems must handle the concurrency that occurs in communications and computing. The concurrency of a SCADA system should be defined in a hierarchical manner. From a high-level perspective, the SCADA system must handle multithreaded and multitasked processes. From a low-level perspective, the field devices must handle multiple inputs and outputs while permitting scalability.

- **Security:** SCADA systems are commonly interconnected to public and enterprise networks. The interconnections subject SCADA systems to inherent threats associated with network communications. Additionally, the minimal processing power of field site components and limited bandwidth prevent the deployment of traditional security protection mechanisms such as anti-virus software. Moreover, SCADA systems have to operate correctly without interruption; the consequences of failure range from loss of revenue to personal injury or death.

Table 1 compares the properties of IT systems and SCADA systems [17].

3.   Publish/Subscribe Paradigm

This section describes the publish/subscribe paradigm used for event correlation.

3.1   Event Correlation Techniques

Individual event analysis methods are typically adopted in order to enhance the security of SCADA systems. An event corresponds to an activity that is used to monitor, supervise or manipulate the system. Examples of events include a measurement uploading process, a remote login action into a field device, and a modification command issued by a system operator. Note that most operations in a SCADA system generate a series of events rather than a single event. For instance, a system operator may wish to check the operational

Table 1. Comparison between IT systems and SCADA systems [17].

Attributes	SCADA Systems	IT Systems
Availability	Extremely high	Low to medium
Integrity	Very high	Low to medium
Confidentiality	Low	High
Authentication	High	Medium
Time Criticality	Critical	Delays tolerated
System Life Cycle	15 years or more	3 to 5 years
Software Maintainability	Rare, informal, not always documented	Frequent, formal, documented
Interoperability	Critical	Not critical
Communications Protocols	DNP3, ICCP, Modbus, Fieldbus, PROFIBUS, BacNet	TCP/IP, UDP
Computing Performance	Very limited with older microprocessors	No limitation with new CPUs
Bandwidth	Limited	Very high
Administration	Centralized/localized	Centralized
Security Attack Impact	Process stability, equipment damage, environmental effects, personnel safety	Business impact

status of an IED located at a remote substation in order to check if the device needs maintenance. The request involves a series of events, such as logging into the master computer, invoking a maintenance application, establishing a communications channel, logging into the remote IED device, uploading history data, invoking the maintenance analysis application and recording the actions in the historical database. Based on these activities, event correlation can be performed to infer system behavior and identify the root causes of a problem or predict future trends.

Although sophisticated cyber attacks are usually stealthy and difficult to detect, they still induce anomalies and underlying events (e.g., abnormal packets, uncommon login attempts and sudden increase in traffic). If these events are analyzed individually, it is difficult to identify potential attacks. By utilizing event correlation techniques, however, an IDS can collect information from associated events to identify seemingly disparate attack actions. For example, when a SCADA system reports a login failure event, an event correlation engine would retrieve related events that occurred within a specified timeframe. If the number of login failures from the same IP address or the same region ex-

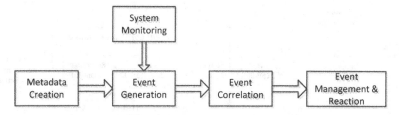

Figure 2. Processing flow in an event correlation system.

ceeds a predetermined threshold, then the event correlation engine can report a potential brute force login attack.

3.2   Event Correlation Flow

The general event correlation process involves a four-stage, pipelined data processing flow (Figure 2). In the first stage, Metadata Creation, distributed sensors create raw data. The remote sensors capture and measure analog signals and the status of systems in real time. Note that the sensors only generate unshaped metadata that is processed by field site components.

In the second stage, Event Generation, the field site components generate system events. In this stage, events are generated according to two situations. First, the field site components may generate events if abnormal behavior is detected in the metadata. The event generation process repackages the metadata according to a predefined event format and reports the events. Second, the field site components monitor the physical attributes of the system as it operates. Based on various requirements and configurations, the event generator identifies normal behavior event characteristics such as successful data transmission.

The third stage, Event Correlation, implements the event correlation engine in the SCADA master. Relying on application servers and database servers, the SCADA master collects all the events from the distributed field site components and uses correlation algorithms to analyze the events.

In the fourth stage, Event Management and Reaction, the event correlation engine sends results to higher-level event management applications. Since the events during this stage are dramatically decreased, only high-risk events are presented. The system operators responsible for interacting with applications perform the appropriate responses in the manual mode or in the automatic unattended mode.

3.3   Event Correlation Engine

Figure 3 shows the architecture of an event correlation engine. The engine has four main components: event queue, format decoder, event correlator, and rearrangement and output module.

When the dispersed events arrive at the event correlation engine, they are buffered to enable concurrent evaluation. Since SCADA systems have real-time

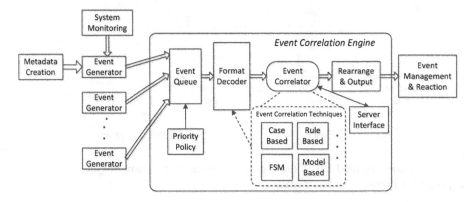

Figure 3. Event correlation engine architecture.

requirements, a priority management scheme is applied for high-risk events to ensure an adequate response time for emergencies. An event format decoder then extracts the effective segments from the primary event messages. After extraction, information is sent to the event correlator for analysis by event correlation algorithms. The event correlator interfaces with application servers and data servers to facilitate the retrieval of historical events. The event rearrangement and output module reformats the correlation results, packages statistical information and sends it to higher level applications.

3.4　　　Publish/Subscribe Mechanism

Event correlation techniques merge related events for evaluation. However, efficiency is a challenge for an event correlation engine. Commercially-available correlation engines (e.g., HP ECS, SMARTS and NerveCenter) typically have complex designs and user interfaces [9, 14, 18]. A primary reason is the requirement that a correlation engine must communicate continuously with every remote sensor. When remote field components upload primary events to an event correlation server, the event correlation engine buffers are filled with primary events, typically exhausting the resources.

We propose a publish/subscribe paradigm shown in Figure 4 to improve processing efficiency. The key aspect of the publish/subscribe paradigm is the integration of an authorized third party certification process in the event subscriber server. The event subscriber server alters the connections between the event correlation engine and the remote event generators from direct connections to subscription-oriented connections. This is a non-invasive online event correlation mechanism, which prevents interruptions of the remote field devices and event correlation server.

The publish/subscribe paradigm provides the possibility that the entire computing workload can be reduced by an order of magnitude. In this architecture, the distributed remote devices are considered to be event publishers and the event subscriber server is considered to be the subscriber. The event console

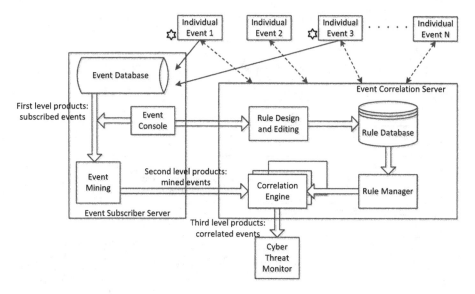

Figure 4. Automated publish/subscribe paradigm.

subscribes necessary information from different remote individuals and decisions can be made manually or automatically. Note that only the subscribed event publishers, marked with stars in Figure 4, are authorized to publish routine events to the event subscriber. This action decreases the amount of data transmitted, resulting in the more efficient use of the SCADA network. Additionally, partial workloads are allocated to remote devices, enhancing the computing performance of the event correlation server.

The event database is constructed and maintained as a two-dimensional data structure to simplify the event mining procedure. Patterns of the events that must be filtered are selected. Ultimately, a group of three-level hierarchical event correlation flows are constructed:

- **First Level Products:** Subscribed events.

- **Second Level Products:** Mined events.

- **Third Level Products:** Correlated events.

4.   Temporal-Spatial SCADA Events Correlation

A two-dimensional (temporal and spatial) event correlator mechanism is incorporated to improve correlation accuracy. Note that temporal-spatial event correlation techniques have been used successfully in IT infrastructures [2, 7]. However, existing event correlation techniques are not well-suited to SCADA systems due to timing and availability requirements.

Figure 5 shows a two-dimensional temporal-spatial event correlator. In the temporal dimension, the event correlator tracks the unusual events within a

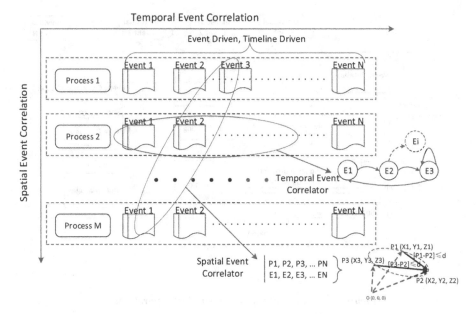

Figure 5. Two-dimensional (temporal and spatial) event correlator.

process using a sequential state machine $\{E1, E2, \ldots, EN\}$. As long as the state machine matches the predefined sequential rule patterns and reaches a final state Ei, the correlation engine triggers an event report to the correlator. For example, consider a scenario where the temporal event correlator is monitoring a repeat login attack where the attacker is attempting to access an account. The temporal event correlator enforces a limit on the number of failed attempts while abstracting the behavior as a state transition. When the sequential state machine reaches the final state, an alarm is triggered to indicate that the intrusion behavior has reached a high-risk level.

In the spatial dimension, the event correlator monitors the events that occur in the various processes and constructs multi-dimensional vectors $\{(P1, E1), (P2, E2), (P3, E3), \ldots, (Pi, Ej)\}$. Note that different processes can run on the same processor or different locations. Many attacks (e.g., distributed denial-of-service attacks) require coordinated actions. If the correlator were to detect the events individually, it would not trigger an event alarm. The proposed spatial event correlator, however, generates an index for each specific event and categorizes them into different security levels. The temporal-spatial event correlator automatically combines the two-dimensional process into a joint correlation procedure that prioritizes the tracking events.

5.   Implementation

We designed and implemented the event correlation tools and integrated them in a server-based platform. The experimental SCADA system shown in Figure 6 was constructed to analyze the effectiveness of the publish/subscribe

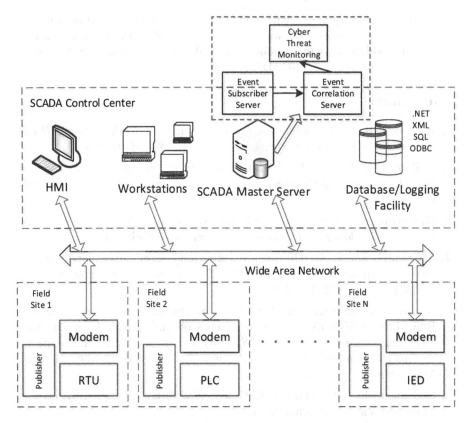

Figure 6. Experimental SCADA system.

temporal-spatial event correlation system. The experimental system deployed the publish function in every field device. The event subscriber server, the event correlation server and the cyber threat monitor module were implemented in the SCADA master server. Low-level communications between the SCADA master server and the distributed field sites were instantiated as TCP/IP. However, other SCADA-specific protocols such as DNP3 and IEC61850 could be implemented using software packages. The generality of the architecture enables the platform to be used as a dedicated SCADA testbed to assess network vulnerabilities and the effects of cyber attacks.

6. Conclusions

Event correlation is an effective mechanism for detecting cyber attacks. However, higher order event correlation requires detailed information about lower order monitoring and the event generation architecture. Data correlation is an essential method for evaluating every layer of attack detection, from the raw data layer to the reporting layer. The correlation quality can be improved by combining the temporal and spatial event properties within a joint correlation engine. Based on the design patterns and results, the publish/subscribe paradigm used in conjunction with temporal-spatial event correlation appears to be an effective approach for detecting attacks on SCADA systems. Indeed, we hope that this work will stimulate renewed research focused on dedicated event correlation engines for SCADA systems.

References

[1] A. Bruce, Reliability analysis of electric utility SCADA systems, *IEEE Transactions on Power Systems*, vol. 13(3), pp. 844–849, 1998.

[2] J. Buford, X. Wu and V. Krishnaswamy, Spatial-temporal event correlation, *Proceedings of the IEEE International Conference on Communications*, 2009.

[3] G. Buttazzo, G. Lipari, L. Abeni and M. Caccamo, *Soft Real-Time Systems: Predictability vs. Efficiency*, Springer, New York, 2005.

[4] J. Cannady and J. Harrell, A comparative analysis of current intrusion detection technologies, *Proceedings of the Technology in Information Security Conference*, pp. 212–218, 1996.

[5] K. Erickson, E. Stanek, E. Cetinkaya, S. Dunn-Norman and A. Miller, Reliability of SCADA systems in offshore oil and gas platforms, in *Stability and Control of Dynamical Systems with Applications: A Tribute to Anthony N. Michael*, D. Liu and P. Antsaklis (Eds.), Birkhauser, Boston, Massachusetts, pp. 395–404, 2003.

[6] N. Falliere, L. O'Murchu and E. Chien, W32.Stuxnet Dossier, Symantec, Mountain View, California, 2011.

[7] G. Jiang and G. Cybenko, Temporal and spatial distributed event correlation for network security, *Proceedings of the American Control Conference*, vol. 2, pp. 996–1001, 2004.

[8] R. Kalapatapu, SCADA protocols and communication trends, presented at the *Instrumentation, Systems and Automation Society Conference*, 2004.

[9] LogMatrix, NerveCenter 6.0 Release Notes Windows and UNIX Version 6.0.02, NCRN60-02-03, Marlborough, Massachusetts, 2012.

[10] R. McMillan, Siemens: Stuxnet worm hit industrial systems, *Computerworld*, September 14, 2010.

[11] I. Nai Fovino, M. Masera, M. Guglielmi, A. Carcano and A. Trombetta, Distributed intrusion detection system for SCADA protocols, in *Critical Infrastructure Protection IV*, T. Moore and S. Shenoi (Eds.), Springer, Heidelberg, Germany, pp. 95–110, 2010.

[12] National Communications System, Supervisory Control and Data Acquisition (SCADA) Systems, Technical Bulletin 04-1, Arlington, Virginia, 2004.

[13] A. Patcha and J. Park, An overview of anomaly detection techniques: Existing solutions and latest technological trends, *Computer Networks*, vol. 51(12), pp. 3448–3470, 2007.

[14] K. Sheers, HP OpenView event correlation services, *HP Journal Online*, article no. 4, 1996.

[15] Star Controls, Reliability and Availability of SCADA Systems, Shanghai, China (`www.star-controls.com/Files/ReliabilityandAvailabilityofSCADASystems.pdf`), 2010.

[16] K. Stouffer, J. Falco and K. Kent, Guide to Supervisory Control and Data Acquisition (SCADA) and Industrial Control Systems Security, NIST Special Publication 800-82, National Institute of Standards and Technology, Gaithersburg, Maryland, 2006.

[17] J. Weiss, *Protecting Industrial Control Systems from Electronic Threats*, Momentum Press, New York, 2010.

[18] D. Williams and D. Curtis, Magic Quadrant for IT Event Correlation and Analysis, Gartner RAS Core Research Note G00208774, Gartner, Stamford, Connecticut, 2010.

[19] B. Zhu and S. Sastry, SCADA-specific intrusion detection/prevention systems: A survey and taxonomy, *Proceedings of the First Workshop on Secure Control Systems*, 2010.

III

INFRASTRUCTURE SECURITY

Chapter 7

PROTECTING INFRASTRUCTURE ASSETS FROM REAL-TIME AND RUN-TIME THREATS

Jonathan Jenkins and Mike Burmester

Abstract   Real-time availability with integrity is a crucial security requirement for critical infrastructure assets – delays in reporting device states or computations may result in equipment damage, perhaps even catastrophic failure. However, it is also necessary to address malicious software-based threats. Trusted computing (TC) is a security paradigm that enables application platforms to enforce the integrity of execution targets. A TC architecture can be combined with a real-time access control system to help protect against real-time availability and malware threats. However TC architectures offer only static (load-time) protection, so it is still necessary to address the possibility of run-time (execution) attacks. This paper focuses on the protection afforded by TC platforms to critical infrastructure assets. The paper defines a threat model, analyzes vulnerabilities, proposes services and tools that guarantee real-time availability with integrity, and demonstrates how they can be used to protect communications of an IEC61850-90-5-compliant substation automation system in an electricity grid. Also, it discusses the impact of run-time attacks on TC-compliant critical infrastructure assets.

Keywords: Trusted computing, real-time threats, power grid communications

1. Introduction

The Stuxnet worm has demonstrated the effectiveness of cyber attacks on industrial facilities. The potentially devastating effects of such attacks are of great concern and highlight the need for solutions that provide effective protection for industrial facilities and, in particular, critical infrastructure systems. The crucial nature of the services provided by critical infrastructure systems and the vulnerabilities found in these systems necessitate an approach to security that focuses on both real-time availability and malware threats. New

J. Butts and S. Shenoi (Eds.): Critical Infrastructure Protection VII, IFIP AICT 417, pp. 97–110, 2013.

technologies that are based on the trusted computing paradigm are needed to augment trust in emerging infrastructure systems and to mitigate threats from intentional and unintentional actors.

Trusted computing (TC) as defined by the Trusted Computing Group [26] is a technology that: (i) supports application platforms for securing distributed systems using trust engines that attest to the integrity of the systems; (ii) provides sealed storage; and (iii) enforces the expected behavior of the systems. This prevents the execution of untrusted (potentially malicious) software and also addresses insider threats. However TC architectures offer only static (load-time) protection, so the possibility of run-time (execution) attacks still has to be addressed.

In a critical infrastructure environment, it is vital that plant operators can access system state information in real-time – correct messages delivered at the wrong time can lead to erroneous responses and system failure. Communications must, therefore, be subject to real-time constraints with availability guaranteed within strict time bounds, a fact that renders most commonly-adopted cyber security paradigms inapplicable.

The three primary cyber security goals are confidentiality, integrity and availability. However, in the case of critical infrastructure systems, real-time availability with integrity is a primary goal, with privacy often only a secondary goal. This leads to a new security paradigm in which robustness in real-time is the main goal. This impacts implementation aspects because real-time behavior cannot be captured by traditional security paradigms.

It is difficult to provide effective protection to critical infrastructure systems with current operating systems, at least with regard to real-time availability and run-time integrity. A promising solution is to identify the key vulnerabilities of critical infrastructure systems and use a TC architecture that prevents the exploitation of the identified vulnerabilities.

This paper combines a TC architecture with a real-time access control infrastructure to implement effective protection against real-time availability and malware threats. Run-time threats are analyzed and approaches for mitigating them are discussed. The threats are combated by ensuring that network devices of TC-compliant systems operate with a limited enumerated set of functions and employ dynamic integrity monitoring that satisfies the tight real-time availability constraints of critical infrastructure systems.

2.   Related Work

TC technologies have been used in various applications to augment trust in network devices and platforms (see, e.g., [16]), but there has been very limited work on applying TC to critical infrastructure assets. Metke and Ekl [18] propose the combination of a public key infrastructure with TC to secure critical infrastructure components, but they do not address the problem of run-time threats.

Considerable work has been done on defending systems from run-time attacks such as buffer overflows, but despite all the research, computer systems and networks continue to be vulnerable to these attacks. Some researchers (see, e.g., [9, 10, 20]) have proposed the use of taint analysis and dynamic integrity monitoring of run-time software behavior to identify and track security violations. Various methods exist to enable tracking, such as code instrumentation, binary re-writing and architectural tracking support. Although serious efforts have been made to optimize the performance of monitoring processes [9], the performance overhead associated with dynamic measurements can be very significant. Architectural tracking methods are interesting, but they require expensive extensions to processors.

3.   Trusted Computing

The Trusted Computing Group [26] has published specifications of architectures and interfaces for several computing implementations. Platforms based on these specifications are expected to meet functional and reliability requirements of computer systems that allow increased assurance and trust. As such, they are well suited to support and protect critical infrastructure assets. The trusted platform module [24] (TPM) and trusted network connect (TNC) [25] are two components that can help address the security threats of critical infrastructures.

The TPM is a TC architecture that binds data to platform configurations of hardware systems to enhance software security. It has two basic capabilities, remote attestation and sealed storage, and is supported by a range of cryptographic primitives and keys. The TPM architecture is defined in terms of trusted engines called roots of trust that are used to establish trust in the expected behavior of a system. There are three mandatory roots of trust: (i) root of trust for measurement (RTM), which makes reliable integrity measurements; (ii) root of trust for storage (RTS), which protect keys and data entrusted to the TPM; and (iii) root of trust for reporting (RTR), which exposes shielded locations for storing integrity measurements and attests to the authenticity of stored values.

Security is based on an integrity-protected boot process in which executable code and associated configuration data are measured before being executed – this requires a hash of the BIOS code to be stored in a platform configuration register (PCR). For remote attestation, the TPM uses an attestation identity key to assert the state of its current software environment to a third party by signing its current PCR values. Sealed storage is used to protect the cryptographic keys. The keys are released for encryption, decryption and authentication purposes, conditional on the current software state (using current PCR values). The Trusted Computing Group requires TPM modules to be physically protected from tampering. This includes binding the TPM to physical parts of the platform (e.g., the motherboard) so that it cannot be transferred.

The trusted network connect (TNC) is a TC interoperability architecture for trusted access control based on TPMs. TNC is distinguished from other interoperability architectures by the requirement that the operating system configurations of the client and server are checked before a communication channel is established. A trusted link between a client and server is established only if:

- The identities of the client and server are trusted. A distributed public key infrastructure is used to establish trust links between a root authority and the TPMs of the client and server.

- The client is allowed real-time access to the server.

- The identities of the client and server are authenticated. A root of trust on the TPMs of both parties is invoked to release the required keys to execute a handshake protocol [25]. The TPM releases the keys only if the current configuration states of the operating systems of the parties permit the release.

- The handshake protocol is properly executed.

- The integrity and (if necessary) the confidentiality of the communicated data are enforced by the TPM.

4.   Security Framework and Threat Model

The TPM prevents compromised components of TC-compliant systems from executing. As a result, if run-time threats are excluded, then malicious (Byzantine) threats are reduced to denial-of-service (DoS) threats. This is a radical departure from the traditional threat model for computer systems because, unlike Byzantine faults, DoS faults are overt – they are self-revealing and, hence, are detectable.

Critical infrastructure assets can be protected from such faults using reliability mechanisms such as replication and redundancy. It is well-known that tolerating f Byzantine faults in a distributed system requires $(2f + 1)$ redundancy (with reliable broadcast) [12]. For a DoS threat model, the faults are overt. Therefore, tolerating f DoS faults requires only $(f + 1)$ redundancy.

Two kinds of faults may affect a TC-compliant critical infrastructure: natural faults (including accidents) and adversarial (intentional, malicious or insider) DoS faults (excluding run-time attacks). Natural faults can be predicted in the sense that an upper bound on the probability of the events can be estimated. Redundancy can then be used to reduce the probability to a value below an acceptable threshold.

Malicious DoS faults cannot be predicted. However they are overt and, because of the TPM and TNC integrity verification, must be physical (e.g., involve the tampering of the TPM chip). Thus, there is a cost involved and one way to thwart such faults is to make the cost high enough to prevent them. Several security approaches use economics and risk analysis based on replication and redundancy [17] to address threat models with overt faults. These approaches assume a bound on adversarial resources and the presence of an architecture with sufficient redundancy to make DoS attacks prohibitively expensive.

Our approach for critical infrastructure protection assumes an architecture with sufficient redundancy such that: (i) the probability that the system will fail due to a natural fault is negligible (e.g., less than 2^{-20}); and (ii) the cost of a successful DoS attack by compromising system components is prohibitive for a resource-bounded adversary.

Our security framework for a critical infrastructure C comprises:

- A real-time model that captures its functionality, including a faults distribution $\mathcal{F}$ on components.

- A set S of specifications, policies, constraints and security requirements that identify the vulnerabilities V that must be addressed.

- An S-profiler that emulates the behavior of C in real-time subject to the specifications S. The profiler is defined by a software program that runs in real-time.

- A proof that the S-profiler adheres to the security requirements specified by S in real-time in the presence of faults/disasters, accidents and malicious behavior.

This framework captures integrity and confidentiality and addresses availability in real-time. The S-profiler is used to measure the actual time required to protect system resources. Note that traditional approaches based on formal methods or security models do not capture real-time availability.

4.1   Security Framework

Let C be a real-time S-compliant critical infrastructure with faults distribution $\mathcal{F}$, specifications S and vulnerabilities V. Then, C is modeled by a finite hybrid real-time automaton with faults [8]: $C = (\tau, A, Q, q_0, D, \mathcal{F})$ with a time schedule $\tau : t_1, t_2 \ldots$; a finite set of actions A that includes a special symbol $\perp$; a finite set of states $Q \neq \emptyset$ that is partitioned into safe states Q_s, critical states Q_c and terminal states Q_t; an initial state $q_0 \in Q_s$; and a time-triggered transition function $D \subset Q \times Q \times A$. D is deterministic when $a \in A \backslash \{\perp\}$ and probabilistic when $a = \perp$; in this case, the posteriori state is selected by nature according to $\mathcal{F}$.

The parties involved in a critical infrastructure are specified by S, e.g., intelligent electronic devices, operators, the adversary and nature (environment). Nature controls the temporal and spatial aspects of all events, schedules state transitions in a timely manner according to τ using the distribution $\mathcal{F}$ to select a strategy for component failure, and resolves concurrency issues by linking events to their actual start times.

For our application involving secure electricity grid communications, the transition frequency $\delta = t_{i+1} - t_i$ is 4 ms, which is the latency specified by IEC 61850-90-5 [13]. It is important that the critical infrastructure protection mechanisms adhere to the time-frame τ because command/control information that arrives late may result in the system transitioning to a critical/terminal state.

A semantic security threat model is extended to capture real-time events. The threat model restricts the adversary to exploiting the system vulnerabilities V specified in S, in particular, those identified by system policies, vulnerability assessments and gray-box penetration testing. The vulnerabilities involve system components such as control systems, embedded systems and communication channels.

4.2　　The Good, the Bad and the Ugly

The inclusion of TC results in a threat model with significant benefits and unique limitations. This section provides an analysis of the effects of TC on the threat model.

The Good.　The TPM is an interface that protects system components from behaving in an unexpected way during a malicious attack. This is achieved by having an integrity-protected boot process and using protected capabilities to access shielded locations for: (i) PCRs to verify integrity; and (ii) cryptographic keys for integrity and confidentiality.

Before an authorized program is executed, an integrity check of its state against a stored PCR configuration is performed. If the check fails, the program is assumed to have been compromised and is not executed by the operating system.

The Bad.　The TPM allows only authorized software programs to execute. Therefore, the integrity of system software, which includes the operating system, is a fundamental requirement for ensuring trust in the computing infrastructure. The system software must be well designed, and not have security holes, backdoors or other vulnerabilities that could be exploited by an adversary.

A vulnerability in the operating system may allow an adversary to bypass the protection offered by the TPM. There are many reasons why software programs used in critical infrastructures may have faulty designs. A major reason is the complexity and architectural constraints of the execution environment (i.e., operating system and hardware). Other reasons are poor software development practices and inadequate applications security. With such systems, a dynamic approach is typically used in which program flaws are addressed with patches. However, this approach does not work for critical infrastructures.

The Ugly.　The TPM provides integrity verification only at load-time, not at run-time. By exploiting a vulnerability in the operating system, an adversary may be able to change the execution flow of a program, e.g., by using a buffer overflow attack. Several run-time attacks [1], such as those that use metamorphic malware (e.g., the self-camouflaging Frankenstein [19]) or more generally, return-oriented programming (ROP) [21], require the adversary to be able to control the flow of execution on the stack. However, there are ways to prevent this [11]. Unfortunately, these approaches do not combat run-time attacks that exploit system vulnerabilities.

5.   Real-Time Availability Threats

Real-time availability threats exploit the time required to deliver system resources. For example, in an electrical grid, controllers must have access to state transition information in real-time. In substation automation systems, synchrophasor streams are sent to controllers via local networks. Protecting such streams from threats involving deletion (availability), corruption (integrity) and privacy is crucial. Typically, the synchrophasor reporting latency should be less than 10 ms to prevent cascading faults [13].

Real-time availability faults occur when the time taken to deliver information is longer than the specified latency. Real-time faults may be natural (e.g., critical state information may get dropped or not arrive in time to be processed) or malicious (e.g., an insider may corrupt synchrophasor data). Note that quality of service (QoS) is not a protection mechanism for critical infrastructures: an average delay less than the latency requirement may still result in a real-time failure if the real delay exceeds the requirement.

5.1   Access Control Systems

Access control systems are trust infrastructures that manage access to computer and network resources. Early approaches include the Bell-LaPadula model [2] that enforces confidentiality policies and the Biba model [4] that enforces integrity policies. These are not dynamic and attempts to make them dynamic are not scalable. In role-based access control (RBAC) [22], roles are assigned to access permissions and users are assigned roles. RBAC scales better than the earlier models, but it is not suitable for highly dynamic systems. Extensions such as the temporal RBAC [3] and the generalized temporal RBAC [15] allow the periodic enabling of roles. However, when the numbers of subject and object attributes become large, the number of roles grows exponentially [27].

The attribute-based access control (ABAC) model [27] assigns attributes to subjects and objects. Authorization is defined for subject descriptors consisting of attribute conditions. These may include environment attributes such as time, day and temperature.

ABAC encompasses the functionality of RBAC by treating roles and security labels as attributes. It captures dynamic environmental and temporal attributes. However, in highly dynamic real-time applications the event space that determines the attribute values can get very large, making any attempt to capture real-time availability scenarios not scalable.

5.2 Enforcing Need-to-Get-Now Policies

The communications systems of critical infrastructure are often bandwidth-constrained. As such, it is important to have an access control mechanism that can guarantee real-time availability to high-priority packets. The Internet Engineering Task Force has proposed two networking architectures, differentiated services (DiffServ) [5] and integrated services (IntServ) [6], that statically partition the bandwidth among different classes of traffic to offer quality of service. However, these architectures do not guarantee real-time availability. Protecting critical infrastructure assets from real-time availability threats requires that packets with the highest priority are guaranteed to be delivered. Consequently, the network bandwidth must be: (i) reserved for the highest priority packets and; (ii) sufficient to enable all the highest priority packets to be delivered.

To address this issue, we propose a real-time attribute based access control mechanism that extends the functionality of DiffServ and IntServ. For any subject s, the availability of a resource o at time t_i is determined based on a real-time attribute $attr(x; t_i)$, $x \in \{s, o\}$ with values in a linearly-ordered set $(\mathcal{L}, \succeq)$ of availability labels. $attr(x, t_i)$ is called a priority label when $x = s$ and a congestion label when $x = o$. The availability labels are dynamically determined based on user events, temporal events, context of the requested service and system events.

To enforce real-time availability, the policy is to guarantee that high-priority (critical) packets are forwarded in real-time when there are faults (caused by nature or the adversary). For this purpose, we shall assume that the network infrastructure has sufficient redundancy to guarantee the delivery of high-priority packets at a specified rate. The following packet forwarding protocol is used:

- **Queuing:** Let P be a packet received by an edge router R and Q the queue of P. If $priority(P) \succeq priority(P')$ for some $P' \in Q$ or if $Q = \emptyset$, then put P in Q and drop all packets $P'' \in Q$ with $priority(P) \succ priority(P'')$. Else, drop P. This implies that all packets in Q have the same priority and, by our earlier assumption, no high-priority packet is dropped.

- **Forwarding:** The first packet P in the queue Q of edge router R is forwarded if and only if $priority(P) \succeq congestion(R)$.

This protocol guarantees the delivery of high-priority packets assuming that the specified rate of high-priority packets is not exceeded.

6. Run-Time Attacks

Run-time attacks involve the imposition of unintended behavior on an executing software target. In an ROP attack [21], there is no need to inject new malicious code – code in local libraries may be used.

The ROP attack overwrites the stack with addresses that point to existing code in a library (e.g., the standard C library libc). Instead of calling a function, it sets return addresses on the stack to the middle of instruction sequences that end with a return instruction. After executing the instructions, the return takes the next address from the stack where execution continues and increments the stack pointer. Thus, the stack pointer acts as an instruction pointer and determines the program control flow. Interested readers are referred to [11, 21] for additional details.

These types of attacks use small instruction sequences (e.g., from libc instead of entire functions). The adversary must be able to control the stack flow to implement the attack, and there are ways to prevent this [11]. However, there are run-time attacks that exploit other vulnerabilities using minimal footprints. There is, therefore, a need to guarantee during run-time that the execution of a program cannot deviate from the prescribed flow path.

One critical characteristic of the TC model is its reliance on digests of static execution targets (software) as key measurements of platform integrity. In order to materially impact the integrity of the trusted platform, the adversary must attack the platform software without requiring the presence of malicious software that would be detected by TC structures. ROP attacks [21] do not require additional malicious code to be injected into a platform, but assume that the attacker has already diverted control of execution. The most salient way to achieve this initial diversion under our constraints is via a network-based attack. If TPM hosts are successfully exploited by run-time network-based attacks, it is possible to alter their behavior in a manner that is not detected by TC methodologies. However, the TNC architecture enables network endpoints to decide based on shared trusted integrity information whether or not to accept connections. Consequently, devices that implement TNC structures and protocols have the capability to restrict network associations to allow only trusted remote entities, thereby limiting the ability of the adversary to launch network-based attacks.

7. Secure Electricity Grid Communications

We demonstrate the effectiveness of our approach by using it to secure communications in an IEC61850-90-5-compliant substation automation system against real-time availability and run-time integrity threats. The IEC 61850 document [14] provides an advanced object-oriented semantics for information exchange in power system automation applications, SCADA systems, substation automation and distribution automation. The IEC 61850-90-5 extension [13] specifies the use of the IP transport protocol with data encapsulated in IP packets and formulated so that they can be distributed in wide area network (WAN) environments. This allows for low-cost wide area monitoring, protection and control.

IEC 61850 and its extension do not address security issues. In this paper, we show how robustness can be achieved using a TC architecture with TPMs. This involves integrating the substation automation system infrastructure with: (i) a TPM interface with built-in non-migratable trust as described in Section 3; (ii) a Kerberos multicast authentication service [7]; (iii) a real-time attribute-based access control system as described in Section 5.2; and (iv) cryptographic services for AES and HMAC (SHA2). Protection from run-time attacks is achieved under the assumption that all trusted software is well-designed and has no flaws or other vulnerabilities (Section 4.2). This assumption is reasonable for critical infrastructure assets with minimal operating systems.

7.1   Trusted IEC 61850-90-5 Profiler

SISCO recently released an open-source software package [23] containing a sample profiler that emulates IEC 61850-90-5 systems. The profiler does not support any security services. However, we use the profiler to demonstrate real-time security for our application involving electricity grid communications.

7.2   Experimental Testbed

The experimental testbed comprised seventeen workstations connected via a Cisco Catalyst 3560G series PoE 48 switch and other switches. The workstations were TPM-enabled and ran Ubuntu Linux and Windows. Eight workstations had an Intel Xeon 5120 1.86 GHz x2 CPU with 2 GB memory and the remaining nine had an Intel Xeon E5506 2.13 GHz x4 CPU and 6 GB memory. A dedicated machine running the krb5 API acted as the Kerberos 5 release 1.10 server, which interfaced directly with the Kerberos API.

7.3   Trusted Substation Automation

A substation automation system consists of multiple substations connected via an intranet. To establish a trusted substation automation system, each component in a zone should be TC-compliant. For trusted interoperability, the TNC platform is used (Section 3). This addresses passive attacks as well as active attacks, including insider attacks. The TPM interface prevents authorized components that are compromised from behaving maliciously, in particular, from contributing to a DoS attack. Furthermore, TNC network access control prevents external DoS attacks.

By using a real-time access control service to manage data feeds, real-time availability is guaranteed for high-priority packets provided that the substation automation network has sufficient redundancy to be resilient when only high-priority packets are sent.

AES was used in the counter mode to generate a stream cipher, with successive values of the counter ctr encrypted with the shared secret key to generate a keystream. The keystream was bitwise XORed with the payload m of the packet. The resulting string c together with the value of the counter ctr comprised the ciphertext.

In the case of decryption, the AES keystream was generated by encrypting ctr with the shared secret key. The result was then XORed with c to get m.

Note that when performing encryption and decryption, the keystream can be computed offline. Only the bitwise XOR operation must be performed online.

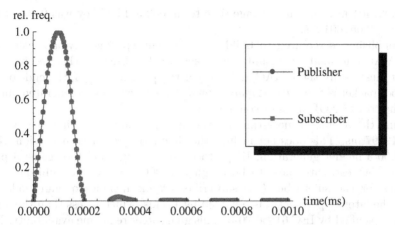

Figure 1. AES counter mode encryption times for publisher and subscriber.

As shown in Figure 1, over the course of 10,000 packet transmissions, the average time needed to generate the keystream at the publisher was 0.0001786 ms with standard deviation $\sigma = 5.37275 \times 10^{-6}$ ms. At the subscriber, the average time was 0.0001133 ms with $\sigma = 0.000229$ ms.

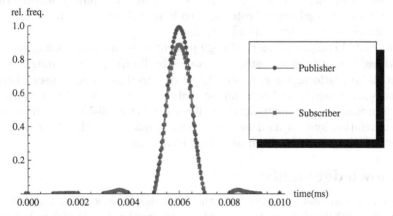

Figure 2. HMAC generation and authentication times for publisher and subscriber.

Authentication was performed by the publisher and subscriber computing HMACs of the ciphertext using SHA2. Over the course of 10,000 packet transmissions the average time at the publisher was 0.006346 ms with $\sigma = 0.001108$ ms; at the subscriber, the average time was 0.007352 ms with $\sigma = 0.002272$ ms (Figure 2).

The average time for generating random numbers was 0.010871 ms with $\sigma = 0.000399$ ms. The average time to lock a TPM key was 0.48788 ms with

$\sigma = 0.021401$ ms, and the average time to unlock a TPM key was 0.36454 ms with $\sigma = 0.051601$ ms.

A publisher is required to build a packet, encrypt the payload, calculate the HMAC and finally transmit the packet. Each subscriber that receives the packet must verify the HMAC and decrypt the payload. Thus, the end-to-end time per packet is $enc + dec + 2mac \approx 2mac$ if the keystream is generated offline and the cost of XORing is discounted.

Using the average time estimates, the average end-to-end time per packet is 0.012697 ms. This does not include the time required for transmission, IEC 61850-90-5 header generation, IP protocol formatting and other general processing. We estimate these to be roughly 0.00069 ms for the publisher and 0.54 ms for the subscriber (the subscriber's value includes queuing delays). Thus, the latency per packet is bounded by 1.3 ms, which is less than the 4 ms latency specified by IEC 61850-90-5. This guarantees real-time availability. If a fresh key is required, then an extra 0.36454 ms is needed to unlock the key and 0.48788 ms to lock it. A random number generator may be used to generate the keys offline.

8.   Conclusions

A trusted computing architecture can be combined with a real-time access control system to help protect critical infrastructure assets against real-time availability and malware threats. However trusted computing architectures offer only static (load-time) protection, so it is still necessary to address the possibility of run-time (execution) attacks.

The trusted computing methodology presented in this paper mitigates run-time threats to critical infrastructure assets by limiting the openings for exploitation on platform software and detecting run-time compromises, thereby guaranteeing integrity and real-time availability. Experimental results involving the protection of communications of an IEC61850-90-5 compliant substation automation system used in power grids demonstrate the effectiveness of the methodology in critical infrastructure environments.

Acknowledgements

This research was supported by the National Science Foundation under Grant No. 1027217. The authors would also like to thank J. D. Allen, V. Chrissikopoulos, S. Easton, R. van Engelen, D. Guidry, J. Jenkins, P. Kotzanikolaou, J. Lawrence, X. Liu, E. Magkos, S. Ty and X. Yuan for helpful discussions and comments.

References

[1] A. Baratloo, N. Singh and T. Tsai, Transparent run-time defense against stack smashing attacks, *Proceedings of the USENIX Annual Technical Conference*, p. 21, 2000.

[2] E. Bell and L. La Padula, Secure Computer System: Unified Exposition and Multics Interpretation, Technical Report ESD-TR-75-306, MITRE Corporation, Bedford, Massachusetts, 1976.

[3] E. Bertino, P. Bonatti and E. Ferrari, TRBAC: A temporal role-based access control model, *ACM Transactions on Information and System Security*, vol. 4(3), pp. 191–233, 2001.

[4] K. Biba, Integrity Considerations for Secure Computer Systems, Technical Report ESD-TR-76-372, MITRE Corporation, Bedford, Massachusetts, 1977.

[5] S. Blake, D. Black, M. Carlson, E. Davies, Z. Wang and W. Weiss, An Architecture for Differentiated Services, RFC 2475, 1998.

[6] R. Braden, D. Clark and S. Shenker, Integrated Services in the Internet Architecture: An Overview, RFC 1633, 1994.

[7] M. Burmester, J. Lawrence, D. Guidry, S. Easton, S. Ty, X. Liu, X. Yuan and J. Jenkins, Towards a secure electricity grid, *Proceedings of the Eighth IEEE International Conference on Intelligent Sensors, Sensor Networks and Information Processing*, 2013.

[8] M. Burmester, E. Magkos and V. Chrissikopoulos, Modeling security in cyber-physical systems, *International Journal of Critical Infrastructure Protection*, vol. 5(3-4), pp. 118–126, 2012.

[9] W. Chang, B. Streiff and C. Lin, Efficient and extensible security enforcement using dynamic data flow analysis, *Proceedings of the Fifteenth ACM Conference on Computer and Communications Security*, pp. 39–50, 2008.

[10] W. Cheng, Q. Zhao, B. Yu and S. Hiroshige, TaintTrace: Efficient flow tracing with dynamic binary rewriting, *Proceedings of the Eleventh IEEE Symposium on Computers and Communications*, pp. 749–754, 2006.

[11] L. Davi, A. Sadeghi and M. Winandy, ROPdefender: A detection tool to defend against return-oriented programming attacks, *Proceedings of the Sixth ACM Symposium on Information, Computer and Communications Security*, pp. 40–51, 2011.

[12] D. Dolev, C. Dwork, O. Waarts and M. Yung, Perfectly secure message transmission, *Journal of the ACM*, vol. 40(1), pp. 17–47, 1993.

[13] International Electrotechnical Commission, IEC/TR 61850-90-5, Edition 1.0 2012-05, Power Systems Management and Associated Information Exchange – Data and Communications Security, Geneva, Switzerland, 2012.

[14] International Electrotechnical Commission, IEC/TR 61850-1, Edition 2.0, Communication Networks and Systems in Substations for Power Utility Automation – Part 1: Introduction and Overview, Geneva, Switzerland, 2013.

[15] J. Joshi, E. Bertino, U. Latif and A. Ghafoor, A generalized temporal role-based access control model, *IEEE Transactions on Knowledge and Data Engineering*, vol. 17(1), pp. 4–23, 2005.

[16] A. Leicher, N. Kuntze and A. Schmidt, Implementation of a trusted ticket system, *Proceedings of the Twenty-Fourth IFIP TC 11 International Information Security Conference*, pp. 152–163, 2009.

[17] M. Lelarge and J. Bolot, Economic incentives to increase security in the Internet: The case for insurance, *Proceedings of the Twenty-Eighth Conference on Computer Communications*, pp. 1494–1502, 2009.

[18] A. Metke and R. Ekl, Smart grid security technology, *Proceedings of the First IEEE PES Conference on Innovative Smart Grid Technologies*, 2010.

[19] V. Mohan and K. Hamlen, Frankenstein: Stitching malware from benign binaries, *Proceedings of the Sixth USENIX Workshop on Offensive Technologies*, p. 8, 2012.

[20] F. Qin, C. Wang, Z. Li, H. Kim, Y. Zhou and Y. Wu, LIFT: A low-overhead practical information flow tracking system for detecting security attacks, *Proceedings of the Thirty-Ninth Annual IEEE/ACM International Symposium on Microarchitecture*, pp. 135–148, 2006.

[21] R. Roemer, E. Buchanan, H. Shacham and S. Savage, Return-oriented programming: Systems, languages and applications, *ACM Transactions on Information and System Security*, vol. 15(1), pp. 2:1–2:34, 2012.

[22] R. Sandhu, E. Coyne, H. Feinstein and C. Youman, Role-based access control models, *IEEE Computer*, vol. 29(2), pp. 38–47, 1996.

[23] SISCO, Cisco and SISCO collaborate on open source synchrophasor framework, Press Release, Sterling Heights, Michigan (`www.sisconet.com/downloads/90-5_Cisco_SISCO.pdf`), 2011.

[24] Trusted Computing Group, TPM Main Specification, Level 2, Version 1.2, Revision 116, Beaverton, Oregon (`www.trustedcomputinggroup.org/resources/tpm_main_specification`), 2011.

[25] Trusted Computing Group, TCG Trusted Network Connect TNC Architecture for Interoperability; Specification 1.5; Revision 3, Beaverton, Oregon (`www.trustedcomputinggroup.org/files/resource_files/28 84F884-1A4B-B294- D001FAE2E17EA3EB/TNC_Architecture_v1_5_r3-1 .pdf`), 2012.

[26] Trusted Computing Group, Trusted Computing Group, Beaverton, Oregon (`www.trustedcomputinggroup.org`).

[27] E. Yuan and J. Tong, Attribute-based access control (ABAC) for web services, *Proceedings of the IEEE International Conference on Web Services*, pp. 561–569, 2005.

Chapter 8

ANOMALY DETECTION IN LIQUID PIPELINES USING MODELING, CO-SIMULATION AND DYNAMICAL ESTIMATION

Saed Alajlouni and Vittal Rao

Abstract   Historically, supervisory control and data acquisition (SCADA) systems have relied on obscurity to safeguard against attacks. Indeed, external attackers lacked knowledge about proprietary system designs and software to access systems and execute attacks. The trend to interconnect to the Internet and incorporate standardized protocols, however, has resulted in an increase in the attack surface – attackers can now target SCADA systems and proceed to impact the physical systems they control. Dynamical estimation can be used to identify anomalies and attempts to maliciously affect controlled physical systems. This paper describes an intrusion detection method based on the dynamical estimation of systems. A generic water pipeline system is modeled using state space equations, and a discrete-time Kalman filter is used to estimate operational characteristics for anomaly-based intrusion detection. The effectiveness of the method is evaluated against deception attacks that target the water pipeline system. A co-simulation that integrates computational fluid dynamics software and MATLAB/Simulink is employed to simulate attacks and develop detection schemes.

Keywords: Liquid pipelines, anomaly detection, dynamical estimation

1. Introduction

SCADA systems are used to monitor and control processes in industrial environments. Typical implementations involve highly distributed operations over large geographical areas, such as the electric grid and pipeline systems. SCADA systems consist of a central control center that issues set-point values and receives measurements and alarm data from distributed controllers. In recent years, utility companies have begun to transition to the Internet and

J. Butts and S. Shenoi (Eds.): Critical Infrastructure Protection VII, IFIP AICT 417, pp. 111–124, 2013.
© IFIP International Federation for Information Processing 2013

standard communications protocols for information exchange and remote control. SCADA systems now face a higher risk of cyber attacks, primarily because their vulnerabilities are more readily exposed [1].

Common attacks that target process control systems are denial-of-service (DoS), deception and stealth attacks. In an example DoS attack, the attacker attempts to prevent the controller from reading sensor data or prevent the actuator from receiving control commands [2]. In a deception attack, the adversary may send false control commands to actuators or inject malicious sensor readings, resulting in control actions based on the false data [8]. A stealth attack is a sequence of deception attacks, where the attacker attempts to cause damage or affect operations without being detected [1, 3]. In a stealth attack scenario, the attacker is assumed to have knowledge of the plant dynamics.

SCADA systems can be abstracted into two interrelated layers: a communications layer and a physical layer. In the case of a pipeline system, the physical layer consists of pipe sections, actuators (e.g., valves and pumps) and measurement sensors (e.g., for flow rate and pressure). The communications layer manages the flow rates and data exchange throughout the physical layer; it incorporates modems, routers, switches and the communications medium. This paper focuses on the physical layer and how dynamical estimation can be utilized to detect anomalies.

The intrusion detection approach is divided into two main steps: (i) modeling the dynamical system; and (ii) applying anomaly-based intrusion detection methods. The first step involves the derivation of a mathematical model that describes the dynamics of the physical system of interest. In the case of a SCADA system, the model can be represented using a non-linear, time-varying differential equation. In the second step, Kalman-filter-based dynamical estimation is used to predict sensor measurement values. If the estimated quantities exceed predetermined thresholds, then an error is detected, which can be attributed either to a system fault or a malicious attack.

The approach is similar to those used to address the well-known problem of "bad data" detection in power grids. However, this paper focuses on how dynamical estimation can be utilized to detect anomalies, whereas approaches for bad data detection in power grids rely on static estimation. The primary difference is that dynamical estimation relies on differential equations to estimate current values and to predict future values. Static estimation, on the other hand, uses measurements taken at various time instances to determine estimates of the current system state without predicting future states.

Compared with the electric power grid, pipeline systems typically have slower dynamics. This provides the proposed detection scheme with more time to detect and respond to malicious attacks without being concerned about system damage during the detection phase. Nevertheless, it is important to note that a critical requirement of the proposed scheme is adequate computational power to implement estimation and anomaly detection in real time. As such, the order of the model and the selected anomaly detection algorithm are both contributing factors to the feasibility of performing real-time anomaly detection. This paper

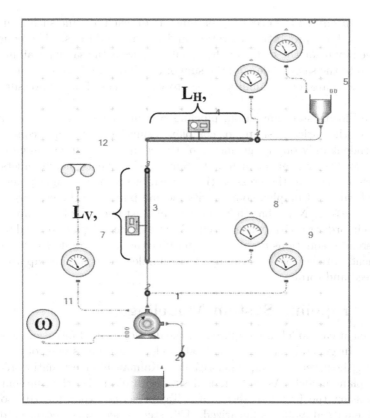

Figure 1. Generic water pipeline system.

makes the case that the availability of dynamical models, necessary computing power, and the relatively slower dynamics of pipeline systems are factors that facilitate dynamical estimation for real-time anomaly detection.

2. Modeling and Simulation

Figure 1 shows a schematic diagram of a generic water pipeline system. It consists of a water transportation system that distributes water from a well to an overhead tank. The pipeline consists of two sections: a vertical section with length (L_v) and diameter (d_v), and a horizontal section with length (L_H) and diameter (d_H). The non-linear dynamical response of the system is simulated using the Flowmaster software package [6]. This computational fluid dynamics software is used to discern the pressure surge, pressure drop, flow rate, temperature and system response times. Flowmaster transient analysis is similar to the simulation approach introduced by Miller [9].

A pipeline network may be represented as a number of modules connected at nodes. The modules consist of pipe sections and other components such as valves, tanks, accumulators and pumps. Pipeline network equations are generated after specifying the necessary parameters for each module such as friction parameters, fluid properties, elevation and initial conditions. The equations are formed by using the fact that the nodal pressure is the same for all modules connected to the same node, and the sum of the flow rates is zero at each node. The equations are solved simultaneously to yield values of nodal pressures and flow rates.

In the Flowmaster simulation, pipeline system components can be categorized as mathematically simple or complex. Equations for simple components are dependent only on the geometry of the component, while complex components involve dynamic elements [9]. Simple components include inlets from reservoirs, changes in the cross-sectional area, orifice plates, rigid pipes, dead ends and valves. Complex components include pumps, turbines, surge tanks and surge vessels. Note that there must be at least one complex component in a system in order to initiate a transient. Numerical techniques are used to solve the differential equations in order to determine the head and flow in a complex component. In the case of a pump, for example, the equations approximate flow, speed and torque.

2.1   Pipeline System Modeling

Mathematical models are required for the development of intrusion detection methods. In general, the mathematical model of a process control system is non-linear; however, the implementation of Kalman filter estimation requires a linear plant model. As such, it is desirable to discretize the mathematical relation using the first two terms of a Taylor series expansion [10] so that the mathematical model is linearized. This step is necessary because a digital controller is used to control the plant.

2.2   Linear Model

For the pipeline system shown in Figure 1, a second-order, linear time-invariant state space model was derived after selecting the state vector $x = [P_t, Q]^T$, where P_t is the pressure at the bottom of the overhead tank, Q is the volumetric flow rate and T is the time. The state space model has the form $\dot{x}(t) = Ax(t) + Bu(t)$ and can be expressed as:

$$\begin{bmatrix} \dot{P_t} \\ \dot{Q} \end{bmatrix} = \begin{bmatrix} 0 & \frac{\rho g}{A_t} \\ \frac{-1}{I_{eq}} & \frac{-R_{eq}}{I_{eq}} \end{bmatrix} \begin{bmatrix} P_t \\ Q \end{bmatrix} + \begin{bmatrix} 0 \\ \frac{1}{I_{eq}} \end{bmatrix} P_{pump} \qquad (1)$$

where I_{eq} is the fluid total inertance in the system, A_t is the cross-sectional area of the tank, R_{eq} is the total fluid resistance in the system, and P_{pump} is the pressure at the pump outlet and the input to the system.

The total inertance I_{eq} is analogous to an inductance in an electronic circuit [4]. It is expressed as:

$$I_{eq} = \frac{4\rho}{\pi} \left(\frac{L_V}{d_V^2} + \frac{L_H}{d_H^2} \right).$$

Table 1. Relationships between friction models and Reynolds Number [6].

Option	Laminar Flow $Re \leq 2000$	Transition Zone $2000 < Re < 4000$	Turbulent Flow $Re \geq 4000$
Colebrook-White	$f_l = \frac{64}{Re}$	$f = x f_t + (1-x) f_l$	$f_t = \frac{0.25}{[\log(\frac{k}{3.7D} + \frac{5.74}{Re^{0.9}})]^2}$
Hazen-Williams	$f_l = \frac{64}{Re}$	$f = x f_t + (1-x) f_l$	$f_t = \frac{1014.2 Re^{-0.148}}{C_{HW}^{1.852} D^{0.0184}}$
Fixed	f_l	f	f_t

The fluid resistance R_{eq} is analogous to a resistor in an electronic circuit [4]. It is expressed as:

$$R_{eq} = \frac{128\mu}{\pi}\left(\frac{L_V}{d_V^4} + \frac{L_H}{d_H^4}\right).$$

R_{eq} is the result of applying the Darcy-Weisbach equation to calculate the pressure drop due to friction in a pipeline. The relationship between the pressure drop due to friction P_f and the flow Q is linear when the flow is laminar. It is expressed as:

$$P_f = R_{eq} \times Q.$$

The following assumptions and operational limitations render the derived pipeline equations simple and linear:

- The fluid used is water, which is incompressible. Water is a Newtonian fluid that has a constant dynamic viscosity μ.

- The flow is laminar (i.e., the speed of flow is relatively slow). Specifically, the Reynolds number Re, a dimensionless number that indicates the type of flow in a conduit, satisfies the constraint $Re \leq 2000$. When $2000 < Re < 4000$, then the flow is transitional between laminar and turbulent flow. When $Re \geq 4000$, then the flow is turbulent. As Re changes, the frictional model of the conduit, which accounts for pressure drops due to frictional losses, changes accordingly.

  Table 1, taken from the Flowmaster V7 manual [6], shows the relation between Re and friction models. Note that, when $Re > 2000$, the relationship between pressure drop due to friction and flow rate ceases to be linear.

- A Newtonian fluid with a laminar flow has a parabolic velocity profile. However, for a relatively long pipe section, the flow profile can be approximated as a uniform velocity profile.

- Dynamic changes due to heat transfer effects are negligible.

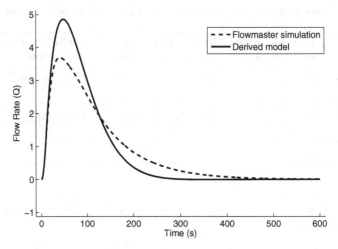

Figure 2. Normalized flow rate.

- Adiabatic changes in water density (i.e., elastic effects of water) may be ignored because heat transfer is negligible.

- Elastic effects of the pipes may be ignored because they are made of rigid steel and have high resistance to deformation.

- Pump speed increases gradually with no abrupt pressure changes. This guarantees laminar flow and preserves the linearity of the mathematical model.

2.3   Discretization

A suitable sampling period must be chosen in order to accurately capture the system dynamics after discretization. The sampling period T_s is selected such that $T_s = \frac{0.1}{|\lambda_{max}|}$, where $|\lambda_{max}|$ is the absolute maximum of the real part of the system eigenvalues.

The discretized version of Equation (1) can be expressed using zero-order hold for the input signal P_{pump}:

$$x_{k+1} = Fx_k + Gu_k \tag{2}$$

where $F = e^{AT_s}$ is the state transition matrix calculated over the sampling period T_s and $G = A^{-1}\left(e^{AT_s} - I\right)B$, where I is the identity matrix.

Using the Flowmaster software simulation as a representation of the actual non-linear dynamics of the pipeline system, the accuracy of the discretized linear model shown in Equation (2) can be evaluated. Figures 2 and 3 compare the pipeline states against the Flowmaster simulation results for the flow rate and pressure at the bottom of the overhead tank, respectively.

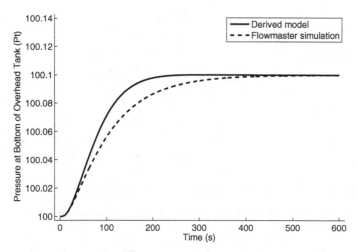

Figure 3. Normalized pressure.

Upon inspecting Figures 2 and 3, it can be seen that the discretized mathematical model in Equation (2) is sufficiently accurate for representing the dynamic behavior of the pipeline. For estimation purposes, however, the response differences between Equation (2) and the Flowmaster simulation are modeled as process disturbances (discussed in Section 4).

3. Co-Simulation

The simulation capabilities of MATLAB/Simulink and Flowmaster software can be integrated to produce a co-simulation. The purpose of a co-simulation is to perform simultaneous simulations and data exchange between a dynamical system model in MATLAB/Simulink and a fluid or electromechanical model in Flowmaster. Note that variables for the controllers and gauges can be transferred into and out of the Flowmaster model [5].

In the context of the pipeline system, co-simulation facilitates a Flowmaster simulation of the non-linear behavior of the pipeline system and the ability to transfer sensor measurements to MATLAB/Simulink to perform state estimation. In addition, the MATLAB/Simulink environment can be used to design a digital controller that sends control signals to the pipeline process in Flowmaster. Malicious attacks on the pipeline system can be simulated using a real-time, co-simulation process between MATLAB/Simulink and Flowmaster. For example, during a co-simulation, MATLAB/Simulink can be programmed to inject malicious data into the true sensor measurements that originate from the Flowmaster simulation. The flexibility enables the simulation of attack scenarios involving DoS, deception and stealth attacks that target sensor measurements.

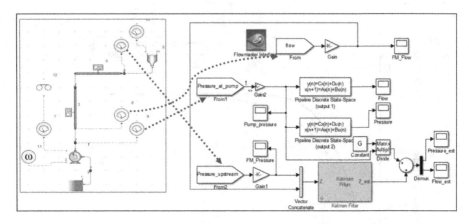

Figure 4.   Variable exchange during the co-simulation process.

Figure 4 illustrates the co-simulation process. The figure shows how measurements from the Flowmaster software can be transferred to MATLAB/Simulink to conduct dynamical estimation and to simulate malicious attacks.

4.   Anomaly Detection

Statistical methods have been used very effectively to detect anomalies in dynamical systems. For example, Cardenas, *et al.* [1] have used hypothesis testing in an evaluation of the Tennessee-Eastman plant. Their results demonstrate the ability to model changes in behavior of the underlying physical system. Interested readers are referred to [7] for an overview of hypothesis testing schemes that can be used in anomaly detection.

The discrete Kalman filter is used to estimate pipeline states at each sampling time. When one or more sensor measurements are compromised by the injection of malicious data, Kalman filtering and prediction results can be used to detect anomalies. Note that successful detection requires the careful selection of alarm threshold levels, which will be examined in future work.

As stated previously, the response differences between the discretized linear mathematical model and the Flowmaster simulation can be modeled as process disturbances. To incorporate a process disturbance, the pipeline state space model specified by Equation (2) is updated as follows:

$$x_{k+1} = Fx_k + Gu_k + w_k$$

$$z_{k+1} = Hx_k + v_k$$

where z_{k+1} is the sensor measurement equation, H is the measurement matrix that relates system states to sensor measurements through a linear relationship, w_k is the process disturbance, and v_k is the sensor measurement noise. Note that both w_k and v_k are assumed to be Gaussian white processes with zero means.

Table 2. Co-simulation cases for pipeline system under attack.

Simulation Case	Flow Rate Integrity	Pressure Integrity
Case I	Not Compromised	Compromised
Case II	Compromised	Not Compromised
Case III	Compromised	Compromised

Since the process disturbance covariance $E[w_k, w_k^T] = Q$ and the measurement noise covariance $E[v_k, v_k^T] = R$ denote the statistical expectation, the Kalman filter equations may be written as [11]:

$$P_{k+1|k} = FP_{k|k}F^T + Q$$

$$K_{k+1} = P_{k+1|k}H^T\left[HP_{k+1|k}H^T + R\right]^{-1}$$

$$\hat{x}_{k+1|k} = F\hat{x}_{k|k} + Gu_k$$

$$\hat{x}_{k+1|k+1} = \hat{x}_{k+1|k} + K_{k+1}[z_{k+1} - H\hat{x}_{k+1|k}]$$

$$P_{k+1|k+1} = [I - K_{k+1}H]P_{k+1|k}$$

where $\hat{x}_{k+1|k+1}$ is the estimated state vector, $\hat{x}_{k+1|k}$ is the predicted state vector, $P_{k+1|k+1}$ is the covariance of the estimation error, and $\hat{z}_k$ denotes the estimated sensor measurements with $\hat{z}_k = H\hat{x}_{k|k}$. The filter initialization is expressed as:

$$\hat{x}_{0|0} = E[x_0]$$

$$P_{0|0} = E\left[\left(x_0 - \hat{x}_{0|0}\right)\left(x_0 - \hat{x}_{0|0}\right)^T\right].$$

4.1 Attack Scenario

For demonstration purposes, we consider a deception attack scenario where the attacker is able to compromise at least one sensor measurement in the pipeline system. In addition, we assume that the attacker has knowledge of the maximum and minimum sensor readings that are pre-defined by the pipeline SCADA system and the alarms that are triggered when the sensor readings are outside the permissible ranges.

The two sensor measurements that are compared against the estimation results are the flow rate and the pressure at the bottom of the storage tank. Under normal operating conditions, the dynamical estimation of each sensor reading based on one or both sensor readings yields results that are comparable with the actual sensor readings. However, there are clear differences between the dynamical estimation results and sensor readings in the case of integrity attacks. Table 2 summarizes the conditions underlying the simulated attack scenarios.

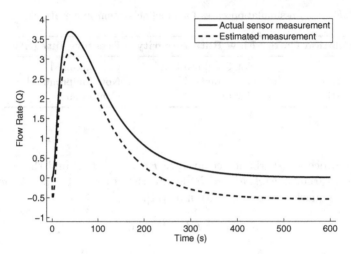

Figure 5. Case I: Flow rate observations.

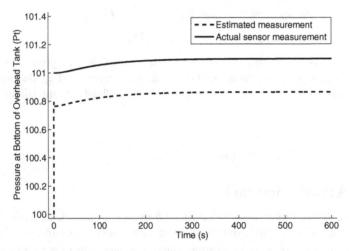

Figure 6. Case I: Pressure observations.

4.2   Anomaly Detection Results

Figures 5 through 10 show the results obtained for the flow rate and pressure measurements using the estimation algorithm. Figure 5 shows the differences in the flow rate for Case I. Figure 6 shows the differences observed in the same attack scenario for the pressure readings at the bottom of the overhead tank.

In Case II, launching a deception attack on the flow measurement reading produces no significant difference between the estimated and actual flow rates (Figure 7). The attack, however, produces a significant difference between

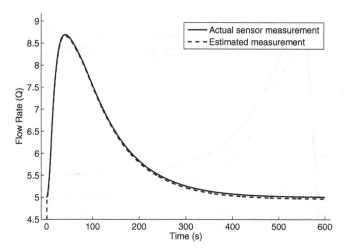

Figure 7.   Case II: Flow rate observations.

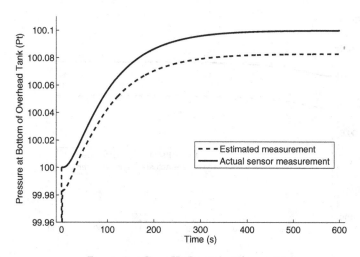

Figure 8.   Case II: Pressure observations.

the estimated pressure and the actual pressure readings as shown in Figure 8. The results are due to the characteristics of the particular pipeline system and emphasize the importance of multiple measurement points.

In Case III, the integrity of both measurements are compromised. The results, shown in Figures 9 and 10, reveal significant differences between the estimated and actual sensor measurements.

The results demonstrate notable differences between the estimates under normal operating conditions and those when sensor readings are compromised. Note that the modeled pipeline system is a non-linear dynamical system sim-

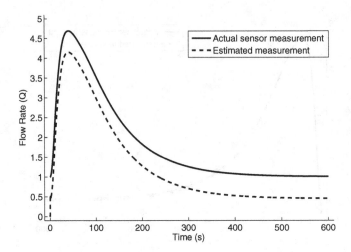

Figure 9.   Case III: Flow rate observations.

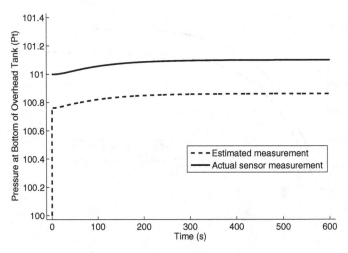

Figure 10.   Case III: Pressure observations.

ulated in Flowmaster. If the nominal operating trajectory of the non-linear system changes such that the flow becomes turbulent or transitional between laminar and turbulent, then the derived linear model in Equation (1) becomes a less accurate representation of the actual pipeline dynamics. However, small changes in the nominal operating point can be modeled as process disturbances in the Kalman filter equations. In other words, as the nominal operating point of the non-linear system changes slightly, the process disturbance covariance matrix Q can be increased to account for modeling differences between the linear equations and the non-linear operating point. Increasing Q involves the trade-off of making the Kalman estimator less sensitive to detecting anomalies, specifically when the attacker tries to shift the behavior of the system over a relatively long period of time. Indeed, to maintain sufficient accuracy, the linear model used in the Kalman estimation should be updated to reflect changes in the point of operation of the non-linear system. Continuous updates can be readily implemented using an extended Kalman filter [11].

5. Conclusions

The anomaly-based intrusion detection method for process control systems presented in this paper uses dynamical state estimation techniques. The water pipeline example demonstrates the utility of the method and the application of co-simulation techniques. The integration of Flowmaster and MATLAB/Simulink software is a promising approach for simulating attacks when developing and refining anomaly detection techniques. The experimental results reveal significant differences between normal operating conditions and scenarios involving the injection of sensor data. The experimental results also demonstrate the feasibility of developing practical intrusion detection algorithms based on dynamical state estimation.

Acknowledgement

This research was supported by the National Science Foundation under MRI Grant No. ECCS-1040161.

References

[1] A. Cardenas, S. Amin, Z. Lin, Y. Huang, C. Huang and S. Sastry, Attacks against process control systems: Risk assessment, detection and response, *Proceedings of the Sixth ACM Symposium on Information, Computer and Communications Security*, pp. 355–366, 2011.

[2] A. Cardenas, S. Amin and S. Sastry, Research challenges for the security of control systems, *Proceedings of the Third USENIX Conference on Hot Topics in Security*, article no. 6, 2008.

[3] G. Dan and H. Sandberg, Stealth attacks and protection schemes for state estimators in power systems, *Proceedings of the First IEEE Conference on Smart Grid Communications*, pp. 214–219, 2010.

[4] C. De Silva, *Mechatronics: An Integrated Approach*, CRC Press, Boca Raton, Florida, 2005.

[5] Flowmaster, FlowmasterLink for MATLAB V2.0.1, Schaumburg, Illinois (`www.flowmaster.com/flowmaster_flowmasterlink_matlab.html`).

[6] Flowmaster, Flowmaster V7 Overview, Schaumburg, Illinois (`www.flow master.com/flowmaster_overview.html`).

[7] T. Kailath and H. Poor, Detection of stochastic processes, *IEEE Transactions on Information Theory*, vol. 44(6), pp. 2230–2259, 1998.

[8] Y. Liu, P. Ning and M. Reiter, False data injection attacks against state estimation in electric power grids, *Proceedings of the Sixteenth ACM Conference on Computer and Communications Security*, pp. 21–32, 2009.

[9] D. Miller, *Internal Flow Systems*, British Hydromechanics Research Association, Cranfield, England, 1990.

[10] W. Rugh, *Linear System Theory*, Prentice Hall, Upper Saddle River, New Jersey, 1995.

[11] D. Simon, *Optimal State Estimation: Kalman, H_∞ and Nonlinear Approaches*, John Wiley, Hoboken, New Jersey, 2006.

Chapter 9

FACTORS IMPACTING ATTACKER DECISION-MAKING IN POWER GRID CYBER ATTACKS

Aunshul Rege

Abstract   For several years, security experts and government officials have been warning about a "Cyber Pearl Harbor" – a cyber attack on the nation's power grid. Current cyber security research focuses on the tactical aspects of infrastructure attacks and views attackers as passive agents, downplaying their strategies. The research only minimally incorporates the human element, which limits the understanding of cyber attacks on the critical infrastructure.

This paper explores attacker decision-making with regard to power grid cyber attacks from a criminological perspective. It presents the findings from a survey that explored the technical and non-technical factors influencing attacker decision-making. A total of 330 participants from the ethical hacker community and the power industry were surveyed. Nine factors influencing attacker decision-making emerged and were organized to create the PARE RISKS framework: prevention measures (P); attacks and alliances (A); result (R); ease of access (E); response (R); interconnectedness and interdependencies (I); security testing and audits (S); knowledge and research (K); and system weaknesses (S). This paper makes the case that infrastructure attackers are intelligent, active actors who plan strategic attacks and adapt to their environments. The paper also offers recommendations for cyber security policy, focusing on improved security practices, education programs and mandatory security budgets.

Keywords: Industrial control systems, cyber attacks, attacker decision-making

1.   Introduction

The U.S. power grid is a complex networked system that serves more than 300 million people, comprises more than 200,000 miles of transmission lines, and is valued at over $1 trillion [25]. Grid operations are now automated, use

J. Butts and S. Shenoi (Eds.): Critical Infrastructure Protection VII, IFIP AICT 417, pp. 125–138, 2013.

industrial control systems (ICSs) and are connected to the Internet; these have helped improve operations, efficiency and reliability [22, 25]. The increased connectivity, however, has made the grid more vulnerable to (remote) cyber attacks [22, 25]. Former Defense Secretary Panetta warned that cyber attacks on critical infrastructures, such as the power grid, from nation states or extremist groups could be as devastating as the 9/11 terrorist attacks [2, 3, 24]. The grid is considered to be "target number one" for cyber attacks because power disruptions impact other dependent critical infrastructures and have significant economic ramifications, with industry downtime costs exceeding U.S. $6 million per day [1, 21, 25, 30]. Unfortunately, the power sector is not prepared for cyber attacks [27, 29, 30].

In general, research has focused on power grid vulnerabilities and security, attack methods, simulations and analysis [9, 16, 17]. The research is mostly technical in nature and primarily addresses the tactical aspects of cyber attacks on the critical infrastructure. Very little research integrates or even considers the human factors underlying attacks.

Attackers are active agents and they plan and conduct strategic cyber attacks against the critical infrastructure [15, 27]. Understanding how attackers make decisions is important because attack strategies determine the tactics employed in power grid cyber attacks [27].

The criminological discipline provides a framework to investigate the strategic aspect of cyber attacks. One theoretical branch of criminology, the rational choice perspective, views attackers as intelligent individuals who learn from their experiences, adapt to their settings and employ an evolving decision-making process [23, 27]. Using this criminological approach in conjunction with technical research provides a better understanding of how attackers make decisions regarding target selection, exploiting criminal environments, and planning, designing and executing attacks. Such an understanding can help articulate and manage preventative and reactive measures.

This paper explores power grid cyber attacks from a criminological perspective to understand attacker decision-making. It identifies nine factors, technical and non-technical, that impact attacker decision-making. Using the perceptions of power grid representatives and ethical hackers, the paper demonstrates that attackers are indeed active agents who engage in dynamic cyber attacks.

2.   Attacker Decision-Making

Four research areas were examined to identify the factors that influence attacker decision-making in power grid cyber attacks. First, the ICS literature was reviewed, which provided information on system components that constitute targets. Second, the literature on ICS vulnerabilities was examined, which offered insight into system design and architectural flaws that are exploited in attacks. Third, the literature on threat agents was reviewed, which identified the assortment of attackers based on type, skill and motivation. Finally, twelve case studies involving malicious acts against the power grid were examined to understand the nature, diversity and intensity of attacker skills and strategies. The factors that influence attacker decision-making were then extracted and combined to create a PARE RISKS framework: prevention measures (P); attacks and alliances (A); result (R); ease of access (E); response (R); interconnectedness and interdependencies (I); security testing and audits (S); knowledge and research (K); and system weaknesses (S).

3. (Criminological) Theoretical Framework

Routine activity theory (RAT) focuses on the essential elements that constitute a crime. RAT states that three conditions must be met for crime to occur: (i) a likely or capable offender; (ii) a suitable target; and (iii) the absence of a capable guardian [5]. RAT is relevant to this research because it addresses the elements necessary for cyber attacks against the power grid to occur. The potential offenders are cyber attackers who have varying levels of skill and sophistication. Poorly-designed ICSs are suitable targets, and weak real-time intrusion detection systems (IDSs), for instance, represent the absence of capable guardianship. When these three elements coincide in space and time, cyber attacks are more likely to occur. Thus, it is necessary to focus on attack events as well as attacker analyses of the situations, which resonates with the active nature of attackers.

Rational choice perspective (RCP) views criminality as an outcome of the continual interaction between a criminal's desires and preferences, and the opportunities and constraints to commit crime; the attacker is a strategic decision-maker [6]. This theoretical perspective is useful for capturing attacker decisions on tactical measures and assessing whether countermeasures implemented by defenders are strong enough to deter attackers. According to RCP, attackers are rational and intelligent actors who conduct cost-benefit analyses before launching attacks; if the benefits outweigh the costs, an attacker is more likely to target the power grid.

RAT and RCP complement each other because an attacker engages in rational calculations based on the suitability of the target and the absence of capable guardianship. Thus, if a target is suitable (easy to access with exploitable loopholes) and the guardianship is weak or non-existent (poor real-time intrusion detection), then the attacker would perceive the risk to be minimal. The benefits of the attack (service disruption) would outweigh the risk, making the power grid cyber attack more likely to occur.

4. Research Methods

This research used methodological triangulation. Specifically, it used multiple data collection methods (surveys and interviews) to study attacker decision-making regarding cyber attacks on ICSs [8, 14]. Methodological triangulation was used to obtain a more complete, "holistic and contextual portrayal of the unit(s) under study" [13]. The use of different methods uncovered some unique findings that would not have been discovered by a single method [13]. Triangulating surveys and interviews also enabled new concepts to emerge [13]. While the surveys helped identify factors that influence attacker decision-making, the interviews revealed rich insights into the factors as well as the domain of cyber security.

4.1   Sampling Strategy and Data Collection

While it would have very useful to obtain information from actual attackers, this population was impossible to reach because they belong to an underground culture that is unknown or inaccessible. The vast majority of attacks on the power grid are not publicized. The few cyber attacks that have been publicly disclosed were often through the media, not from official government, security or industry sources; this raised issues of credibility, accuracy and completeness. Moreover, when the sources of attacks were disclosed, they were often foreign-based or nation-sponsored, which prevented jurisdictional access and hindered the identification of the specific source(s) and accountable individual(s).

Survey data for the hacker community was obtained during the 2010 DEF CON Hacker Conference, which had approximately 8,000 attendees with varying levels of knowledge about hacking techniques and attack trends. A total of 202 hacker respondents were sampled. Survey data from the power industry was collected from four sources. The survey was advertised and promoted through the North American Electric Reliability Corporation (NERC), the System Administration, Networking and Security (SANS) Infrastructure Conference, and the EnergySec and SCADASEC mailing lists. A total of 121 industry responses were received.

Some survey participants from the hacker community and from industry identified control system experts, specifically, system penetration testers, who were willing to participate in the interviews. These individuals are known as ethical hackers, who are engaged by the power industry to mimic malicious attackers. They possess the technological savvy to test systems, exploit vulnerabilities and evaluate preventative measures. Moreover, they employ similar decision-making processes as actual attackers when targeting systems.

4.2   Survey and Interview Design

The surveys were administered in paper and online formats. The survey items were categorized to reflect the PARE RISKS framework. A cross-sectional survey was employed to collect hacker and industry perceptions on the factors that influence attacker decision-making. The survey content was based primarily on National Institute of Standards and Technology (NIST) Special Publication 800-82 [26], and included additional items regarding attacker motivations, alliances, research and development, and resources.

The interviews helped identify additional factors that contribute to the attacker decision-making process. Telephone interviews were used to collect data from penetration testers and industry personnel. The interviews lasted approximately one hour and thirty minutes, and like the surveys, were anonymous and approved by the university's ethics committee.

Table 1. Regrouping of PARE RISKS to SPAARR.

SPAARR	PARE RISKS	Items	Subject to Item Ratio
System	Ease of Access + System Weaknesses	38	11:1
Preventative	Preventative Measures + Security Testing, Assessments and Audits	10	32:1
Attackers	Attacks and Alliances + Knowledge, Skills, Research and Development	23	14:1
Attacks	Attacks and Alliances + Knowledge, Skills, Research and Development	18	18:1
Reactive	Response and Recovery	21	15:1
Result	Results + Interconnectedness and Interdependencies	22	14:1

5. Analysis and Results

Exploratory factor analysis (EFA) was conducted to help determine whether measured variables could be explained by any underlying factors (latent variables) [7, 11]. The literature suggests that, when conducting EFA, there should be approximately ten cases per survey item [7, 10]. Unfortunately, this was not feasible in the research. The survey had 122 items, which would have required a data set of 1,220 cases, but only 322 cases were available. To ensure that the subject to item ratio was at least 10:1, the PARE RISKS factors were logically regrouped into hypothetical categories, SPAARR, which are shown in Table 1.

The principal axis factoring extraction method was used in SPSS. The factors that preceded the last major drop of the scree plot were retained [7, 11]. The direct oblimin method with the default delta (0) value was used, which allowed the factors to correlate [7]. Factor loadings greater than 0.3 were reported; this cutoff is conventionally regarded as a "meaningful loading" [18]. While the retained factors accounted for most of the variance, the remaining factors also accounted for some variance and, as such, a second EFA was conducted that forced all the items to load on the retained factors. Table 2 lists the factors that were retained from the second EFA. A value between 0.7 and 0.8 is an acceptable value for Cronbach's alpha (scale reliability) and was, thus, kept for the EFA [10].

As noted earlier, survey items were predominantly informed by the existing literature, which was technical in nature. Other, non-technical factors were only minimally addressed in the ICS cyber security research. Interviews complemented and supplemented the survey because they had the potential to identify new factors and add more depth to the EFA-retained factors.

The NVivo 9 software was used to code the interview transcripts. NVivo 9 classifies, sorts and arranges information by creating nodes (themes) and subnodes (sub-themes) as they emerge [19, 20]. The transcripts were scanned to

Table 2.　Factors retained from exploratory factor analysis.

Grouping	Factors
System	Network security and monitoring; Lack of redundancy; Non-cyber/physical access; Remote access; Authentication
Preventative	Protection updates; Security testing and vulnerability assessment frequency; Ease of bypassing IDSs
Attackers	Commercial; Political; Leisure; Business-financial
Attacks	Information-seeking techniques; Installation techniques; Non-technical techniques; Attack-in-progress techniques
Result	Human health; Information; Environment and health; Order and finance; Plant operations

identify common themes that emerged in the interview transcripts. Three main themes emerged: attacker, target and dynamics.

Table 3.　Factors retained from the interview analysis.

Theme	Sub-Theme	Further Sub-Themes
Attacker	Resources	Skills; Money; Time
	Organization	Alliance; Division of Labor
	Attacks	Research; Technique
Target	Accessibility	Electronic; Physical
	Prevention	Existence/Quality; Vendor; Detection
	Weaknesses	COTS; Architecture; Updates/Testing
Dynamics	Cost-Benefit Analysis	Attack Plan; Decision Trees
	Response	Type: Isolation; Reconnaissance; Feed False Data
		Body: Industry; Public-Private; National; International
	Counter-Response	Alternate Access; Alternate Tactic
	Exit	Delete Evidence; Tracking Complexity

While the interviews yielded rich details on several factors that influence attacker decision-making, all the details cannot be provided here. Table 3 presents a summary of the factors retained from the interview analysis. Only the attacker-related resource factors are discussed here: skills, money and time. These resources are considered to be crucial for the successful planning and execution of cyber attacks on ICSs:

> If anything, some **very very good virus writing**, but more importantly **a very very very deep understanding** of the vulnerabilities

for that system, how to exploit those vulnerabilities, how to do things with a payload ... *Penetration Tester 2 (Skills)*

From a monetary investment, ... about **$100,000 for a single zero-day** with an exploit mind you. OK. So they put **4 of them ... Black Market value for a digital cert is b/w a 100K and 200K**... So what does that tell you? It tells you that it was funded. **Quite well-funded** in fact. *Penetration Tester 1 (Money)*

To me, I would put it at skills, I'd put it at preparation time. I mean, this is **months worth of planning and preparation**, this isn't just a payable coding that's done in a couple of weeks. *Penetration Tester 3 (Time)*

6.   Study Limitations

This section discusses the limitations of the study and the revisions made to PARE RISKS.

6.1   Comparing Attack Perceptions and Reality

The study was exploratory in nature and based on hacker and industry perceptions. As such, there was concern if the perceptions reflected reality. Did the PARE RISKS framework, which is based on hacker and industry perceptions, parallel other cyber security studies? Did this framework contribute to industry vulnerability assessments? If so, how?

Two industry assessments served as comparison points. The first report pertained to ICS cyber security assessments conducted by the Idaho National Laboratory (INL) [12], which identified vulnerabilities that could put the critical infrastructure at risk from cyber attacks. The second report was produced by the Control Systems Security Program [28] of the U.S. Department of Homeland Security. This report offers eighteen security assessments of ICS products and installations from 2004 to 2010. Both the reports were based on actual ICS assessments, the former focusing on power grid ICSs and the latter more general ICS vulnerability assessments. The results of the criminological study parallel the two assessment studies very well. Increased access and connectivity, poorly protected networks, weak authentication protocols and infrequent security and patch updates are findings that also emerge from the criminological study.

However, as noted earlier, the INL and DHS assessments were mostly technical in nature. According to RAT, three elements must coincide in space and time for crime to occur: capable offender, suitable target and capable guardian. The INL and DHS assessments focused on the second and third elements of RAT. The criminological study made the case that the first element, the capable offender, should also be considered to obtain a fuller picture of power grid cyber attacks, which require moving beyond the technical knowledge base.

First, power grid cyber attacks involve human (attacker) aspects, such as available resources and research, which can be non-technical. A capable attacker can engage in social engineering tactics that trick power grid employees into divulging sensitive information. Control system documentation and blueprints are often found online, which attackers can use to extensively study their targets and design system-specific cyber attacks. Also, attackers can physically access corporate networks, bypass firewalls and connect directly to ICSs. These issues, while non-technical, can also contribute to the occurrence of the ICS cyber attacks. Yet, they are not fully addressed in the ICS cyber security assessments.

There are other limitations with this study given the methodology chosen. Selection bias is an unavoidable survey limitation. In this particular context, the hacker and industry respondents may not have had the knowledge necessary to complete the survey. Participants may have been unaware of all the threats and cyber attack scenarios, and may have possessed varying levels of technical expertise. This limitation, however, could not be avoided given the exploratory nature of the research, and that there was no publicly-available list of power grid cyber security experts from which the survey respondents could have been solicited. This shortcoming was managed by comparing the survey responses with the technical vulnerability assessments conducted by INL and DHS, and similar results were found (as discussed above). Selection bias was not an issue for the interviews because participants were experts with more than twenty years of experience in power grid cyber security. As such, they had inside information about prior grid cyber attacks and extensive knowledge about current trends, and the techniques and strategies used by attackers.

6.2   PARE RISKS Revisions

The EFA and interview analysis each yielded several factors that influence attacker decision-making. What did this imply for the original PARE RISKS framework? Was it an adequate framework? Table 4 shows that each of the factors that was retained by the analysis is easily mapped to the nine factors from the original framework.

It is important to note, however, that some of the elements originally included for a few PARE RISKS factors did not emerge in the analysis. EFA sifted through the original PARE RISKS elements and condensed them into a new set of factors. Thus, despite the clean mapping back to the PARE RISKS framework, some of the factors now had fewer items. For instance, the "Response and Recovery" factor was now simply "Response;" the "Recovery" component did not seem to impact the attacker decision-making process. Nor did this component emerge in the interview analysis as a relevant factor that influences how ICS attackers make decisions.

Although the original framework was adequate to address attacker decision-making, new elements still need to be incorporated, such as physical access to ICSs. Other new elements included how attackers manage industry responses; for instance, alternate access and techniques could be used to continue the attack. Another addition incorporated the attacker's need for well-designed attack plans, where all possible attack scenarios are mapped out with possible courses of action. Finally, the "Exit Strategy" was also a new addition to the

Table 4. Revised PARE RISKS framework.

Factors	Items (New items are italicized)
Preventative Measures	Protection updates
	Ease of bypassing IDSs
	Existence/quality
	Vendor-based
	Network security and monitoring
Attacks and Alliances	Attacker Type: Commercial; Political; Leisure; Business-financial
	Organization: Alliances; Division of labor
	Attack Technique: Information-seeking techniques; Installation techniques; Non-technical techniques; Attack-in-progress techniques
	Resources: Skills; Money; Time
Results	Data modification; Plant operations
Ease of Access	Electronic/remote; *Physical*
	Weak authentication
Response	Type of Response: Isolation; Reconnaissance; Feed false data
	Responding Body: Industry; Public-private; National; International
	Counter-Response: Alternate access; Alternate tactic
	Exit Strategy: Delete evidence; Tracking complexity
Interconnectedness and Interdependencies	Human health; Environment; Civic order; Finance
Security Testing and Audits	Security testing and vulnerability assessment frequency
Knowledge and Research	Research and development
	Attack Plan
System Weaknesses	Commercial-off-the-shelf software
	Architecture/legacy systems
	Inadequate redundancy

PARE RISKS framework. Attackers could delete logs or evidence that could be traced back to them, and they could also hop through several transit points in cyber space to mask their digital footprints.

7.   Policy Implications

While this study is based on the perceptions of hackers and industry personnel, the policy implications offered here are based on their extensive knowledge base and experience. All the implications cannot be discussed due to space constraints. However, the four most important implications for ICS cyber security policy and practice are presented.

7.1   Better Security Practices

- IDSs may not be the most effective means to detect malicious activity. Human resources for monitoring IDSs and reviewing entry/exit logs are minimal; improving real-time detection mechanisms is a must.

- Poor authentication practices permit malicious entities to easily access ICSs. Better password practices, such as encrypting passwords when they are stored and when they are transferred through internal networks, using complex passwords, frequently changing passwords, and not sharing passwords, can all help minimize unauthorized access to ICSs.

- ICS information can be obtained through various means; malicious entities share this information in online hacking forums and use it to design attacks. While industry cannot control the information released in hacking forums, it can regulate the amount of ICS information (e.g., blueprints, passwords, system versions and vulnerabilities) that is released to unauthorized entities. This would make it harder for malicious entities to study targets and design appropriate attacks, thereby making it more difficult to target ICSs.

- Situational crime prevention focuses on reducing crime opportunities instead of identifying potential attackers based on their characteristics. Situational crime prevention offers 25 crime prevention techniques based on five principal categories of action: (i) increasing the effort required by the attacker to commit the crime by hardening targets; (ii) increasing the risks of detection; (iii) reducing the rewards of critical infrastructure attacks; (iv) removing excuses by educating employees; and (v) reducing provocations by setting formal regulatory policies [4]. Situational crime prevention principles can help design security measures that extend beyond the existing technical solutions.

7.2   Definition (In)Consistency

Hackers and industry personnel feel that there is a lack of consensus regarding how threats, vulnerabilities, risks and consequences are defined. Furthermore, both hackers and industry personnel believe that there is no consensus on these terms within their communities.

> [People] will **confuse threat, vulnerability, and risk and not actually understand what it is** . . . but the problem is that the reason we don't understand how to really define risk is because **there is no consensus on how we define threat, vulnerability, and consequence**, which is funny as hell. . . *Penetration Tester 2*

The different definitions of these terms are problematic because, if there is no clear understanding about the terms and how they are connected, then the identification of security issues and risks are flawed because they are based on different definitions. The (multiple) incorrect views lead to security (and prevention) measures that are grossly ineffective. One approach for reducing inconsistencies in definitions is to develop a concise set of definitions of threats, vulnerabilities, risks and consequences that are uniformly used and practiced throughout industry. This would minimize confusion about the definitions, allow a common context to compare incidents and help design effective vulnerability assessments, security testing protocols and prevention strategies.

7.3 Education Programs

The hacker and industry groups both believe that stovepiping knowledge impacts the security of ICSs. Industry members who are not involved in security and/or penetration testing activities generally possess limited technical expertise to comprehend the importance of vulnerability assessments and security testing.

> And it **took quite a lot to help educate those guys on what risks are**. I mean, the initial discussion with those guys was "hey – this is regulatory stuff called FERC and NERC, and you know – what do we need to worry about" - I'm like "oh good grief – oh god" – OK people – let's do little bit of education first. *Penenetration Tester 3*

> The SCADA industry professionals have **relatively limited technical expertise at implementing security controls**. Their employers have not put a lot of effort into changing that situation. *Power Grid Representative 4*

Building the knowledge bases of non-technical industry personnel can be done through education programs. These programs should educate company executives and management on the basic ideas of threats, vulnerabilities, risk, and consequences, how they are related, and why they are important.

7.4 Mandatory Security Budgets and Programs

The power sector and the ICS vendor community should have mandatory security budgets. Each power utility should be required to set aside funds dedicated to continuous security monitoring, frequent and rigorous security testing, vulnerability assessments and audits. ICS vendors should be required to follow suit. The interview data revealed that the hacker and industry groups both agree that only a handful of ICS vendors engage in (poorly developed) testing practices, which undermines the effectiveness of their products. Furthermore, vendors need to continue to support their products even after industry updates security measures.

> The problem again is that this goes back to the vendor who says "well, hey, **we won't support your system unless you were at this version**," and well that version is vulnerable to an attack, so what are we supposed to do? So you have to find **different mitigations or risk, becoming unsupported by the vendor by putting a host of firewalls into your system**. *Penetration Tester 1*

> For most ICSs, **the introduction time frame for a new item of software is umm. . . the earliest at about three months, typically is six months, twelve months are not unusual**. . . you don't want the change . . . to cause more harm than the change you were trying to defend against. [Updating] is a pretty **slow process**, and only in the rarest case does it happen in less than three months. . . pressure from some of the larger utilities, **some vendors do testing**. Vendor industry is very **immature . . . and their testing is not particularly effective. . . Some of the vendors don't do any testing at all**. *Penetration Tester 4*

If the vendor software development cycle is indeed a slow process, the power industry should not have to choose between security and support. Instead, security practices and vendor support should be performed synchronously.

8. Conclusions

This study makes the case that power grid cyber attackers are active decision-makers who are influenced by several technical and non-technical factors. Future studies should further explore the complex temporal, interactive and causal relationships underlying attacker decision-making. This study has focused exclusively on the power grid. Future research should test the generalizability of the PARE RISKS framework to other infrastructures, which will help refine the framework and enhance its applicability.

An unexpected, yet important, finding that emerged is that attackers engage adaptive decision-making processes. The participant interviews revealed the temporal and dynamic nature of ICS attacks by focusing on the pre-attack and attack-in-progress periods. The temporal aspect of ICS attacks suggests that ICS attackers engage in extensive research and planning to study the target and its weaknesses before proceeding with an attack. The dynamic property of ICS attacks further supports the notion that attackers are not passive; they learn from their experiences, adjust to their environments and engage a constantly-changing decision-making process. Five distinct stages of the crime script emerge from the interview data: preparation, entry, initiation, attack dynamics and exit. Future research should study these stages, which can help project attacker moves and, in turn, identify the most effective countermeasures.

References

[1] S. Baker, S. Waterman and G. Ivanov, In the Crossfire: Critical Infrastructure in the Age of Cyber War, McAfee, Santa Clara, California, 2009.

[2] A. Beatty, U.S. cybersecurity chief warns of "market" in malware, *Agence France-Presse*, June 17, 2009.

[3] E. Bumiller and T. Shanker, Panetta warns of dire threat of cyberattack on U.S., *New York Times*, October 11, 2010.

[4] R. Clarke, Situational crime prevention, in *Environmental Criminology and Crime Analysis*, R. Wortley and L. Mazerolle (Eds.), Willan Publishing, Portland, Oregon, pp. 178–194, 2008.

[5] L. Cohen and M. Felson, Social change and crime rate trends: A routine activity approach, *American Sociological Review*, vol. 44(4), pp. 588–609, 1979.

[6] D. Cornish and R. Clarke (Eds.), *The Reasoning Criminal: Rational Choice Perspectives on Offending*, Springer-Verlag, New York, 1986.

[7] A. Costello and J. Osborne, Best practices in exploratory factory analysis: Four recommendations for getting the most from your analysis, *Practical Assessment, Research and Evaluation*, vol. 10(7), pp. 173–178, 2005.

[8] N. Denzin (Ed.), *Sociological Methods: A Sourcebook*, McGraw-Hill, New York, 1978.

[9] N. Falliere, L. O'Murchu and E. Chien, W32.Stuxnet Dossier, Symantec, Mountain View, California, 2011.

[10] A. Field, *Discovering Statistics Using SPSS*, Sage Publications, London, United Kingdom, 2013.

[11] N. Grant and L. Fabrigar, Exploratory factor analysis, in *Encyclopedia of Measurement and Statistics*, N. Salkind (Ed.), Sage Publications, Thousand Oaks, California, pp. 332–335, 2007.

[12] Idaho National Laboratory, NSTB Assessments Summary Report: Common Industrial Control System Cyber Security Weaknesses, INL/EXT-10-18381, Idaho Falls, Idaho, 2010.

[13] T. Jick, Mixing qualitative and quantitative methods: Triangulation in action, *Administrative Science Quarterly*, vol. 24(4), pp. 602–611, 1979.

[14] N. King and C. Horrocks, *Interviews in Qualitative Research*, Sage Publications, Thousand Oaks, California, 2010.

[15] McAfee, Advanced Persistent Threat, Santa Clara, California (`blogs.mcafee.com/tag/advanced-persistent-threat`).

[16] National Security Telecommunications Advisory Committee, Electric Power Risk Assessment, Washington, DC (`www.solarstorms.org/ElectricAssessment.html`), 2000.

[17] P. Oman, E. Schweitzer and J. Robert, Safeguarding IEDS, substations and SCADA systems against electronic intrusions, *Proceedings of the Western Power Delivery Automation Conference*, 2001.

[18] E. Pedhazur and L. Schmelkin, *Measurement, Design and Analysis: An Integrated Approach*, Taylor and Francis, New York, 1991.

[19] QSR International, NVivo 9 Features and Benefits, Melbourne, Australia (`www.qsrinternational.com/products_nvivo_features-and-benefits.aspx`).

[20] QSR International, What is Qualitative Research? Melbourne, Australia (`www.qsrinternational.com/what-is-qualitative-research.aspx`.

[21] R. Rantala, Cybercrimes Against Businesses, 2005, Special Report NCJ 221943, Bureau of Justice Statistics, U.S. Department of Justice, Washington, DC, 2008.

[22] A. Rege, Cybercrimes against critical infrastructures: A study of online criminal organizations and techniques, *Criminal Justice Studies*, vol. 22(3), pp. 261–271, 2009.

[23] A. Rege, Offender decision-making in industrial control systems cybercrime, presented at the *Cyber Infrastructure Protection Conference*, 2012.

[24] S. Sloane, The U.S. needs a cybersecurity czar now, *Bloomberg Businessweek*, August 13, 2009.

[25] Staff of Congressmen Edward J. Markey (D-MA) and Henry A. Waxman (D-CA), Electric Grid Vulnerability: Industry Responses Reveal Security Gaps, U.S. House of Representatives, Washington, DC, 2013.

[26] K. Stouffer, J. Falco and K. Scarfone, Guide to Industrial Control Systems (ICS) Security, NIST Special Publication 800-82, National Institute of Standards and Technology, Gaithersburg, Maryland, 2012.

[27] L. Tinnel, O. Saydjari and D. Farrell, Cyberwar strategy and tactics: An analysis of cyber goals, strategies, tactics and techniques, *Proceedings of the IEEE SMC Workshop on Information Assurance*, pp. 228–234, 2002.

[28] U.S. Department of Homeland Security, Common Cybersecurity Vulnerabilities in Industrial Control Systems, Washington, DC, 2011.

[29] U.S. Government Accountability Office, Protection of Chemical and Water Infrastructure: Federal Requirements, Actions of Selected Facilities and Remaining Challenges, Report No. GAO-05-327, Washington, DC, 2005.

[30] B. Wingfield, Power-grid cyber attack seen leaving millions in dark for months, *Bloomberg*, January 31, 2012.

Chapter 10

TIMELY DELIVERY OF MESSAGES IN POSITIVE TRAIN CONTROL

Andre Bondi, Damindra Bandara, Michael Smith, Rajni Goel and Duminda Wijesekera

Abstract   In the railway infrastructure, positive train control (PTC) is an automated method for controlling and monitoring train movements to ensure safe travel by enforcing safe braking distances and speed limits, even if the locomotive driver fails to act within the specified guidelines. Obviously, it is vital to assure the timely delivery of control messages to the on-board computer system that implements PTC for a locomotive. In particular, the parameters for the timely delivery of control messages must be evaluated and specified. The delivery times of the control messages are directly impacted by the locomotive speed and braking characteristics. Train braking is characterized by braking curves that express speed as a function of distance or position. This paper utilizes numerical techniques to convert braking curves into functions of time to specify safety-driven requirements for the upper bounds on message delivery delays. Message delivery time requirements are combined with the requirement that the probability of erroneously stopping a train is very small. Rules are derived for scheduling re-transmissions of train control messages to ensure timely train braking in the event of driver error.

Keywords: Railroad security, positive train control, control messages

1. Introduction

The United States has mandated that positive train control (PTC) must be implemented in railroads that carry passengers, freight and hazardous materials by 2015 [7]. PTC enables the control and monitoring of train movements to enhance collision avoidance, enforce line speed and provide alerts about temporary speed restrictions. Trains receive information about their locations and where they are allowed to travel in a safe manner, also known as movement

J. Butts and S. Shenoi (Eds.): Critical Infrastructure Protection VII, IFIP AICT 417, pp. 139–152, 2013.

authorities. The equipment on board the trains then enforces specified policies to prevent unsafe movements.

In order to assess PTC vulnerabilities, the engineering properties of the infrastructure must be considered and analyzed. Indeed, the timely delivery of train control messages in automated signaling systems is essential to assuring the safety of railway travel. The locomotive driver must receive notice of a stop signal early enough to allow the manual application of the brakes, or the automated system must apply emergency braking in the event that the driver fails to act in a timely manner. Equally important is the timely delivery of green signals and authorities to proceed. The requirements make it imperative to understand the performance requirements of automatic signaling systems and, in particular, the performance of mechanisms that deliver messages to on-board automatic train control systems.

PTC ensures that trains do not pass stop signals or exceed speed restrictions, even if locomotive drivers do not obey them. Various systems have been proposed for PTC implementation, including ACSES (used by Amtrak) and Interoperable Train Control-PTC (ITC-PTC) [10]. This paper focuses on ITC-PTC, which has been developed by four major freight railroads under the auspices of the American Association of Railroads. In ITC-PTC, a wayside interface unit (WIU) wirelessly transmits beacon messages containing information about the status of wayside equipment (e.g., signals, switches, grade crossing barriers and track condition sensors) to on-board control systems.

The timing requirements for delivering control messages to a train are dependent on its speed and braking properties. To ensure the safe operation of control equipment, it is important to understand the performance requirements of the control system. In previous work [4], we provided a brief overview of the performance and security aspects of train identity management as trains move from one railroad to another. This paper presents an analysis of braking properties as they relate to performance requirements. Train braking properties are typically evaluated using braking curves, which specify train speed as a function of distance. Train speeds are represented as functions of time because braking directly impacts the requirements for message delivery delays.

The clarity of radio signals is also a factor that affects the timely delivery of control messages from a WIU to a locomotive. In the presence of heavy interference, the locomotive may not receive messages often enough to operate safely. In such a scenario, fail-safe braking procedures are invoked to bring the train to a stop, whether or not it is otherwise safe to proceed. The probability of such an invocation, when it is otherwise safe to proceed, should be minimal to avoid the costs imposed by unnecessary braking. Using repetitive beaconing, rather than single messages, allows the loss probability of wayside status messages (WSMs) to be rather large, while maintaining safety. This requires beaconing to be robust when radio interference is severe enough to prevent the delivery of a sizable portion of the WSMs.

This paper shows that the braking times can be used to derive guidelines for setting beaconing intervals between the transmissions of WSMs sent by WIUs.

The remainder of this paper is organized as follows. First, the details of ITC-PTC are provided. Then, an analysis of braking curves is employed to derive delay requirements for control message delivery. A rule is then specified for configuring the times between the transmissions of beaconed WSMs based on the probability of losing packets in the beaconing stream. This rule accounts for railroad guidelines related to the maximum acceptable delay of WSMs. Finally, the operational impact of the findings is discussed.

2. ITC-PTC Overview

The ITC-PTC version of PTC incorporates the existing signaling, switching and track monitoring systems. The basic components of ITC-PTC include the wayside interface unit (WIU), on-board unit (OBU) and back office server (BOS) [4]. The locomotive driver's control panel is equipped with a display that shows the status of wayside equipment on the line ahead, including the signal aspects, switch positions and indicators of track defects.

WIUs are positioned at various locations along the track. Each WIU monitors the settings of a defined set of signals and switches, as well as the status of grade crossing barriers and track defect monitors. WIUs beacon the status of wayside equipment to all trains within their broadcast ranges at regular intervals. Note that beaconing may occur continuously in congested areas. In lightly traveled areas, however, WIUs rely on battery power and only beacon the status upon receiving requests from approaching trains to conserve power.

Each locomotive is equipped with an OBU containing a track database that identifies the signals, switches and permanent speed restrictions that it may encounter. The messages received by the train provide information about signal aspects (e.g., stop, proceed slowly, proceed with moderate speed and clear), switch alignment, track conditions and special notifications (e.g., work crews present on the track). Note that the track database is consulted to select only the status fields that relate to the designated path [2]. The OBU enforces signal-based and form-based movement authorities along with speed restrictions by automatically intervening to apply the brakes if they are ignored by the locomotive driver. The shorter the time available for a train to come to rest, the quicker the response to changes in wayside equipment status.

The BOS is responsible for speed restriction, track geometry and OBU configuration. The BOS provides the track database, along with form-based movement authorities, dispatch messages, crew authorities and track directives. Additionally, it sends notices of temporary speed restrictions. If a locomotive is not within the range of a WIU, it can register to receive change-of-status messages from the BOS [8]. The OBU relays the train speed and position to the BOS, along with other information specified by the railroad [1].

3. Key Parameters

This section discusses the key parameters, which include braking curves, braking distance, stopping times and train speed.

The performance requirements for the delivery time of movement authorities and stop messages must take into account the braking characteristics. In the current PTC specifications, the requirements are based on the notion that braking on freight trains is a binary activity [9]. For trains with non-binary braking, the performance requirements are based on the maximum tolerable loss of speed (and by extension, kinetic energy) should a movement authority arrive after brake application has commenced.

Because the performance requirements for delivering control messages to a train are expressed in terms of time, braking is computed using braking curves, which provide train speed in terms of the distance traveled. In previous work [4], we derived and illustrated a numerical method for computing deceleration curves and stopping times from braking curves. Under PTC, brakes are applied by the OBU if an infraction has occurred. Emergency braking is invoked when the penalty brake does not sufficiently reduce train speed to a level below the braking curve.

On a freight train, once the air brakes are applied, they cannot be partially released because brake application entails the release of air pressure within the braking system. Note that for emergency braking, the release of air pressure is more rapid than for penalty braking. As a result, the brake is either applied or not applied. Thus, the braking of freight trains is a binary activity. The degree of brake application is more refined with electronic controls that manage the release of air pressure, but this is not currently the vision for freight trains operating under PTC. Nevertheless, we discuss the performance requirements for both cases.

The time required for a train to respond to a command depends on the following conditions:

- The current distance from the train to the point at which the train must execute the command. This is referred to in the railroad industry as the "point of protection."

- The reaction time of the driver.

- The speed of the train.

- The time required for PTC to intervene if the driver has not acted on a signal.

- The braking capabilities of the train as described by the shape of the braking curve.

The braking curve represents the speed of the train as a function of distance traveled under expected actions, such as the application of brakes. The message delivery time requirements can be derived using the braking curve as a basis for computing the time to decelerate by a given speed [4].

Leveraging the work described in [5], we illustrate the concept of a braking curve for a train with an initial speed of 40 mph and an anticipated stopping distance of 6,000 feet from the point of initial brake application. Note that these

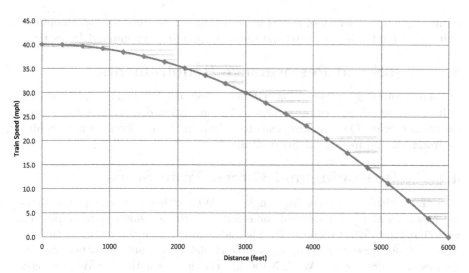

Figure 1. Synthetic braking curve.

conditions are consistent with long freight train operations. Figure 1 shows a braking curve associated with these conditions.

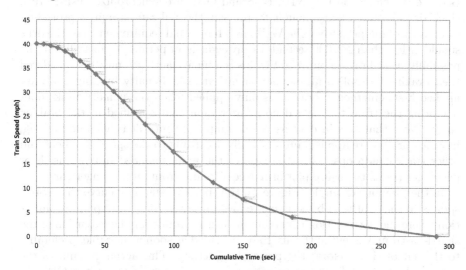

Figure 2. Train speed as a function of time.

Figure 2 shows the corresponding curve for speed as a function of time. The point of inflection in the speed versus time curve occurs because the curve is continuous and the acceleration is zero before brake application. Since the acceleration is non-positive, there must be an instant at which it reaches a local minimum. Figure 2 shows that it takes approximately five minutes to bring the train to a complete stop. To limit the amount of deceleration that occurs as a result of the late delivery of a WSM, a limit can be specified for the acceptable reduction from the initial speed and the corresponding maximum delivery time.

4.   QoS and Performance Requirements

Factors affecting timely message delivery from the WIU to the OBU include radio interference, processing delays and propagation delays. Our focus is on quality of service (QoS) requirements to include message delivery in a beaconing environment and message delivery delays.

4.1   Beaconing and Forced Train Stops

A train within the receiving range of a WIU either passively receives status messages at regular intervals or receives status messages in response to a getWIUstatus (5201) request [2]. The messages contain the status of the signals, switches, grade crossing sensors, track defect sensors and other wayside devices monitored by the WIU. Note that the devices notify the WIU directly whenever their status changes.

The OBU classifies a wayside status message as current or stale. The wayside status message is considered to be stale if it is received more than time T_w seconds after the preceding message, invoking the fail-safe stopping procedure. Because the clocks on the WIU, BOS and OBU are synchronized using GPS, clock drift is not severe enough to prevent the fail-safe stopping procedure from functioning properly. The WIU has a functional requirement that the drift should be less than $\pm 2,000$ seconds in any eight-hour period [3]. In addition, the possibility that braking on freight trains is a binary activity must be considered (i.e., braking is applied all at once or not at all). Penalty braking is always applied first; emergency braking is only applied when the penalty brake does not bring the train to a speed no greater than that specified in the braking curve. Note that this in contrast with computer controlled dynamic braking, in which brakes are applied automatically according to the speed, gradient and other track conditions, as in the case of the more nuanced braking used for passenger trains to ensure platform access to and from all passenger cars.

In the previous example (Figure 2), the speed versus time curve that corresponds to the synthetic braking curve has a negative slope and point of inflection where the deceleration is maximum. It is desirable for the extension of the signal-based movement authority to be provided as soon as possible, preferably to the left of (i.e., before) the point of inflection. This action minimizes the speed reduction while the permission to proceed is en route to the OBU. It is unlikely that the permission to proceed is rescinded for operational reasons; however, a penalty braking curve requires invocation as quickly as possible.

To ensure timely delivery, the following two conditions require consideration.

- If the permission to proceed is granted after brake application, then the message delivery time should be short enough to prevent a slowdown greater than a specified level.

- If the permission to proceed is rescinded or a stop or restrictive signal is sent, then the corresponding message delivery time should be short enough to prevent the train from traveling a specified distance before it stops.

In both cases, the time between beacon transmissions t_b must be less than the maximum chosen value of $t_D - t_0$, where t_D is the time at which notification occurs and t_0 is the time at which monitoring for brake enforcement starts.

Subject to calculations, the foregoing suggests that the higher the speed of an approaching train and/or the heavier the train, the shorter the maximum required time between beacons. If the train is subject to binary braking, the train requires a receive status message to stop or proceed at least T seconds before it arrives at the point of automated brake application. For example, if the train is traveling at 40 mph, a delivery time requirement of ten seconds would result in the train moving 0.1111 miles before the commencement of brake application. If the train is subject to a more refined braking policy with a requirement that it lose no more than 5 mph from its initial speed of 40 mph, then the delivery of a message to proceed should arrive no more than 37 seconds after brake application based on the quadratic braking curve shown in Figure 2. Note that the performance requirement is specified in terms of time, not distance. As demonstrated in Figure 2, the time required to reduce the speed from 40 mph to 35 mph is just under 50 seconds, with the distance traveled equating to approximately 2,800 feet.

4.2   QoS Models

Suppose that a railroad decrees that the maximum permissible time between successful wayside status message arrivals is T_w and that the configured time between WIU beacon transmissions is $t_b < T_w$. Thus, the maximum number of beacon transmissions that can occur without being received before the brakes are automatically applied is $N_B = \lfloor \frac{T_w}{t_b} \rfloor$. Note that T_w should be chosen with respect to the braking curve properties that determine the distance between the point of earliest reception of a wayside status message and the point at which braking must commence.

The probability that beacon messages may be lost must also be considered. Taking into account that a wayside status message may be lost or corrupted because of radio interference or other reason (e.g., buffer overflow, jamming or a replay attack), it can be assumed that the number of beacons transmitted before the successive message arrives at the train has a geometric distribution, with parameter p equal to the probability of wayside status message loss. The following probabilities further characterize message arrival:

- The probability that two successive beacon messages are successfully received without interruption is $1 - p$.

- The probability that one beacon message is not received between two successful arrivals is $p(1 - p)$.

- The probability that two successive beacon messages are not received between two successful arrivals is $p^2(1-p)$.

- The probability that k successive messages are not received between two successful arrivals is $p^k(1-p)$ where $k < N_B$.

- The probability that the train comes to a stop because at least N_B successive messages have failed to arrive between two successful arrivals is given by:

$$
\begin{aligned}
p_{stop} &= 1 - (1-p) \sum_{k=0}^{N_B-1} p^k \\
&= 1 - (1-p)\frac{(1-p^{N_B})}{(1-p)} \qquad (1)\\
&= p^{N_B}.
\end{aligned}
$$

Equation (1) leads to the specification of the probability of a message being lost. If the probability that a train needlessly comes to a stop is less than a specified quantity ϵ, then a constraint on the probability is discerned that specifies message loss due to radio interference or other cause $p^{N_B} < \epsilon$, such that:

$$
p < \sqrt[N_B]{\epsilon}. \qquad (2)
$$

For example, suppose the probability that a train is stopped unnecessarily because of radio interference is less than 10^{-6} (i.e., $\epsilon = 10^{-6}$). If the wayside status messages are sent one second apart with the allotted time between successful transmissions set to twelve seconds, then $N_B = \frac{12}{1} = 12$ and $p < \sqrt[12]{10^{-6}} = 0.316$.

This example demonstrates the requirement of a low probability for stopping can be met with a maximum allowed time of twelve seconds if message transmissions occur every second, even if one-third of all WIU status messages are lost. This makes the communication method quite robust in the face of a very high probability of message loss. If the constraint on the message loss probability cannot be met, then the railroad must tolerate a larger value of ϵ. In operational terms, this means that, if the probability of message loss due to interference is too high, then the railroad must tolerate a larger probability of unnecessarily stopping a train because a permissive message is not received.

Suppose that wayside messages have to be transmitted less frequently due to bandwidth limitations. If the maximum allowed time of a wayside status message is twelve seconds and the messages are transmitted every four seconds (instead of every second), then $N_B = \frac{12}{4} = 3$ and the corresponding probability of non-delivery of a valid wayside status message must be less than $\sqrt[3]{10^{-6}} = 0.01$. Note that the required loss probability is non-linear with respect to the ratio of the maximum allowed time between beacon messages. A higher ratio makes the system much more robust, since more beacon messages can

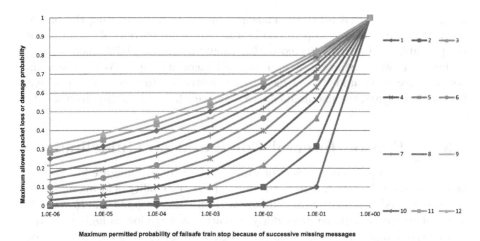

Figure 3. Maximum permitted probability of lost/damaged wayside status messages.

be transmitted during the maximum allowed time, provided that the increased number of beacons does not result in increased message loss because of radio interference or excessive bandwidth use.

Since the number of consecutive transmissions that are unsuccessful is geometrically distributed with parameter p, the mean number of consecutive unsuccessful transmissions is $\frac{p}{(1-p)}$. As such, $p = 0$ is considered to represent pure transmission. Alternatively, if $p = 1$, then every message transmission is unsuccessful and wayside status messages do not reach their destinations. Interestingly, the expected number of consecutive successful transmissions of beacons is the reciprocal of the expected number of unsuccessful transmissions (i.e., $\frac{(1-p)}{p}$). Note that if $p = 1 - p = \frac{1}{2}$, the expected consecutive number of either successful or unsuccessful beacon transmissions is one, meaning that on the average every other message is successfully received.

The results demonstrate that PTC is fairly robust in the face of radio interference considering the transmission interval and timeout value for automatic brake application. Even if the probability of losing a wayside status message is 0.5 (an indicator of severe interference), fewer than three in 10,000 trains would be stopped when braking is triggered by twelve consecutive losses. Normal operations can continue if the risk level of unnecessary delay is deemed tolerable.

Figure 3 shows the maximum permitted probability of a wayside status message not being received by the OBU as a function of the probability that a fail-safe stop must be invoked given that the train does not have to stop, for different numbers of successive lost messages between arriving messages. The plot shows that allowing large numbers of consecutive lost messages increases the maximum allowed probability of losing a message, regardless of the probability that a train is stopped because of consecutive message losses, as might be expected. The degenerate case of allowing erroneous stops without restriction

($p_{stop} = 1$) means that all status messages can be lost. Restricting the probability of an unnecessary stop to one in a million train movements means that the probability of an undelivered packet should not exceed 0.32 when braking occurs after twelve consecutive undelivered beacon messages. When the number of consecutive undelivered messages is restricted to three messages sent four seconds apart, the maximum allowed message loss probability decreases to 0.01.

4.3   Beacon Interval Configuration Guidelines

Equation (2) provides a guide for railroad planners to configure beacon frequency based on known or estimated values of the probability of losing messages and the desired maximum probability of a train being stopped due to wayside status message loss. If the probability of status message loss is high, then the risk of erroneously stopping a train because of message loss can be reduced by shortening the interval t_b between beacons. This increases the number of wayside status messages sent within time T_w. For example, if the probability that a valid wayside status message is not delivered within twelve seconds is 0.3, then the odds of an erroneous stop is approximately one in a million if beacons are sent at intervals of $t_b = \frac{12}{12} = 1$ every second. The odds are one in a thousand if the interval is $t_b = \frac{12}{6} = 2$ seconds and one in ten if the interval is $t_b = \frac{12}{2} = 6$ seconds. Note that the choices of t_b and T_w also create the requirement that the OBU should process incoming wayside status messages at a rate that is no less than $\frac{1}{t_b}$ messages per second. If the OBU is designed to meet the requirement of processing one wayside status message every T_C seconds, then $T_C < t_b$.

4.4   Delay Requirements for Message Delivery

The numerical method suggested in [4] can be used to compute the message delivery and other delay requirements for a train approaching a WIU that guards an entrance to PTC territory. Since the train is PTC-enabled, it is aware of the existence and position of the WIU and listens for the status beacon or issues a getWIUstatus request when it is within range of the WIU radio transmitter. After the locomotive is within range, the following events occur:

- The locomotive authenticates the identity of the WIU; this requires time t_a. Note that, if HMAC is the sole means of authentication, as is the case for ITC-PTC, then this step is performed for every message.

- The WIU sends a beacon at regular intervals, or the locomotive issues a getWIUstatus request to start the beacon. The time taken to receive a beacon is the expected time between successful beacon transmissions t_s plus the time t_g taken for the WIU to respond to a getWIUstatus request. If the WIU is beaconing steadily without waiting for a BeaconRequest message, then $t_g = 0$.

- The locomotive driver takes time t_R to react to the OBU display or wayside signal or, if the signal indicates danger and the driver ignores it, then the OBU begins to activate the brakes according to the braking curve, which takes time t_{OBU}.

United States Government regulations 49 CFR 236.563 and 49 CFR 236.831 state that if a train is required to stop, the time elapsed from when the on-board apparatus detects a more restrictive indication until brake application commences shall not exceed eight seconds [6]. Hence, $t_{OBU} < 8$ seconds. For a probability of failed beacon transmission p, the expected time to receive a successful beacon is the expected time between successful transmissions or, equivalently, the expected number of failed transmissions multiplied by the beacon interval time, plus the expected time to the next beacon emission $\frac{t_b}{2}$. Thus,

$$
\begin{aligned}
t_s &= \frac{(p \times t_b)}{(1-p)} + \frac{t_b}{2} \\
&= \frac{(1+p)t_b}{2(1-p)}.
\end{aligned}
\tag{3}
$$

For safety reasons, the time between successful receptions of beacon transmissions cannot be greater than the maximum permitted reception time of a wayside status message. Thus, $t_b < T_W$ or equivalently,

$$
t_b < \frac{2T_w(1-p)}{1+p}.
\tag{4}
$$

When $p = 0$, the expected time to successfully receive a wayside status message is $\frac{t_b}{2}$. Alternatively, when $p = 1$, the expected time is infinite because all WIU transmissions fail, as one would intuitively expect. Note also that, when $p = 0$, the requirement for the time between beacons is less than twice the maximum allotted time of a wayside status message T_W.

Consider the track distance from the initial point of a train when a wayside status message is received to the point at which brakes are applied B. Additionally, assume that the train is traveling with constant speed v. If the braking curve is followed and the train is to be stopped before the signal of interest, then:

$$
v(t_a + t_s + t_g + t_R + t_{OBU}) < B.
\tag{5}
$$

If $x_R = v \times t_R$ is the distance traveled during the driver's reaction time, during which time the speed of the train is assumed to be constant, then the following upper bound on the time is obtained for a locomotive to activate the brakes in response to a WIU status message:

$$
t_a + t_s + t_g + t_{OBU} < \frac{(B - x_R)}{v}, \quad x_R < B.
\tag{6}
$$

This equation shows that a long reaction time decreases the maximum permissible time to activate the brakes according to the braking curve, and that the maximum allowable activation time is inversely proportional to the speed of the train. Moreover, the reaction distance must be less than the distance such that the train speed must follow the braking curve. Interpreted another way, if the brake activation time cannot be reduced, then either the speed v in the approach zone to the PTC-controlled track must be decreased accordingly or the braking distance B must be increased accordingly. Combining Equations (2) through (6) provides a relationship between the successful transmission probability, the desired probability of the train braking incorrectly, speed and braking distance. Substituting for p yields:

$$t_a + t_{OBU} + \frac{1 + \sqrt[N_R]{\epsilon}t_b}{2(1 - \sqrt[N_R]{\epsilon})} + t_g < \frac{B - x_R}{v}, \ x_R < B. \tag{7}$$

If the inequality in Equation (7) cannot be satisfied by a reasonable set of parameters, the train cannot be brought to a stop within the requisite distance while keeping the probability of an erroneous stop below the desired level.

If the train is eligible to proceed in a more permissive manner than is enforced by the PTC mechanism, it is desirable that the OBU be notified as early as possible so that enforcement can be rescinded. This minimizes the adverse effect of unnecessary braking, especially in the case where braking is a non-binary as opposed to a binary activity. It is desirable to rescind enforcement either before the application of the brakes, or as soon as possible after their application. If brake application begins after enforcement, cancellation should occur at the earliest point at which the absolute value of the intended acceleration (i.e., the slope of the speed with respect to time) is as small as possible. Put another way, the desire is to minimize the loss of kinetic energy due to unnecessary braking by setting the maximum desired message delivery time $t_D - t_0$ to ensure that the change in kinetic energy $\frac{1}{2}m(v_0^2 - v_D^2)$ is as small as possible.

5.   Impact on Engineering and Operations

The preceding discussion shows that the braking properties, beacon transmission quality requirements and the desired probability of erroneously stopping a train are closely related. The impact of this relationship is that transmission quality cannot be engineered independently of service and braking properties, or vice versa. Competing stakeholders and entities that coordinate their activities must weigh the tradeoffs between the bandwidth associated with the frequent transmission of wayside status messages, the cost of engineering braking capability to accommodate radio interference and the cost of minimizing radio interference. The braking properties of a train are dependent on its composition, how slippery the tracks are, whether the approach to a signal is on a curve or slope and the characteristics of the brakes themselves.

The effects of radio interference can be mitigated by broadcasting wayside status messages to trains more frequently. Determining how often to broadcast wayside status messages allows a railroad to transmit messages less frequently when higher radio interference is present and to choose the lowest rate of transmission that meets safety needs, while containing the risk of stopping a train when there is no need to do so. It should be noted that the causes of radio interference may be outside the control of the railroad. Moreover, interference could have seemingly mundane and unexpected causes, such as the presence of a refrigerator with poor electrical grounding or other undesirable properties in the locomotive cab. The possibility of unexpected and/or uncontrolled causes of message loss implies that wayside status messages should be transmitted more often to increase their chances of reception by the OBU, to the extent that bandwidth is not exhausted.

6.   Conclusions

Ensuring the timely delivery of control messages is vital to creating a safer and more efficient railway infrastructure. In particular, the guidelines derived in this paper for configuring the operating parameters of a positive train control specification help contain the risk of unnecessarily braking locomotives. By associating message delivery time requirements with a low probability of erroneously stopping a train, the rules derived for scheduling control message transmission rates ensure timely braking. Another key contribution is the demonstration of the need to consider operating conditions and braking properties when formulating performance and QoS requirements for control message delivery. By utilizing numerical techniques to convert braking curves into functions of time, it is possible to specify safety-driven requirements for the upper bounds on message delivery delays. As a result, railroad authorities can assess message delivery rates to minimize unnecessary braking while enhancing safe travel.

The opinions, findings and conclusions or recommendations expressed in this paper reflect the views of the authors, who are responsible for the facts and the accuracy of the data presented. The contents do not necessarily reflect the official view or policies of the Federal Railroad Administration, the U.S. Department of Transportation or the United States Government and shall not be used for advertising or product endorsement purposes. Neither the United States Government, nor any of its employees, make any warranty, express or implied, including the warranties of merchantability and fitness for a particular purpose, or assume any legal liability or responsibility for the accuracy, completeness or usefulness of any information, apparatus, product or process disclosed, or represent that their use would not infringe privately owned rights.

Acknowledgements

We wish to thank Dan Paulish of Siemens Corporate Technologies and Peter Torrellas and Aleksandar Isailowski of Siemens Mobility for their assistance with this research. This research was supported by the Federal Railroad Administration under Grant No. FR-TEC-0006-11-01-00/20.321.

References

[1] Association of American Railroads, Interoperable Train Control Office-Locomotive Interface Control Document, S-9352A, Washington, DC, 2010.

[2] Association of American Railroads, Interoperable Train Control Wayside-Locomotive Interface Control Document, S-9352B, Washington, DC, 2011.

[3] Association of American Railroads, Interoperable Train Control Wayside Interface Interface Unit Requirements, Standard S-9202, Washington, DC, 2012.

[4] D. Bandara, A. Bondi, R. Goel, N. Pilapitiya and D. Wijesekera, Developing a framework to address performance and security protocol concerns in identity management for interoperable positive train control systems, *Proceedings of the ASME Joint Rail Conference*, pp. 389–396, 2012.

[5] B. Ede and J. Brosseau, Development of an Adaptive Predictive Braking Enforcement Algorithm, Technical Report PB2009-115671, Federal Railroad Administration, Washington, DC, 2009.

[6] Federal Railroad Administration, Rules, Standards and Instructions Governing the Installation, Inspection, Maintenance and Repair of Signal and Train Control Systems, Devices and Appliances, Title 49, *Code of Federal Regulations*, Part 236, Subpart I, Washington, DC, 2012.

[7] Federal Railroad Administration, Positive Train Control Overview, Washington, DC (`www.fra.dot.gov/Page/P0621`), 2013.

[8] Meteorcomm, ITCC Overview, Renton, Washington (`www.fra.dot.gov/Elib/Document/2218?`), 2012.

[9] Railway Technical Web Pages, Air Brakes (`www.railway-technical.com/air-brakes.shtml`), 2013.

[10] J. Stagl, PTC: Railroads attempt to get a better handle on positive train control implementation, *Progressive Railroading*, November 2011.

IV

INFRASTRUCTURE MODELING AND SIMULATION

Chapter 11

MODELING SERVICE MIGRATION AND RELOCATION IN MISSION-CRITICAL SYSTEMS

Yanjun Zuo

Abstract   Mission-critical information systems are commonly used in critical infrastructure assets such as the electric power grid, telecommunications networks, healthcare systems, water management systems and national defense. Damage or disruption of these systems could result in the loss of services and potentially serious societal consequences. Therefore, it is important to ensure that the essential services provided by these systems are reliable and dependable. This paper presents a modeling framework for service migration and relocation, which can dynamically transfer critical services from a compromised platform to other healthy platforms. The mechanism guarantees that vital services are continuously available despite malicious attacks and system failures. When the compromised platform has recovered, the services can be moved back to the platform. The modeling framework provides a means for studying the important factors that impact service migration and relocation, and how an assured service migration mechanism can be designed to increase confidence about the reliability of mission-critical information systems.

Keywords: Mission-critical systems, migration, reliability, availability

1.   Introduction

Mission-critical systems provide vital services and must, therefore, be reliable and dependable despite malicious attacks and system failures. Their use in critical infrastructure assets such as the electric power grid, telecommunications networks, healthcare systems, water management systems and national defense raises serious concerns about their ability to withstand hardware and software failures, operator errors, power outages, environmental disasters and attacks by adversaries [9].

J. Butts and S. Shenoi (Eds.): Critical Infrastructure Protection VII, IFIP AICT 417, pp. 155–170, 2013.
© IFIP International Federation for Information Processing 2013

Despite the best efforts of system developers and security practitioners, it is infeasible to assure that a mission-critical system will be invulnerable to well-organized attacks and unpredictable system failures. Indeed, the scale and complexity of mission-critical systems make it almost impossible to build completely secure and reliable systems. Consequently, it is prudent to prepare for the worst-case scenarios involving security incidents and system failures while ensuring that critical services continue to be available.

This paper focuses on service migration and relocation as a means for ensuring critical service availability. Informally, service migration is a process that suspends a critical service on its current faulty platform and moves its core programs and data to a clean, healthy platform where the service is resumed from where it left off. At a later time, after the compromised platform has recovered and the environment has been sanitized, the critical service is relocated to the original platform and its execution is resumed. Such migration and relocation is incorporated in the architectures of many safety-critical systems [6].

Compared with other survivability approaches, service migration is a viable solution to ensure that the most critical services are available in a challenging environment. Techniques such as fault tolerance/masking and damage avoidance are often too expensive or infeasible for large and complex mission-critical systems. In situations where faults are extensive and non-maskable, system operations cannot be continued, even when the system has multiple redundancies. Reconfiguration [7, 10] can avoid intensive replication, but it requires a change in the functional specifications of the platforms that are in operation. Dynamically reconfiguring a system is not always possible, especially when system components have been compromised and only untrustworthy components are available for reconfiguration. Unlike these techniques, strategic migration allows critical services to be continuously provided by other healthy platforms without incurring expensive resource duplication or attempting to reconfigure a system that is not trustworthy.

This paper presents a modeling framework for service migration and relocation in mission-critical systems. A stochastic process algebra, i.e., the Performance Evaluation Process Algebra (PEPA) [5], is used to represent the activities and components of a complete service migration and relocation procedure. Since critical services are essential, minimal time and effort should be required to move the mission-critical services and relocate them back after the original platform has recovered. This paper studies how important factors such as the probability of severe damage on a platform and the probability and duration of viable migration scheduling can impact the effectiveness and efficiency of service migration and relocation. The resulting model can be used to determine the important factors and how they impact service availability. Also, it can reduce the magnitude of service interruptions by helping deploy the most effective and efficient service migration and relocation mechanisms.

2.   Related Work

Migration has been studied for a number of purposes, including application and service survivability, improvement of the quality of services, resource optimization, system agility and network virtualization. Migration has been proposed at a variety of levels, including services, system components, operating system processes, program threads and applications (e.g., mobile agents).

Choi, *et al.* [2] have proposed a methodology for run-time software component migration for application survivability in distributed real-time systems. Two properties are necessary for fast component migration: lightweight service and data transfer and proactive resource discovery. Choi and colleagues developed middleware to support prompt software component migration and identify the available resources to complete the migration. Experimental results demonstrate that the approach takes much less time compared with techniques based on reactive resource discovery.

Amoretti, *et al.* [1] have studied service migration in SP2A-based clouds (SP2A is a framework and middleware for peer-to-peer service-oriented architectures). They propose a framework and middleware for highly dynamic and adaptive clouds, characterized by peer providers and services that can be replicated by code mobility mechanisms.

Another service migration mechanism [4] moves the computational services of a virtual server to other available servers for adaptive grid computing. This enables computations to be resumed on a remote server without service reinstallation. The mechanism is incorporated in DSA, a Java compliant distributed virtual machine that accommodates adaptive parallel applications in grids.

Cohen, *et al.* [3] have proposed a service migration approach for enterprise system architectures. Instead of locating and delivering data to a processing site as in the case of traditional systems, services are delivered to the data sites for efficiency and higher levels of service availability. This approach extends the notion of a service-oriented architecture and is particularly effective when massive volumes of data (in terabytes) have to be processed. However, the approach requires new technical infrastructures and policies for client and server systems.

Li, *et al.* [8] have presented a service migration protocol that supports multimedia transfer in single-user, multiple-device scenarios. Data sessions are grouped by users and can seamlessly migrate to devices associated with the same user. A proxy is used to bridge a client and a server and a protocol is used to retain the current client and server operations while placing new functions at the proxy through naming and control and data plane designs.

The migration approaches described above are very specific and are defined at the lower level of system processes. Our methodology complements these approaches with the objective of providing a general analytic framework that can model and simulate service migration and relocation. Furthermore, it helps users identify the factors that influence the effectiveness and efficiency of service migration and relocation.

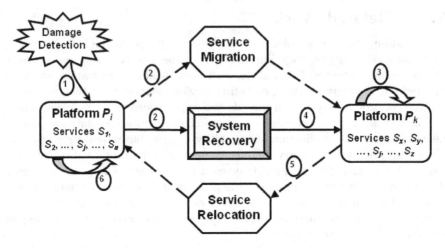

Figure 1.   Workflow of a service migration and relocation process.

3.   Service Migration and Relocation

Let SYS be a distributed system that provides critical services S_1, S_2, ..., S_n. SYS is composed of a set of computing platforms P_1, P_2, ..., P_m. Each service S_j is executed on one platform at any time and operates as a set of programs. It is assumed that service S_j is executed in a virtualized container and is, thus, self-contained, i.e., the service programs, data and processes can be referenced within its namespace. Technically, it is possible to move a service from its current platform P_i to a new platform P_k in a situation where P_i has been severely damaged. In such a case, allowing the platform to continue to perform mission-critical functions could be disastrous. To ensure that the critical services can be provided continuously and to avoid further losses, the services must be transferred to other healthy platforms that are immune to the same types of attacks that compromised the original platform.

Figure 1 shows the workflow of a service migration and relocation process. We assume that a set of services S_1, S_2, ..., S_n are currently executing on platform P_i. Suppose that abnormal behavior is detected on P_i and reported as shown in Step 1. This event triggers a thorough investigation and analysis of P_i by the security systems of SYS. If the damage assessment indicates that P_i has been severely damaged and service migration is the most appropriate strategy, then a service migration and relocation process initiates. For simplicity, we discuss the migration and relocation of one critical service S_j.

After a migration decision is made, two actions are taken concurrently as indicated by Step 2. The first action is to halt service S_j appropriately, e.g., by freezing the service processes, recording global data (service configuration and state), recording the states of individual processes and terminating the entire service program. As part of the second action, a migration scheduler attempts to generate a service migration arrangement for service S_j to be migrated from

P_i to a new, healthy platform P_k. The new platform must be able to support the core functions of S_j and should be immune to the same types of attacks suffered by P_i. Since a suitable platform may not always be available (e.g., in an environment in which resources are limited), we use a stochastic process to quantify the probability of whether or not an appropriate platform is available. If a platform is not available, the scheduler is modeled to constantly repeat the scheduling process – on the chance that a new platform becomes available at a later time when the operating environment has improved.

The service migration process is composed of three sub-processes [11]: (i) migration preparation, which saves the service programs and data in a resume-able image in a self-contained format with header, global data, internal process dependencies and shared resources (task structure and open files); (ii) service and data transfer, which synchronizes data copies, withdraws transactions, establishes recovery points and disseminates the packed service programs and data to the new platform P_k; and (iii) service setup on P_k, which creates a new namespace and restores the service configuration and state. Since some data associated with S_j may have been damaged, the system must provide supplemental data or generate fuzzy data to support the continuity of service S_j. When S_j is executed on the new platform P_k, the compromised platform P_i is immediately repaired. A recovery process in the model covers fault diagnosis and damage repair.

In Step 3 in Figure 1, after the service and data are set up on the new platform P_k, the execution of S_j is resumed. S_j may continue to execute on P_k to completion. However, for a long-running service, if the previously damaged platform P_i has recovered, then S_j must be moved back to P_i. This relocation is necessary for several reasons [11]: (i) it improves data access locality by relocating a service closer to the data; (ii) it provides better system response time by relocating the service closer to users; and (iii) it makes for better load balancing by relocating the service to its initial platform based on an optimal resource assignment scheme.

In Step 4, a repair completion notification is sent by the recovery manager to P_k when P_i is fully recovered. In Step 5, the relocation manager arranges to move S_j back to P_i. Service relocation is composed of three sub-actions similar to the migration process, but with one major difference – any fuzzy data used by S_j when it is running on P_k is meant to be used only temporarily while P_i is being repaired. A correctional recovery must be performed when S_j is relocated back to P_i so that the data items reflect the exact values instead of inaccurate, albeit acceptable, values. Finally, in Step 6, S_j runs to completion on the repaired platform P_i.

To ensure that critical services are provided with minimal interruption, we examine how important factors, such as various system security and functional properties, affect the activities that support an effective and efficient migration and relocation process. For example, the probability (or frequency) of severe damage to a platform significantly impacts the normal operations of the critical services on the platform. Intuitively, if a system has a strong security baseline, few vulnerabilities, efficient intrusion detection and high levels of fault tolerance and masking abilities, then the probability of a platform being severely damaged would be low. Consequently, the critical services can operate on their original platforms most of the time. In such situations, the need for service migration and relocation is minimized. Even in a worst-case scenario, when a migration is necessary, it is necessary to ensure that some key system properties, if satisfied, will provide for effective and efficient service migration. For example, a new platform must be available to host the services when damage is detected to the original platform. Halting the services on the compromised platform and setting them up on the new platform must be completed as quickly as possible. The service priority, response time and throughput must be ensured both during and after the service migration. As will be seen below, these factors are expressed as model parameters (e.g., activity rates) in a simulation because we are interested in learning how the parameters affect the normal execution of critical services.

4.   Service Migration and Relocation Modeling

We use the PEPA model [5] to express and simulate the activities and behavior of system components in a service migration and relocation process. PEPA introduces delays and probabilistic occurrences to process algebras. The timing behavior of a system is quantified by associating a random variable with each activity, which represents its duration. Behavior uncertainty is determined by probabilistic branching – the probabilities of occurrence of some activities are determined by race conditions between the enabled activities. The model represents service migration and relocation activities as stochastic actions that are non-deterministic and whose occurrence or non-occurrence are predicted by one or more random variables (i.e., activity rates).

Figure 2 shows the PEPA model representing a system SYS. The system SYS is modeled in terms of interactions between the service migration and relocation components (i.e., a migrating scheduler, a platform supporting a critical service and a relocation manager) and the damage recovery components (i.e., a fault diagnosing agent and a damage repairer). The model has eleven processes (components) representing the entire procedure for service S_j to migrate from a compromised platform P_i to a new platform P_k and relocate from P_k to P_i after P_i has recovered. The model also includes the recovery procedure of the compromised component. The PEPA processes and their activities are described below.

Process $Execution_{i\_j}$ models the behavior of platform P_i where service S_j is executed. It either executes normally or needs to be investigated if the intrusion detection system (implicitly modeled) reports suspicious (or abnormal) behavior. Correspondingly, P_i behaves either as $(monitor\_anomaly, p_1).(alarm, al)$ $.Contingency_i$ or $(monitor\_normal, p_2).(executing_{i\_j}, f).Execution_{i\_j}$ in the PEPA model. The former describes the situation where the system reports damage symptoms (represented by the PEPA activity $monitor\_anomaly$). In this case, an alarm is trigged (represented by the PEPA activity $alarm$) and P_i enters a contingency state (represented by the PEPA process $Contingency_i$),

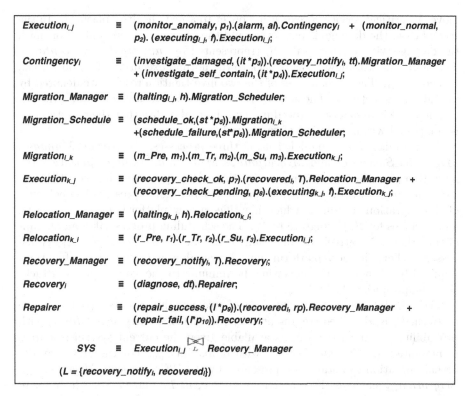

Figure 2. PEPA model of service migration and relocation.

where the symptoms are further analyzed. The latter represents the case when no abnormal symptom is detected (represented by the PEPA activity *monitor_normal*). Therefore, S_j is continuously executed on P_i (represented by $executing_{i-j}$). The probabilities of occurrence of the two cases are denoted by p_1 and p_2, respectively. In our model, *monitor_anomaly* and *monitor_normal* have default activity rates of one; *alarm* and $executing_{i-j}$ have the rates al and f, respectively, indicating that the two activities have durations that are negatively exponentially distributed with parameters al and f, respectively. The probabilities that *alarm* and $executing_{i-j}$ occur within a period of time length t are $1 - e^{-al*t}$ and $1 - e^{-f*t}$, respectively.

The PEPA process $Contingency_i$ represents the investigation of platform P_i for advanced analysis given the reported suspicious behavior. Based on the investigation results, $Contingency_i$ behaves either as $(investigate\_damaged, (it * p_3))$.$(recovery\_notify_i, tt)$.$Migration\_Manager$ or $(investigate\_self\_contain, (it * p_4))$.$Execution_{i-j}$. In the first case, the investigation reveals that P_i is severely damaged (represented by the PEPA activity *investigate_damaged*). Thus, a recovery notification ($recovery\_notify_i$) is sent to $Recovery\_Manager$ in order to arrange for P_i to recover. Furthermore, the system starts the service migration process (represented by the PEPA process $Migration\_Manager$) to move the critical service S_j executing on P_i to a new, healthy platform. In the second case, the damage is not severe and the system can self-contain or mask the damage without disrupting S_j (represented by $investigate\_self\_contain$). Therefore, the workflow transits back to the normal execution of S_j on P_i, i.e., $Execution_{i\_j}$. The probabilities of the two investigation results are denoted by p_3 and p_4, respectively. The activity rate it probabilistically determines the duration of the investigation procedure, i.e., the probability that the investigation is completed within a period of time t is $1 - e^{-it*t}$.

Service migration is modeled using three processes: $Migration\_Manager$, $Migration\_Scheduler$ and $Migration_{i\_k}$. $Migration\_Manager$ initializes the migration procedure by halting service S_j on P_i (represented by the PEPA activity $halting_{i\_j}$ with a rate h). $Migration\_Scheduler$ represents the behavior of the migration scheduler, which identifies a new platform P_k, if one exists, and arranges for S_j to migrate to P_k. The scheduling process takes an amount of time that is negatively exponentially distributed with parameter st. As discussed earlier, the new platform must be capable of providing the functions required by S_j and in the meantime be immune to the same types of attacks that compromised platform P_i.

The scheduling process yields one of two possible results: (i) a suitable platform P_k is identified (represented by the PEPA activity $schedule\_ok$) with probability p_5; and (ii) no P_k is available given the current system resources (represented by $schedule\_failure$) with probability p_6. For the first case, the actual migration can start as represented by the PEPA process $Migration_{i\_k}$. $Migration_{i\_k}$ engages three activities m_Pre, m_Tr and m_Su, which correspond to migration preparation, service and data transfer, and setup on the new platform P_k, respectively. Their corresponding PEPA activity rates are m_1, m_2 and m_3. However, if the scheduling process does not identify a suitable P_k, then the workflow returns to $Migration\_Scheduler$ for rescheduling (hopefully a suitable platform will be available the next time).

The PEPA process $Execution_{k\_j}$ represents the execution of service S_j on the new platform P_k. Depending on whether the compromised platform P_i has recovered or not, P_k behaves differently. As discussed above, S_j has to be relocated when P_i has recovered. The first behavior of the process $Execution_{k\_j}$, i.e., $(recovery\_check\_ok, p_7).(recovered_i, T).Relocation\_Manager$ covers this case with a probability p_7 when the status of P_i is periodically checked ($recover$ y_check_ok). Indeed, in this case, P_k synchronizes with the $Recovery\_Manager$ through the activity $recovered_i$. This activity has an unspecified rate (denoted by T and is determined by the repair notification rate rp when the two processes $Execution_{k\_j}$ and $Recovery\_Manager$ are synchronized). Then, the system starts the relocation process $Relocation_{k\_i}$, which moves S_j to its original platform P_i. $Relocation_{k\_i}$ engages three activities r_Pre, r_Tr and r_Su. The second behavior of $Execution_{k\_j}$, i.e., $(recovery\_check\_pending, p_8).(executing_{k\_j},$ $f).Execution_{k\_j}$ represents the continuous execution of S_j on P_k given the condition that P_i is still being repaired (represented by the PEPA activity $recovery\_check\_pending$). The probability of this case is represented by p_8. In terms of time, S_j is executed on P_k (represented by $executing_{k\_j}$) for a duration that is negatively exponentially distributed with a parameter f before the process returns to $Execution_{k\_j}$ for the next cycle of repair checking.

The damage recovery subsystem of SYS is modeled by three PEPA components: (i) *Recovery_Manager*, a coordinator that waits for a recovery notification (represented by $recovery\_notify_i$) and then starts a recovery process; (ii) *Recovery_i*, a local agent responsible for recovering platform P_i; it first performs fault diagnosis on P_i (represented by the PEPA activity *diagnose* with a rate dt) and then develops a plan for repair; and (iii) *Repairer*, a component responsible for the actual repair of P_i. System repair is application-specific and can take various forms, e.g., system restoration, check pointing and rollback, and re-programming. Given the diagnosis information, P_i may be successfully repaired (represented by *repair_success*) with probability p_9 or repair is not possible (represented by the activity *repair_fail*) with probability p_{10}. In the first case, the workflow returns to the PEPA process *Recovery_Manager*, indicating that the damage recovery system has completed the recovery of P_i and is waiting for the next recovery request. In the second case, since the repair attempt has not resulted in successful repair, further diagnosis is necessary. Therefore, the workflow returns to *Recovery_i* for more diagnostic information about the cause and nature of the damage on the promised platform.

Finally, the service migration and relocation enabled system SYS is modeled using the PEPA cooperation operator $Execution_{i\_j} \bowtie_L Recovery\_Manager$ (where $L = \{recovery\_notify_i, recovered_i\}$) to represent the concurrent interactions of the execution of service S_j on platform P_i, and the damage recovery activities in the case of severe damage to P_i, via synchronized participation in the events $Recovery\_notify_i$ and $recovered_i$. While a severe damage event triggers the service migration process, a successful repair results in the migrated service being moved back to the original platform.

5. Simulation Results and Analysis

The PEPA model presented in this paper was solved using the PEPA Eclipse plug-in software [5]. The activity rates used in the model are shown in Table 1. A Bayesian network decision model was used to determine the activity rates. Due to space limitations, the Bayesian network model is not presented in this paper.

5.1 Overview

We conducted several rounds of simulations for steady-state, utilization, passage-time, throughput and experimental analysis in order to study how the important factors influence the effectiveness and efficiency of service migration and relocation.

In order to run the PEPA simulation, the system states corresponding to the underlying continuous time Markov processes were derived and the probability of the system at each state was generated. The PEPA model incorporated 33

Table 1. Parameter settings for the PIPA model.

Parameter	Value	Explanation
p_1	0.001	Probability that an anomaly is detected on platform P_i
al	0.5	Alarm on P_i is fired for two time units
p_2	$1 - p_1$	Probability that the intrusion detection system reports normal activities
it	0.1	Investigation of P_i takes ten time units upon triggering an alarm
f	0.1	S_j is executed on P_i for ten time units before the next intrusion report
p_3	0.1	Probability that P_i is severely damaged
tt	1	Repair notification to the *Recovery_Manager* takes one time unit
p_4	$1 - p_3$	Probability that the damage is not severe and P_i can contain the damage
h	0.2	Service S_j takes five time units to be halted appropriately
st	0.3	Migration scheduling takes about 3.3 time units
p_5	0.8	Probability that a new platform P_k is identified for S_j to migrate
p_6	$1 - p_5$	Probability that no suitable platform is available for S_j to migrate
m_1	0.25	Migration preparation takes four time units
m_2	0.5	Data and service transfer to the new platform P_k takes two time units
m_3	0.2	Setting up service S_j on P_k takes five time units
p_7	0.01	Probability that P_i has recovered while S_j is executing on P_k
p_8	$1 - p_7$	Probability that P_i still has to recover
r_1	0.25	Relocation preparation takes four time units
r_2	0.5	Data and service transfer back to the repaired P_i takes two time units
r_3	0.1	Setting up service S_j on P_i takes five time units
dt	0.1	Diagnosing the nature of the damage to P_i takes ten time units
l	0.001	Attempting to repair P_i takes 1,000 time units
p_9	0.6	Probability that P_i can be successfully repaired
p_{10}	$1 - p_9$	Probability that P_i cannot be repaired (new diagnosis is necessary)
rp	1	Sending a repair completion notification to P_k takes one time unit

global states. Since the model had two top-level PEPA processes, *Execution$_{i\_j}$* and *Recovery_Manager*, a global state had two elements, one for each local state of the corresponding top-level processes. The simulation revealed that

$Execution_{i\_j}$ had seventeen local states while *Recovery_Manager* had four states.

The system activities were represented as non-deterministic stochastic actions whose occurrence or non-occurrence were predicted by one or more random variables. The system SYS was modeled in terms of interactions between the service migration and relocation components and the damage recovery subsystems. The interactions reached a set of steady states after an extended execution time. The term "steady state" means that there was a statistically determined possibility that the system remained in the state.

Our simulations showed that the PEPA states with dominating steady-state probabilities were associated with the two local states $executing_{i\_j}.Execution_{i\_j}$ (0.891) and *Recovery_Manager* (0.981). This was also observed in our utilization analysis, which showed the long-run utilization of each top-level process in the PEPA model. More precisely, the percentage of time that a top-level component $Execution_{i\_j}$ (resp. *Recovery_Manager*) was in the local state $executing_{i\_j}.Execution_{i\_j}$ (resp. *Recovery_Manager*) was 0.891 (resp. 0.981). Since $executing_{i\_j}.Execution_{i\_j}$ represents the normal execution of service S_j on its original platform P_i, maximizing the utilization of this state is the objective of an efficient service migration and relocation process. Therefore, in the following discussion, we focus on how the important factors influence the utilization of $executing_{i\_j}.Execution_{i\_j}$. This utilization rate is denoted by p.

The activity throughput was also studied in the simulations. The throughput analysis yielded the rate at which PEPA actions were performed at steady-state. The two PEPA activities with the highest throughputs were $executing_{i\_j}$ (0.09) and $monitoring\_normal$ (0.09). The former indicates that service S_j was executing on platform P_i and, hence, a higher value is more desirable. The latter indicates that the intrusion detection system reported normal system operations in most cases (i.e., no suspicious behavior was detected). Just as the steady-state analysis focused on the local state $executing_{i\_j}.Execution_{i\_j}$, the throughput of $executing_{i\_j}$ represented the desired behavior of S_j on P_i; therefore, it is another metric of interest.

5.2 Simulation Results

We executed the PEPA model with parameter values in the desired ranges. The experiments were designed to study how system security and functional factors affect the utilization rate of $executing_{i\_j}.Execution_{i\_j}$, i.e., p and the throughput of $executing_{i\_j}$ as mentioned above.

We started with the two factors determined by the security features of system SYS: (i) probability of anomaly detection on a platform P_i (p_1) in an intrusion detection reporting cycle; and (ii) probability that the detected damage is severe (p_3). Intuitively, if a system has strong security mechanisms and the ability to contain and mask potential damage, then the need for the critical services to migrate from their normal executing platforms is low. Hence, the utilization of $executing_{i\_j}.Execution_{i\_j}$ should be higher. The experimental results confirmed this observation.

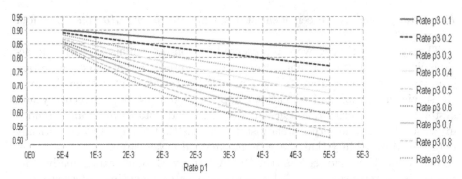

Figure 3. Utilization of $executing_{i\_j}.Execution_{i\_j}$ (p_1 and p_3 values).

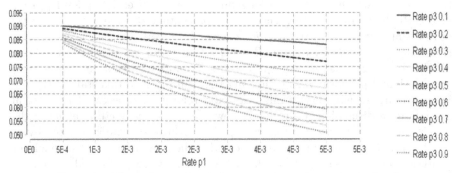

Figure 4. Throughput of activity $executing_{i\_j}$ (p_1 and p_3 values).

Figure 3 shows the utilization of $executing_{i\_j}.Execution_{i\_j}$ for different p_1 and p_3 values. In particular, it shows that p decreases when p_1 and p_3 increase. This clearly indicates that a higher compromise rate for a platform decreases the amount of time that the platform effectively supports the critical services. Furthermore, the quantitative relationship between p and p_1 is roughly linear given a fixed p_3 rate. This implies that a significant improvement in system security results in an almost equal increase in the normal execution of critical services on their original platforms. A similar pattern is observed in Figure 4 for the throughput of $executing_{i\_j}$ for different p_1 and p_3 values.

As discussed earlier, the migration manager is responsible for halting a critical service on a compromised platform, scheduling and arranging a new platform for service migration, moving the data and program space of the service to the new platform, and finally setting up the service on the new platform. In the meantime, the recovery manager diagnoses the faults and attempts to repair the compromised platform. The performance of these two system components clearly affects service migration. Figures 5 and 6 show that a higher probability of a successful migration-scheduling rate (i.e., p_5) and a higher probability of a successful repair of a compromised platform (i.e., p_9) positively affect the utilization of $executing_{i\_j}.Execution_{i\_j}$ (i.e., p). This indicates that effective damage recovery and the availability of healthy platforms increase the overall

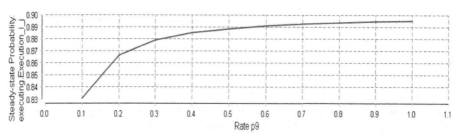

Figure 5. Utilization of $executing_{i\_j}.Execution_{i\_j}$ (p_5 values).

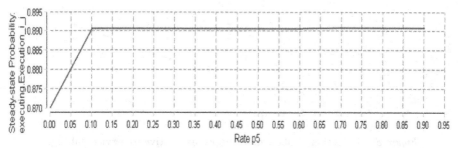

Figure 6. Utilization of $executing_{i\_j}.Execution_{i\_j}$ (p_9 values).

efficiency of service migration, which, in turn, increases the percentage of time that critical services are executed on their normal platforms. However, Figure 6 shows that p becomes stable after p_5 reaches a certain value (0.1 in our simulation). This means that any further improvement in migration scheduling will not improve p significantly. Therefore, migration scheduling is not a significant bottleneck for $executing_{i\_j}.Execution_{i\_j}$ beyond this point.

Next, we examine how the time required to halt a critical service on a compromised platform and the time required to repair the compromised platform affect the utilization of $executing_{i\_j}.Execution_{i\_j}$. Figure 7 shows that when less time is taken to repair a compromised platform (i.e., higher value of l), the probability that S_j is executed on platform P_i is higher. Similarly, the simulation shows that a shorter duration for halting S_j on P_i (i.e., higher value of h) and a shorter duration for migration scheduling to move S_j to a new platform P_k (i.e., higher value of st) both result in a higher value of p. However, both results indicate that the effects of h and l on p are not significant beyond certain points. This implies that further investments in halting and repairing mechanisms may not significantly increase the probability that critical services are executed on their normal platforms.

5.3 Passage-Time Analysis

We also conducted various passage-time analyses, i.e., the distribution of the probabilities that a second event occurs after a given event within a time duration. Figure 8 shows the passage-time analysis results of detecting abnormal symptoms ($monitor\_abnormal$) relative to service halting ($halting_i$).

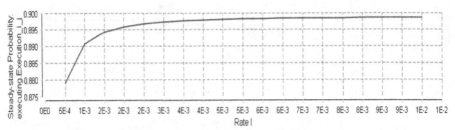

Figure 7. Utilization of $executing_{i\_j}.Execution_{i\_j}$ (l values).

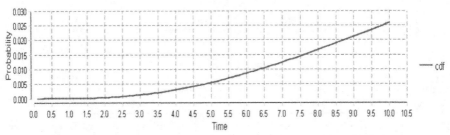

Figure 8. Detection of abnormal symptoms relative to service halting.

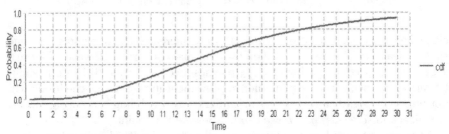

Figure 9. Service setup on a new platform relative to completion.

The results reveal that the occurrence probability of halting service S_j on P_i (i.e., $halting_i$) increases with time relative to the event where P_i is detected as damaged.

The passage-time analysis results in Figure 9 show that the probability of P_i being repaired (i.e., $recovered_i$) increases with time relative to the event that S_j executes on the new platform P_k (i.e., SU_{k_j}). In particular, it is almost certain that the compromised platform P_i will be repaired within about 30 time units after SU_{k_j}.

6.   Conclusions

Service migration and relocation is an effective mechanism for dynamically transferring mission-critical services from a compromised platform to other clean, healthy platforms to ensure that mission-critical services are provided continuously. Service migration is crucial in situations where other security and fault tolerance approaches are infeasible or expensive. In these situations, service migration and relocation is a viable solution for minimizing the impact of malicious attacks and system failures. The process-algebra-based modeling framework presented in this paper provides a foundation for studying how important factors can influence the effectiveness and efficiency of service migration and relocation in mission-critical systems.

Acknowledgement

This research was supported by the U.S. Air Force Office of Scientific Research under Award No. FA9550-12-1-0131.

References

[1] M. Amoretti, M. Laghi, F. Tassoni and F. Zanichelli, Service migration within the cloud: Code mobility in SP2A, *Proceedings of the International Conference on High Performance Computing and Simulation*, pp. 196–202, 2010.

[2] B. Choi, S. Rho and R. Bettati, Fast software component migration for application survivability in distributed real-time systems, *Proceedings of the Seventh IEEE International Symposium on Object-Oriented Real-Time Distributed Computing*, pp. 269–276, 2004.

[3] S. Cohen, W. Money and S. Kaisler, Service migration in an enterprise system architecture, *Proceedings of the Forty-Second Hawaii International Conference on System Sciences*, 2009.

[4] S. Fu and C. Xu, Service migration in distributed virtual machines for adaptive grid computing, *Proceedings of the International Conference on Parallel Processing*, pp. 358–365, 2005.

[5] J. Hillston and S. Gilmore, Performance Evaluation Process Algebra (PEPA), Laboratory for Foundations in Computer Science, University of Edinburgh, Edinburgh, United Kingdom (www.dcs.ed.ac.uk/pepa), 2012.

[6] A. Keromytis, J. Parekh, P. Gross, G. Kaiser, V. Mishra, J. Nieh, D. Rubenstein and S. Stolfo, A holistic approach to service survivability, *Proceedings of the First ACM Workshop on Survivable and Self-Regenerative Systems*, pp. 11–22, 2003.

[7] M. Koester, W. Luk, J. Hagemeyer, W. Porrmann and U. Ruckert, Design optimizations for tiled partially reconfigurable systems, *IEEE Transactions on Very Large Scale Integration Systems*, vol. 19(6), pp. 1048–1061, 2011.

[8] C. Li, I. Pefkianakis, B. Li, C. Peng, W. Zhang and S. Lu, A multimedia service migration protocol for single user multiple devices, *Proceedings of the IEEE International Conference on Communications*, pp. 1923–1927, 2012.

[9] R. Marsh, Critical Foundations: Protecting America's Infrastructures, Report of the President's Commission on Critical Infrastructure Protection, United States Government Printing Office, Washington, DC, 1997.

[10] K. Zick and J. Hayes, Low-cost sensing with ring oscillator arrays for healthier reconfigurable systems, *ACM Transactions on Reconfigurable Technology and Systems*, vol. 5(1), article no. 1, pp. 1.1–1.26, 2012.

[11] Y. Zuo, Moving and relocating: A logical framework of service migration for software system survivability, *Proceedings of the Seventh IEEE International Conference on Software System Survivability*, p. 10, 2013.

Chapter 12

CASCADING EFFECTS OF COMMON-CAUSE FAILURES IN CRITICAL INFRASTRUCTURES

Panayiotis Kotzanikolaou, Marianthi Theoharidou and
Dimitris Gritzalis

Abstract   One of the most challenging problems in critical infrastructure protection is the assessment and mitigation of cascading failures across infrastructures. In previous research, we have proposed a model for assessing the cumulative security risk of cascading threats due to high-order dependencies between infrastructures. However, recent empirical studies indicate that common-cause failures may result in extremely high impact situations, which may be comparable with or even more devastating than the cascading effects of high-order dependencies. This paper presents an extension to our model, which permits the assessment of the risk arising from complex situations involving multiple cascading failures triggered by major or concurrent common-cause events. The paper also discusses a realistic scenario that is used as a test case for the model extension.

Keywords: Infrastructure dependencies, common-cause failures, cascading effects

1.   Introduction

The analysis of cascading failures is an important problem in critical infrastructure protection because, despite the low likelihood of such events, they can result in devastating consequences to multiple critical infrastructures. Examples of such "domino effects" are the electric power disruptions in California in 2001 [15] and the major blackouts in the United States, Canada and Europe in 2003 [1]. However, emphasis has been placed on common-cause failures, primarily because recent statistics [20] indicate that cascading effects are either very rare or are not well documented. Common-cause failures are events that may cause the concurrent disruption of multiple critical infrastructures, which may have no dependency of any type (e.g., cyber, physical, geographi-

J. Butts and S. Shenoi (Eds.): Critical Infrastructure Protection VII, IFIP AICT 417, pp. 171–182, 2013.
© IFIP International Federation for Information Processing 2013

cal, logical or social dependency). They can be caused by an adversary, such as the IP-hijacking of YouTube servers in Pakistan in 2008 and the London bombings of July 7, 2005; or they can be natural disasters, such as the 2005 Hurricane Katrina and the 2008 Mediterranean cable breaks [3]. In addition to their immediate effects, such disruptions also cause wider indirect institutional, political and economic effects. These effects include reduced public trust in government services and in democratic processes (e.g., e-voting [8, 10, 11]).

Although cascading and common-cause failures have been studied by many researchers, the relationships between them have been largely ignored. A common-cause failure can affect multiple infrastructures in different sectors such as government, health, information and communications technology and transportation [16, 17]. Each infrastructure that has failed concurrently due to a common-cause failure may lead – with some probability – to multiple cascading chains of failures in its dependent infrastructures.

This paper focuses on the combination of cascading and common-cause failures. In particular, it attempts to assess the overall risk of common-cause failures that may also result in multiple cascading failures. The combined approach is used to assess a scenario that results in concurrent cascading and common-cause failures. The analysis of such scenarios can assist decision-makers in identifying optimal approaches to mitigate risk.

2.   Related Work

Dependency modeling has been studied extensively, including sector-specific methods (e.g., for gas lines, electric power grids and information and telecommunications systems) and more general methods that are applicable to multiple critical infrastructures. Dependency models can be divided into six broad categories [7, 14, 21]: (i) aggregate supply and demand models, which evaluate the total demand for infrastructure services in a region and the ability to supply services; (ii) dynamic simulation models, which examine infrastructure operations, effects of disruptions and the associated downstream consequences; (iii) agent-based models, which permit the analysis of the operational characteristics and physical states of infrastructures; (iv) physics-based models, which analyze the physical aspects of infrastructures using standard engineering techniques; (v) population mobility models, which examine the movement of entities through geographical regions; and (vi) Leontief input-output models, which, in the basic case, conduct linear, aggregated time-independent analyses of the generation, flow and consumption of commodities in the various infrastructure sectors.

Critical infrastructure disruptions or outages are usually categorized as cascading, escalating or common-cause [15]:

- A cascading failure occurs when a disruption in one infrastructure affects one or more components in another infrastructure, which, in turn, leads to the partial or complete unavailability of the second infrastructure.

- An escalating failure occurs when a disruption in one infrastructure exacerbates an independent disruption in another infrastructure, usually in the form of increasing severity or increasing time for recovery and restoration in the second infrastructure.

- A common-cause failure occurs when two or more (connected) infrastructures are disrupted at the same time and components within each infrastructure fail because of a common cause. This occurs when two infrastructures are co-located (geographic interdependency) or when the root cause of the failure is widespread (e.g., a natural or a man-made disaster).

Statistical data about the three failure types is limited. The principal reason is that infrastructure asset owners and operators are unwilling to report incidents and vulnerabilities. A recent empirical study [20] examined data reported to the media. While there is some skepticism regarding the completeness of the data about reported incidents, some interesting findings emerge. First, the study produced a different categorization of failures from the one presented by Rinaldi, *et al.* [15]. Events are classified as: (i) cascade initiating, an event that causes an event in another critical infrastructure; (ii) cascade resulting, an event that results from an event in another critical infrastructure; and (iii) independent, an event that is neither cascade initiating nor cascade resulting.

Other key findings are that cascading dependencies are restricted to a limited number of critical infrastructure sectors, they occur more frequently than expected and often do not cascade deeply. The most commonly reported initiators of cascading effects are the information and communications technology sector and the energy sector, which is expected because these sectors provide products and services to all the other infrastructure sectors. For example, a large number of infrastructures may rely on a common electricity provider because, in many countries, there are relatively few providers. Likewise, critical infrastructures often have few choices regarding Internet and telecommunications service providers [2, 9].

The limited depth observed with regard to cascading failures is likely due to the fact that infrastructure owners and operators make contingency plans and apply countermeasures to mitigate the risk of the obvious upstream dependencies. Examples include the use of emergency generators to cope with power disruptions, and redundant telecommunications links and service providers. Statistics show that cascading effects usually stop after a few nodes due to the presence of countermeasures and contingency plans. However, most of the time these do not take into account changes in the operational mode of critical infrastructures (e.g., stressed, crisis and recovery modes) [12]. Also, they do not consider the changes in the operational modes of upstream suppliers that may be critical to the infrastructures under consideration.

Two (from among several) documented examples of common-cause failures for the two cascading initiating sectors are the blackouts in the United States, Canada and Europe [1] and the cable break incidents in the Taiwan Strait and the Suez Canal [3]. Both types of failures share the common characteristic that a single event caused disruptions to multiple critical infrastructures (common-cause) that, in turn, caused cascading effects to multiple sectors in large geographical regions.

Table 1. Dependency risk table.

Init. CI	Casc. CI	Dependency Type	Impact Type	Impact Scale	Likeli- hood	Risk
CI_A	CI_E	Cyber: Provides payment services	Public trust	Low	Low	3
CI_B	CI_A	Physical: Provides power services	Economic	Very Low	Low	2
CI_B	CI_C	Physical: Provides power services	Public trust	High	Very Low	4
CI_B	CI_D	Physical: Provides power services	Economic	Very High	Very Low	5
CI_B	CI_E	Physical: Provides power services	Public trust	Low	Low	3
CI_C	CI_E	Cyber: Provides network services	Public trust	Low	Very Low	2
CI_D	CI_C	Physical: Provides connectivity	Public trust	High	Very Low	4

3. Proposed Method

This section presents our approach for assessing the risk arising from complex situations involving multiple cascading failures triggered by major or concurrent common-cause events.

3.1 Preliminaries

We have previously proposed a method for assessing the risk of nth-order dependencies based on the combined results of organization-level risk assessments [4–6]. This method permits the use of existing risk assessment results (e.g., provided by infrastructure operators) that usually document the obvious, upstream dependencies [18].

Following the approach suggested in [19], a risk assessor can construct a dependency risk table as shown in Table 1. The dependency risk table lists the infrastructures that are dependent on each examined infrastructure, which means that it provides information on the cascading risks for each examined infrastructure. For each identified dependency, the table indicates the impact type, impact scale ($I_{i,j}$) and likelihood ($L_{i,j}$) of a disruption. The product of the impact scale and likelihood is defined as the dependency risk $R_{i,j}$ of infrastructure CI_j due to its dependency on infrastructure CI_i. For example, infrastructure CI_B, which belongs to the energy sector, can initiate cascading effects of various levels of risk to four other infrastructures: CI_A (finance sector), CI_C and CI_D (information and communications technology sector) and CI_E (government sector). It is important to note that high-level coordination is required in order to construct a dependency risk table. Risk assessment data

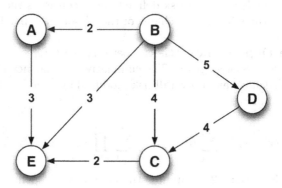

Figure 1. Dependency risk graph.

from all the examined infrastructures must be collected and homogenized (e.g., by government authorities such as sector coordinators).

Dependencies can also be visualized in the form of a graph as shown in Figure 1. An infrastructure is denoted as a circle. An arrow from $X \rightarrow Y$ denotes a risk dependency, i.e., an outgoing risk from infrastructure CI_X to infrastructure CI_Y. A bi-directional arrow $X \leftrightarrow Y$ denotes a cascading risk from CI_X to CI_Y and another cascading risk from CI_Y to CI_X. The number associated with each arrow refers to the level of the cascade resulting risk for the receiver due to the dependency, based on a risk scale from one through nine. For example, in Figure 1, CI_E has a dependency risk $R_{A,E} = 3$ from infrastructure CI_A. This risk value refers to the likelihood that a disruption from CI_A will cascade to CI_E ($L_{A,E}$) as well as the societal impact caused to CI_E if a failure is realized at the source of the dependency CI_A (i.e., $I_{A,E}$). All these parameters ($L_{i,j}, I_{i,j}$ and Ri, j) must be defined in order to assess the risk of the first-order dependencies.

A recursive algorithm is used to estimate the nth-order cascading risks. Let $\mathbb{CI} = (CI_1, ...CI_m)$ be the set of examined infrastructures. Let $CI_{Y_0} \rightarrow CI_{Y_1} \rightarrow ... \rightarrow CI_{Y_n}$ denote a chain of connected infrastructures of length n. The algorithm examines each critical infrastructure as a potential cause of a cascading chain (denoted as CI_{Y_0}) and then computes the dependency risk DR exhibited by CI_{Y_n} due to its nth-order dependency.

Risk of nth-Order Cascading Events: Let $CI_{Y_0} \rightarrow CI_{Y_1} \rightarrow ... \rightarrow CI_{Y_n}$ be a chain of dependencies, $L_{Y_0,...,Y_n}$ be the likelihood of an nth-order cascading event and I_{Y_{n-1},Y_n} be the impact of the $CI_{Y_{n-1}} \rightarrow CI_{Y_n}$ dependency. Then, the cascading risk exhibited by CI_{Y_n} due to the nth-order dependency is computed as:

$$R_{Y_0,...,Y_n} = L_{Y_0,...,Y_n} \cdot I_{Y_{n-1},Y_n} \equiv \prod_{i=0}^{n-1} L_{Y_i,Y_{i+1}} \cdot I_{Y_{n-1},Y_n}. \qquad (1)$$

The cumulative dependency risk defined below considers the overall risk for all the infrastructures in the sub-chains of the nth-order dependency.

Cumulative Dependency Risk: Let $CI_{Y_0} \rightarrow CI_{Y_1} \rightarrow \ldots \rightarrow CI_{Y_n}$ be a chain of dependencies of length n. The cumulative dependency risk, denoted as $DR_{Y_0, Y_1, \ldots, Y_n}$ is defined as the overall risk produced by an nth-order dependency and is computed as:

$$DR_{Y_0, \ldots, Y_n} = \sum_{i=1}^{n} R_{Y_0, \ldots, Y_i} \equiv \sum_{i=1}^{n} (\prod_{j=1}^{i} L_{Y_{j-1}, Y_j}) \cdot I_{Y_{i-1}, Y_i}. \qquad (2)$$

Informally, Equation (2) computes the cumulative dependency risk exhibited by every node in the chain due to a failure realized in the source of the dependency chain. The computation of the risk is based on a risk matrix that combines the likelihood and the incoming impact values of each vertex in the chain. Interested readers are referred to [5] for a detailed analysis of dependency risk estimation.

3.2   Combining Failure Risks

The assessment of cascading failures may reveal hidden, neglected or non-obvious dependencies between critical infrastructures. However, the dependency risk assessed using Equations (1) and (2) only assumes an initiating event (failure) in a single critical infrastructure that causes cascading failures. Thus, it does not capture the overall risk due to large-scale common-cause failures that affect multiple critical infrastructures and potentially initiate multiple cascading chains.

The following method combines common-cause and cascading events in order to assess the potential risk caused by complex situations:

1. **Identify Common-Cause Threats:** Identify every potential threat T_x that may result in a common-cause failure in a critical infrastructure. The potential threats can be accidents, natural disasters or human-initiated attacks.

2. **Assess Likelihood of Threats:** When a potential threat T_x that may cause a common-cause failure is identified, the probability of occurrence L_{T_x} of the threat is assessed. The likelihood of natural disasters can be assessed based on statistics of previous incidents, prognostications and the presence of vulnerabilities. The assessment of the likelihood of adversarial attacks is more complex. These are affected by the motivation and skills of adversaries, as well as the perceived impact of the attacks. Thus, expert opinions coupled with a worst-case approach are commonly used, which results in the maximum valuation of risk.

3. **Assess Cumulative Dependency Risk of Cascading Chains:** For each initiating event (i.e., threat identified in Step 1), Equation (2) is used

to evaluate the nth-order dependency risk for every critical infrastructure that is initially affected by the common-cause threat.

4. **Assess Combined Common-Cause and Cascading Failure Risk:** Let $\mathbb{CI}$ be the set of all examined critical infrastructures. The combined risk of all possible chains of cascading events $CI_{Y_0} \rightarrow CI_{Y_1} \rightarrow CI_{Y_n}$ for each possible source infrastructure $CI_{Y_0} \in \mathbb{CI}$ is computed as the sum of all possible risk chains $DR_{Y_0,...,Y_n}$ for all $Y_0 \in \mathbb{CI}$ multiplied by the likelihood L_{T_x} of each examined threat T_x estimated in Step 2:

$$\sum DR_{Y_0,...,Y_n}(T_x) = L_{T_x} \cdot \sum_{\forall Y_0 \in \mathbb{CI}} DR_{Y_0,...,Y_n} \qquad (3)$$

Informally, Equation (3) combines the likelihood L_{T_x} of each examined threat T_x with all the possible dependency chains that may be triggered by the threat being realized. Every critical infrastructure that is affected by T_x is examined as a possible root of a dependency chain (as CI_{Y_0}) based on the risk dependency table and dependency graph. For each CI_{Y_0}, the cumulative dependency risk is computed by applying Equation (2). The next section uses an example scenario to demonstrate the use of the method.

4. Example Scenario

The example scenario focuses on the information and communications technology sector because, along with the energy sector, it is likely to cause cascading chains. The four-step methodology described in the previous section is applied to the scenario.

1. **Identify Common-Cause Threat:** A communication link failure T_{CLF} can cause multiple (common-cause) failures. Such a failure, e.g., a cable break, can be accidental. Underwater cable breaks are common on intercontinental links. They have been caused by direct physical damage from ship anchors, fishing and dredging, and natural disasters such as earthquakes and currents created by extreme weather [3]. A link failure can also be caused by a power outage and, of course, sabotage.

2. **Assess Likelihood of Threat:** Next, it is necessary to assess the likelihood of a cable break $L_{T_{CLF}}$. Previous accident data provides useful information to estimate the likelihood. In 2007, there were more than 50 undersea failures in the Atlantic alone [3]. If we consider the same threat, but as a human-initiated attack, then additional information would have to be incorporated to assess the likelihood. In particular, it would be necessary to identify a potential adversary and proceed to assess factors such as motivation, available resources to perform the attack and the perceived outcome of the attack. Let us assume that the likelihood that a cable break would occur in a particular region is Medium (M) because there were several incidents in the region during the past year,

i.e., $L_{T_{CLF}} = M$. Also, a resonable assumption based on past incidents is that a cable break in this region affects a maximum of four Internet providers that supply services to two countries.

3. **Assess Cumulative Dependency Risk of Cascading Chains:** In this step, Equation (2) is applied to to evaluate the nth-order dependency risks for each possible cascading chain initiated by each of the four service providers belonging to $\mathbb{CI}$, i.e., $\mathbb{CI} = \{CI_{A_0}, CI_{B_0}, CI_{C_0}, CI_{D_0}\}$. Thus, for each identified critical infrastructure, it is necessary to retrieve existing dependency tables and graphs. The cumulative dependency risk for provider CI_{A_0} is the overall risk caused by a failure chain initiated by CI_{A_0}, e.g., $CI_{A_0} \rightarrow CI_{A_1} \rightarrow \ldots \rightarrow CI_{A_n}$ based on Equation (2). The same procedure is followed for the other three providers. If we assume that, for every critical infrastructure, only one chain of failures is identified, then the result of this step is four different, but comparable, values of dependency risk $DR_{CI_{i_0},\ldots,CI_{i_n}}$; $i = A, B, C, D$.

The dependency risks of these chains may vary based on geography and the presence of redundancies. For example, cable breaks in the Atlantic may occur relatively frequently, but they do not have serious impact because of redundant links. In contrast, cable breaks in the Taiwan Strait or Suez Canal can cause entire geographic regions to lose connectivity [13], resulting in a significantly higher societal impact.

Even within the same region, the cumulative dependency risks of critical infrastructures may differ because they do not share the same mitigation plans. For example, CI_{A_0} may not cause cascading events with a high likelihood and CI_{A_1} may have countermeasures that reduce the impact caused by the disruption of CI_{A_0}. In contrast, CI_{B_0} may be very likely to cause cascading failures to CI_{B_1} and CI_{B_2}, which may consequently cause a high societal impact if CI_{B_2} is affected (e.g., if a large proportion of a nation's population loses Internet connectivity). The cumulative dependency risk for the chain caused by CI_{B_0} is expected to be higher than the chain caused by CI_{A_0}, i.e., $DR_{CI_{B_0},CI_{B_1},CI_{B_2}} > DR_{CI_{A_0},CI_{A_1}}$.

4. **Assess Combined Common-Cause and Cascading Failure Risk:** The final step is to assess the overall risk caused by the initial (common-cause) failure, i.e., the cable break, to the four affected infrastructures. The risk of the communications link failure threat is assessed using Equation (3) and is given by:

$$R_{T_{CLF}} = L_{T_{CLF}} \cdot \sum_{\forall X_0 \in \mathbb{CI}} DR_{CI_{X_0},\ldots,CI_{X_n}}. \tag{4}$$

This measure takes into account the likelihood of the common-cause (i.e., cable break) as well as the cascading risk of this event. In the scenario, four infrastructures are affected initially. According to the conditions that affect the likelihood of a cascading failure and the resulting impact if such a failure spreads, different cumulative dependency risks would be assessed for each chain caused by a failure in the four critical infrastructures.

The approach presented above offers two principal benefits. First, assessing the cascading risk due to n^{th}-order dependencies permits the detection of high societal impacts that would otherwise not appear if only the immediate risks caused by a threat were to be considered. In the cable break scenario, the high societal impact due to the second-order dependency of CI_{B_2} to CI_{B_0} would have been ignored. Second, combining the risks of cascading effects with the common-cause likelihood provides decision makers with a more accurate view of how such threats can affect populations, even at the international level.

In the scenario described above, the assessments would have taken place individually by each of the infrastructure operators and the overall risk of the threat would not have been assessed accurately. Likewise, if the cable break is not considered to be an accident, then the likelihood of occurrence would have been assessed differently, resulting in a different overall risk.

5. Conclusions

Although cascading failures and common-cause failures have been studied by many researchers, the risk deriving from combined failures has not been thoroughly investigated. The method proposed in this paper is a simple and efficient approach for studying the cascading effects caused by large-scale, common-cause events. The combined method can be applied to real-world scenarios to evaluate whether or not common-cause failures can propagate to infrastructures that are not directly affected by the common-cause threat under consideration. This analysis can assist decision-makers in identifying optimal approaches to mitigate risk.

One limitation underlying the proposed method is the combination of risk assessment results at the organizational level. In order to construct a valid dependency risk table, risk assessment data from all the examined critical infrastructures must be collected and homogenized. Thus, the implementation of the methodology requires high-level coordination and management at the national, if not international, level. Another limitation is the identification and evaluation of common-cause threats. This occurs because of the lack of historical data about incidents, largely due to their rarity and the unwillingness of infrastructure owners and operators to provide detailed data. One way to address this problem is to project the consequences of common-cause and cascading effect scenarios by simulating various attack scenarios; this makes it possible to identify the hidden risks and underestimated threats.

Our future work involves the development of an automated tool for implementing and validating the proposed method. The tool will assist risk assessors and decision-makers in gathering information and evaluating the risk of common-cause and cascading events. In addition, the automated tool will help analyze scenarios involving common-cause events (especially, scenarios triggered by low-likelihood events) and identify the underestimated common-cause threats that could result in very high risks. The analysis of these scenarios could also reveal conflicting data obtained during the information gathering phase and help validate input data for future assessments.

Acknowledgement

This research was supported in part by the S-Port (09SYN-72-650) Project funded by the Hellenic General Secretariat for Research and Technology under the Synergasia Programme, and by the Research Funding Program for Excellence and Extroversion (Action 2) of the Athens University of Economics and Business.

References

[1] G. Andersson, P. Donalek, R. Farmer, N. Hatziargyriou, I. Kamwa, P. Kundur, N. Martins, J. Paserba, P. Pourbeik, J. Sanchez-Gasca, R. Schulz, A. Stankovic, C. Taylor and V. Vittal, Causes of the 2003 major grid blackouts in North America and Europe and recommended means to improve system dynamic performance, *IEEE Transactions on Power Systems*, vol. 20(4), pp. 1922–1928, 2005.

[2] J. Iliadis, D. Spinellis, D. Gritzalis, B. Preneel and S. Katsikas, Evaluating certificate status information mechanisms, *Proceedings of the Seventh ACM Conference on Computer and Communications Security*, pp. 1–8, 2000.

[3] C. Johnson, The telecoms inclusion principle: The missing link between critical infrastructure protection and critical information infrastructure protection, in *Critical Information Infrastructure Protection and Resilience in the ICT Sector*, P. Theron and S. Bologna (Eds.), IGI Global, Hershey, Pennslyvania, pp. 277–303, 2013.

[4] P. Kotzanikolaou, M. Theoharidou and D. Gritzalis, Interdependencies between critical infrastructures: Analyzing the risk of cascading effects, *Proceedings of the Sixth International Conference on Critical Information Infrastructure Security*, pp. 107–118, 2011.

[5] P. Kotzanikolaou, M. Theoharidou and D. Gritzalis, Assessing n-order dependencies between critical infrastructures, *International Journal of Critical Infrastructures*, vol. 9(1/2), pp. 93–110, 2013.

[6] P. Kotzanikolaou, M. Theoharidou and D. Gritzalis, Risk assessment of multi-order dependencies between critical information and communication infrastructures, in *Critical Information Infrastructure Protection and Resilience in the ICT Sector*, P. Theron and S. Bologna (Eds.), IGI Global, Hershey, Pennslyvania, pp. 153–172, 2013.

[7] W. Kroger and E. Zio, *Vulnerable Systems*, Springer-Verlag, London, United Kingdom, 2011.

[8] C. Lambrinoudakis, D. Gritzalis, V. Tsoumas, M. Karyda and S. Ikonomopoulos, Secure electronic voting: The current landscape, in *Secure Electronic Voting*, D. Gritzalis (Ed.), Kluwer Academic Publishers, Boston, Massachusetts, pp. 101–122, 2003.

[9] D. Lekkas and D. Gritzalis, Long-term verifiability of electronic healthcare record authenticity, *International Journal of Medical Informatics*, vol. 76(5-6), pp. 442–448, 2007.

[10] L. Mitrou, D. Gritzalis and S. Katsikas, Revisiting legal and regulatory requirements for secure e-voting, *Proceedings of the Seventeenth IFIP International Conference on Information Security: Visions and Perspectives*, pp. 469–480, 2002.

[11] L. Mitrou, D. Gritzalis, S. Katsikas and G. Quirchmayr, Electronic voting: Constitutional and legal requirements and their technical implications, in *Secure Electronic Voting*, D. Gritzalis (Ed.), Kluwer Academic Publishers, Boston, Massachusetts, pp. 43–60, 2003.

[12] A. Nieuwenhuijs, E. Luiijf and M. Klaver, Modeling dependencies in critical infrastructures, in *Critical Infrastructure Protection*, E. Goetz and S. Shenoi (Eds.), Boston, Massachusetts, pp. 205–213, 2008.

[13] A. Popescu, B. Premore and E. Zmijewski, Impact of the Middle East cable breaks: A global BGP perspective, presented at the *Forty-Second North American Network Operators Group Meeting*, 2008.

[14] S. Rinaldi, Modeling and simulating critical infrastructures and their interdependencies, *Proceedings of the Thirty-Seventh Hawaii International Conference on System Sciences*, 2004.

[15] S. Rinaldi, J. Peerenboom and T. Kelly, Identifying, understanding and analyzing critical infrastructure interdependencies, *IEEE Control Systems*, vol. 21(6), pp. 11–25, 2001.

[16] M. Theoharidou, M. Kandias and D. Gritzalis, Securing transportation-critical infrastructures: Trends and perspectives, in *Global Security, Safety and Sustainability and e-Democracy*, C. Georgiadis, H. Jahankhani, E. Pimenidis, R. Bashroush and A. Al-Nemrat (Eds.), Springer, Heidelberg, Germany, pp. 171–178, 2012.

[17] M. Theoharidou, P. Kotzanikolaou and D. Gritzalis, Risk-based criticality analysis, in *Critical Infrastructure Protection III*, C. Palmer and S. Shenoi (Eds.), Springer, Heidelberg, Germany, pp. 35–49, 2009.

[18] M. Theoharidou, P. Kotzanikolaou and D. Gritzalis, A multi-layer criticality assessment methodology based on interdependencies, *Computers and Security*, vol. 29(6), pp. 643–658, 2010.

[19] M. Theoharidou, P. Kotzanikolaou and D. Gritzalis, Risk assessment methodology for interdependent critical infrastructures, *International Journal of Risk Assessment and Management*, vol. 15(2/3), pp. 128–148, 2011.

[20] M. van Eeten, A. Nieuwenhuijs, E. Luiijf, M. Klaver and E. Cruz, The state and the threat of cascading failures across critical infrastructures: The implications of empirical evidence from media incident reports, *Public Administration*, vol. 89(2), pp. 381–400, 2011.

[21] E. Zio and G. Sansavini, Modeling interdependent network systems for identifying cascade-safe operating margins, *IEEE Transactions on Reliability*, vol. 60(1), pp. 94–101, 2011.

Chapter 13

A PLATFORM FOR DISASTER RESPONSE PLANNING WITH INTERDEPENDENCY SIMULATION FUNCTIONALITY

Abdullah Alsubaie, Antonio Di Pietro, Jose Marti, Pranab Kini, Ting Fu Lin, Simone Palmieri and Alberto Tofani

Abstract   Catastrophic events can result in great loss of lives and property. Planning an effective disaster response to minimize associated losses is a fundamental challenge for decision makers. The planning process can be improved by simulating interdependent critical infrastructures and evaluating system behavior during disaster scenarios. This paper describes a disaster response planning simulation platform that supports decision making based on the interdependencies existing between a power grid and a supervisory control and data acquisition (SCADA) system. By considering the physical constraints on the power grid and SCADA network, a set of feasible configurations is presented to disaster responders. The utility of the platform is demonstrated using an example scenario involving power distribution to a hospital during a disaster event.

Keywords: Disaster response, interdependencies, simulation

1.   Introduction

Implementing disaster response for critical infrastructures is difficult due to their size and complexity. Indeed, developing an effective response plan requires the identification of the associated infrastructure interdependencies. This can be accomplished using simulators to model interactions and assess infrastructure behavior in disaster scenarios.

Interdependency simulators support emergency decision making by modeling system interactions to determine resource requirements and distribution. Consider, for example, a situation where energy is supplied to an electrical load. The system is limited by the maximum current level of the corresponding

J. Butts and S. Shenoi (Eds.): Critical Infrastructure Protection VII, IFIP AICT 417, pp. 183–197, 2013.

electrical feeder and cannot exceed a physical threshold. An interdependency simulator can model the physical characteristics to evaluate the impact at the system level under varying conditions. By simulating each physical system independently (e.g., power grids, telecommunications networks, water distribution and transportation systems), the impact of potential disaster scenarios can be evaluated and response plans developed accordingly.

In earlier work [11], we proposed the adoption of the Disaster Response Network Enabled Platform (DR-NEP), a universal simulation network that integrates heterogeneous user interfaces and software. By linking the Infrastructure Interdependencies Simulator (I2Sim) [12] with a power grid simulator, DR-NEP enables the validation of resource allocation in the electrical domain. I2Sim is an event-driven, time-domain simulator that models resource flow among different infrastructures to determine how the output of one infrastructure is affected by its physical properties and the availability of input resources. The power grid simulator uses a web-service-based distributed simulation platform (WebSimP) and simulates the electrical infrastructure at the functional level.

This paper focuses on the additional resource allocation for a supervisory control and data acquisition (SCADA) communications infrastructure. This is accomplished using a telecommunications simulator along with WebSimP. The approach is demonstrated using a scenario modeled with I2Sim, which involves a power grid and an associated SCADA network that serves a hospital and other loads in a disaster area. The results demonstrate the utility of the interdependency simulator and provide an avenue for future work in disaster preparedness.

2. Related Work

Following Hurricane Katrina, researchers and government agencies began focusing on decision support frameworks to assist emergency planners in visualizing the real-time cascading effects of multiple infrastructure failures in the event of a natural disaster [5, 10]. Such frameworks include disaster support systems that optimize decision making during time-sensitive situations [2, 7, 16]. However, existing disaster support systems do not take into account the important effects of infrastructure interdependencies. Indeed, as disaster responders face increasingly difficult decisions due to the growing size and complexity of critical infrastructures, simulators are needed to evaluate the impact of interdependent systems.

Researchers have adopted a variety of techniques (e.g., agent-based systems, input-output inoperability, system reliability theory, nonlinear dynamics and graph theory) to model different types of interdependency phenomena [4, 14]. Rinaldi, et al. [14] have demonstrated that it is possible to distinguish physical, social, logical, geographical and cyber interdependencies. Satumitra, et al. [15] have categorized the various interdependency modeling approaches. Ghorbani, et al. [8] have presented a classification and comparison of agent-based interdependency modeling and simulation tools. Our work leverages I2Sim [12], a cell-channel model framework. I2Sim uses an integrated interdependency simulator as the underlying framework for infrastructure recovery and coordination [13]. Decision makers can use the framework to verify different resource allocation strategies and to simulate the effects of different event sequences. In turn, I2Sim uses domain-specific simulators to verify the feasibility of resource allocation strategies.

In our simulation, we consider scenarios that involve dependencies between an electrical power grid and a SCADA system. A proprietary network and a public telecommunications network represent a typical communications infrastructure for a SCADA system. As noted in [1], such a solution guarantees adequate performance with respect to transmission bandwidth, but it introduces a number of potential failure points that did not exist previously. Several approaches have been proposed in the literature to better understand the potential vulnerabilities and risks. As an example, the hierarchical holographic modeling approach [9] expresses a complex system at different hierarchical levels, including the physical, organizational and managerial levels. This approach has been applied to SCADA systems in order to evaluate the risk of cyber attacks on controlled critical infrastructures [6]. One of the most promising tools for investigating SCADA system interdependencies is the Virtual Control System Environment, a hybrid simulator that is used to analyze the effects of cyber security vulnerabilities of control systems used in the power grid [18].

There is growing interest in modeling and simulation frameworks for investigating the dependencies existing between SCADA systems, the controlled infrastructure (e.g., oil and gas distribution networks and power grids) and the underlying telecommunications infrastructure. Bobbio, *et al.* [1] have proposed a general framework that shows how the power supply to customers depends on the availability of SCADA services that, in turn, depend on the availability of a communications network. Each network is expressed using by a stochastic modeling formalism that helps evaluate assumptions made about failure and recovery mechanisms.

Ciancamerla, *et al.* [3] have computed quality of service indicators for a fault isolation and system restoration procedure applied to a realistic power grid and SCADA system. The procedure detects and isolates faults in the power distribution grid and reconfigures the grid to reconnect isolated customers. This paper focuses on fault isolation and system restoration procedures for managing a damaged power grid with the objective of maintaining power to most of the critical infrastructures in the area (e.g., hospitals).

3.   Disaster Response Planning Platform

The disaster response planning platform is intended to assist emergency responders in planning effective responses based on the interdependencies existing between a power grid and a SCADA network. The platform has three main components: (i) Disaster Response Network Enabled Platform (DR-NEP); (ii) Infrastructure Interdependency Simulator (I2Sim); and (iii) Web-Service-Based Simulation Platform (WebSimP).

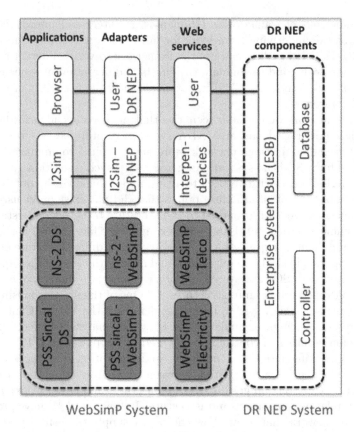

Figure 1.   DR-NEP architecture.

3.1   DR-NEP Architecture

DR-NEP is a web service platform that enables different simulators to communicate results to each other via a common enterprise service bus (ESB) and a database. A distributed computing architecture (Figure 1) is employed to support decision making. Every simulator is connected to DR-NEP using an adapter that listens on the ESB for instructions about running simulations, gathers inputs from the other simulators and the database and pushes results from the simulators to the database. After the simulators and adapters are configured, a controller in the ESB pushes input to the simulators at predefined intervals.

DR-NEP also offers web pages and mapping services for researchers and disaster responders to support coordination, resource flow visualization and infrastructure operability.

3.2   I2Sim

I2Sim is an event-driven, time-domain simulator that is used to model infrastructure interdependencies. I2Sim uses a cell-channel approach, which provides a multi-system representation at multiple hierarchical levels (e.g., local, municipal and provincial). The simulator assesses in real time the effects of resource allocation decisions during disasters [12]. The DR-NEP platform enables I2Sim to exchange inputs and outputs with other domain simulators via software adapters.

3.3   WebSimP

WebSimP enables the domain simulators that are integrated with DR-NEP to be invoked separately through web service technologies. Such a service-based platform offers many benefits over other types of distributed computing architectures in terms of interoperability and ubiquity. As shown in Figure 1, WebSimP allows the simulation of the electrical and telecommunications domains.

Each simulation layer incorporates three software components: (i) a web service that receives operation requests to execute a particular simulation; (ii) a software adapter that implements the details of each requested operation and oversees command execution in the simulator and output data post-processing; and (iii) a simulator (e.g., discrete/continuous, deterministic/stochastic) that executes a simulation model for a certain domain.

Electrical Adapter. The electrical adapter is a software component that is responsible for invoking operations in a pre-existing model. The possible operations are: (i) network configuration (e.g., disconnecting electrical lines to simulate line damage and closing breakers to simulate load shedding actions); and (ii) constraint computation (e.g., maximum available power). The simulator determines the loads that the grid may support without damaging the infrastructure by considering physical limits on parameters such as current and voltage. The PSS Sincal [17] electrical simulator is used; it supports network planning for power transmission and distribution networks (e.g., load flow calculations, dynamics and network protection).

Telecommunications Adapter. The telecommunications adapter is a software component that is in charge of invoking operations in a pre-existing telecommunications simulation model. The possible operations are: (i) network configuration (e.g., disconnecting telecommunications and SCADA elements to simulate damage events); (ii) constraint computation (e.g., communications bandwidth); and (iii) electrical network reconfiguration time computation (e.g., response time required to send and execute specific commands). The telecommunications simulation uses ns-2, a discrete event simulator that allows the modeling and simulation of communications protocols, routing and multicast protocols over wired and wireless networks.

4.   Resource Allocation Process

The DR-NEP platform presents decision makers with a set of feasible options. The three simulators, I2Sim, PSS Sincal and ns-2, are used to model disaster events.

I2Sim models a disaster event at a high level and assesses the effects of resource allocation. In a disaster scenario, I2Sim maximizes the functionality of critical infrastructures (e.g., hospitals) by optimizing resource allocation. Different resources can be incorporated in I2Sim models, such as electricity, water, medicine and transportation. This paper focuses on the determination of the distribution of electricity using power grid and SCADA network (domain) simulators.

The power grid is modeled using PSS Sincal, which simulates the status of the power system during a disaster event and examines the feasibility of possible configurations. The possible configurations include the power required to supply a load, electrical equipment used, power grid limits, and control elements of the SCADA communications network.

Resource allocation begins with I2Sim suggesting the desired resource distribution required to supply a specific amount of electricity to a critical load (e.g., a hospital). Decisions are determined based on the I2Sim optimization process, which considers other resources and critical infrastructures. PSS Sincal and ns-2 simulate the possible configurations that can accommodate an I2Sim request and return a feasible configuration via the WebSimP adapter. Note that the feasible configuration may or may not satisfy the initial request made by I2Sim. If all the conditions are not satisfied, I2Sim updates its model and selects another request. PSS Sincal and ns-2 then simulate the configurations once again and return a feasible solution. The process continues iteratively to optimize the power distribution to critical infrastructures based on the power grid and SCADA network constraints.

5.   Sample Scenario

The sample scenario involves a disaster event where the power and SCADA infrastructures place constraints on the resource allocation process. The main objective in the scenario is to maximize the operability of a hospital by providing the required electricity and water resources. The I2Sim simulates the interdependencies between the hospital and the water pumping station. PSS Sincal and ns-2 simulate the physical constraints introduced by the power and SCADA networks.

In more complex situations, the failure of a power provider would affect multiple critical infrastructures. However, for demonstration purposes, we consider a small set of infrastructure entities. Note that the DR-NEP platform can be readily extended to run a simulation scenario where multiple infrastructures concurrently depend on a single power provider.

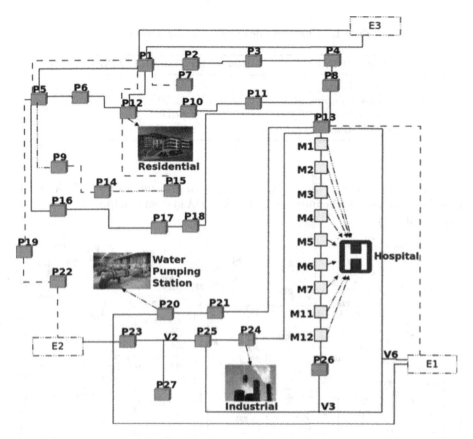

Figure 2. Power distribution grid.

5.1   Infrastructure Simulation Models

This section describes the power distribution grid, SCADA system and I2Sim simulation models.

Power Distribution Grid. The power distribution grid shown in Figure 2 incorporates 165 buses, 22 circuit breakers and 46 loads. E_i nodes represent the power transmission grid substations, P_i nodes represent high voltage (HV) 150 kV buses, M_i nodes represent the medium voltage (MV) 20 kV buses, and physical links between two buses represent electrical lines. Each substation supplies energy to different types of loads/customers: (i) public loads/customers for the hospital, including emergency and intensive care units with very high criticality (M_{11} and M_{12}) and other hospital units ($M_1, \ldots, M_7$); (ii) industrial loads/customers for a water pumping station and an industrial load (P_{20} and P_{24}); and (iii) residential loads/customers for domestic users (P_{12}).

In normal conditions, hospital loads are supplied by P_{13} and P_{26} through intermediate nodes M_i. In the event of a physical failure of P_{13}, the hospital

Table 1.   Electricity demand for loads/customers.

Physical Entity	Electricity Demand (MW)
Hospital	13.47
Water Pumping Station	52.50
Industrial	9.47
Residential	120.91

is fed only through P_{26}. Since P_{26} can supply a maximum of 9.50 MW, load shedding actions must be initiated by the SCADA system to supply the hospital loads (Table 1).

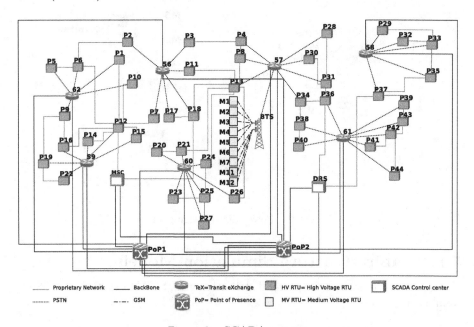

Figure 3.   SCADA system.

SCADA System.   Figure 3 shows the SCADA system that controls the power distribution grid. The SCADA system includes: (i) a main SCADA control (MSC) center that controls and supervises the power distribution grid; (ii) a disaster recovery SCADA (DRS) center that assumes control and supervision in case of MSC failure; (iii) 44 remote terminal units (RTUs) (P_i nodes) located at HV substations; and (iv) nine RTUs (M_i nodes) located at MV substations. RTUs receive commands through the SCADA communications network from the MSC and DRS centers to perform local actions on the power grid (e.g., closing circuit breakers).

Table 2. SCADA network model assumptions.

Link Type	Proprietary Network	PSTN	Backbone
Capacity	0.5 Mbps	0.5 Mbps	1 Mbps
Source-Destination Nodes	$MSC - P_i$, $DRS - P_i$, $P_i - P_j$, $P_i - M_j$, $M_i - M_j$	$TeX_i - P_j$	$PoP_i - PoP_j$, $PoP_i - TeX_j$, $MSC - PoP_i$, $DRS - PoP_i$
Traffic Type	CBR over TCP	CBR over TCP	CBR over TCP
Traffic Bit Rate	255 B/30 sec	255 B/30 sec	255 B/30 sec

The SCADA communications network comprises two networks:

- The default proprietary network (DPN) connects the SCADA control centers to RTUs at the HV and MV substations. DPN nodes can also communicate with each other through the public switched telephone network (PSTN) to provide backup capabilities.

- The PSTN network models the public backup telecommunications network that connects the MSC and DRS to the HV RTUs. Two virtual private networks (VPNs) are established between the MSC and DRS via two high data rate digital subscriber line connections that employ two points of presence (PoPs), PoP_1 and PoP_2.

Communications between the MSC and DRS and the RTUs are modeled with ns-2 using TCP agents located at the source and destination nodes. Traffic is generated at a specified constant bit rate (CBR). Table 2 summarizes the main assumptions.

I2Sim Model. The I2Sim model provides a high-level abstraction of the physical components. The detailed topological configurations of the power and SCADA networks are modeled using the domain simulators, PSS Sincal and ns-2, respectively. In the I2Sim ontology, physical infrastructure entities are modeled as cells connected by channels that transport resources (e.g., electricity and water). In the model shown in Figure 4, eight cells are used to represent interdependent infrastructures at the disaster site, consisting of four electrical substations, a water pumping station, a hospital, residential loads and industrial loads. Note that a backup power supply, which is typically used in a hospital, can be modeled but is not included in this scenario.

The WebSimP electrical adapter and telecommunications adapter implement the mappings between the three models using the DR-NEP database. The database has three primary components: (i) models; (ii) physical entities; and (iii) ports. A model has one or more physical entities, with every physical entity having input and output ports. In our implementation, three models

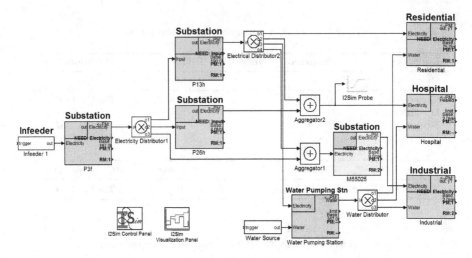

Figure 4. I2Sim model.

are defined in the database, one for each simulator. The output ports of one simulator serve as inputs to the other simulators. After the setup is complete, the port replication module implemented in DR-NEP uses these definitions and automates the process of mapping outputs to inputs at each time-step during the simulation. Note that this reduces the complexity of feeding and collecting data manually in large interconnected systems.

5.2   Simulated Scenarios

Three scenarios are simulated to illustrate the utility of the DR-NEP platform. All three scenarios involve a transformer failure in the power grid. However, two of the scenarios, Scenario 2 and Scenario 3, are more severe in that they also involve failures of SCADA network components.

- Scenario 1: A failure in the power grid (transformer) only.

- Scenario 2: A failure in the power grid (transformer) with a failure in the SCADA network (RTU).

- Scenario 3: A failure in the power grid (transformer) with two failures in the SCADA network (RTU and communications node).

Table 3 shows the sequence of events for the three scenarios. At time T2, failures are introduced: a transformer in Scenario 1; a transformer and an RTU in Scenario 2; and a transformer, RTU and communications node in Scenario 3. At time T3, a desired configuration of the power grid, selected by I2Sim, is sent to the domain simulators for verification. Note that the desired configuration is selected based on optimality, experience and pre-determined feasibility of the power grid and SCADA networks.

Table 3. Sequence of events for the simulated scenarios.

No.	Time	Event	Effect
1	T1	Normal operation	Hospital and water pumping station have full supply of electricity and water
2	T2	Equipment failure is detected	Hospital loads lose 6.2 MW of supply
3	T3	Feasible power grid configuration is implemented	Hospital and water pumping station loads are partially supplied
4	T4	Affected equipment is restored	Full supply can be restored
5	T5	Normal operation configuration is restored	Hospital and water pumping station have full supply of electricity and water

The I2Sim ontology defines operability in terms of available resources in human readable tables with five levels: 100%, 75%, 50%, 25% and 0%. Note that the hospital and water pumping station require 100% power supply for full operability. However, 100% power supply may not be possible during disasters due to damage to the physical systems. In such situations, different combinations of the distributions of available resources can be deployed (e.g., 75% power supply to the hospital and 50% power supply to the water pumping station).

In the three scenarios, the distribution of electricity between the hospital and the water pumping station is determined based on the physical constraints of the power grid and SCADA networks. For example, Table 4 shows the feasible configurations for 100% power supply to the water pumping station and different power supply percentages to the hospital.

5.3   Simulation Results

Based on the five levels in the human readable tables, there are $5 \times 5 = 25$ possible combinations for electricity distribution between the hospital and the water pumping station. However, the failures in the power grid and SCADA networks limit the set of feasible configurations. Table 5 compares the decision spaces for the three simulated scenarios in terms of the number of feasible configurations available for each scenario. The rows represent the levels of power supplied to the hospital and the columns represent the levels of power supplied to the water pumping station. The boldface **X** symbols denote the feasible combinations for electricity distribution. In Scenario 1, for example,

Table 4.   Feasible configurations for 100% power supply to the water pumping station.

No.	Power Supply	Feasible Configurations
1	100%	**Configuration 1:** Breakers P_{10}, P_{13} and P_{26} closed; Breakers $M_1 - M_{12}$ closed
2	75%	**Configuration 2:** Breaker P_{13h} open; Breaker P_{26} closed; Breakers $M_1, M_2, M_5, M_6, M_{11}, M_{12}$ closed; Breakers M_3, M_4, M_7 open **Configuration 3:** Breaker P_{13} open; Breaker P_{26} closed; Breakers $M_1, M_2, M_3, M_5, M_{11}, M_{12}$ closed; Breakers M_4, M_6, M_7 open **Configuration 4:** Breaker P_{13} open; Breaker P_{26} closed; Breakers $M_5, M_6, M_7, M_{11}, M_{12}$ closed; Breakers $M_1 - M_4$ open
3	50%	**Configuration 5:** Breaker P_{13} open; Breaker P_{26} closed; Breakers M_1, M_2, M_{11}, M_{12} closed; Breakers $M_3 - M_7$ open
4	25%	**Configuration 6:** Breaker P_{13} open; Breaker P_{26} closed; Breakers M_{11}, M_{12} closed; Breakers $M_1 - M_7$ open
5	0%	**Configuration 7:** Breakers P_{13} and P_{26} open

a maximum 75% power supply can be delivered to the hospital and the water pumping station.

Table 6 presents the results of the resource allocation process. Note that EF denotes electrical feasibility, SF denoted SCADA feasibility, GF denotes global feasibility and Rt denotes reconfiguration time. Configuration 1 in Scenario 1 is not electrically feasible because feeder P_{13} is isolated from the network by the transformer failure and the power needed to supply all the M_i loads cannot be provided through feeder P_{26} because of the electrical constraints (P_{26} cannot exceed 9.50 MW capacity).

On the other hand, Configuration 2 in Scenario 1 has global feasibility (marked with a boldface **Yes**). This means that all the components of the power grid are within their physical limits and a communication path between the MSC and RTUs is available.

The time required for reconfiguring the power grid was computed by considering the physical time needed to open/close breakers plus the SCADA message round trip time (RTT). The simulated scenarios show that the RTT is negligible with respect to breaker operation. The open/close operations take 50 seconds for MV breakers and 100 seconds for HV breakers.

Table 5. Decision spaces for the three scenarios.

| | Scenario 1 | | | | |
	100%	75%	50%	25%	0%
100%	X	X	X	X	X
75%	X	**X**	**X**	**X**	**X**
50%	X	**X**	**X**	**X**	**X**
25%	X	**X**	**X**	**X**	**X**
0%	X	**X**	**X**	**X**	**X**
	Scenario 2				
	100%	75%	50%	25%	0%
100%	X	X	X	X	X
75%	X	X	**X**	**X**	**X**
50%	X	X	**X**	**X**	**X**
25%	X	X	**X**	**X**	**X**
0%	X	X	**X**	**X**	**X**
	Scenario 3				
	100%	75%	50%	25%	0%
100%	X	X	X	X	X
75%	X	X	X	X	X
50%	X	X	X	X	X
25%	X	X	X	X	X
0%	X	X	X	X	**X**

Table 6. Simulation results.

Scenario	Configuration	EF	SF	GF	Rt (sec)
Scenario 1	1 (100%)	No	Yes	No	–
	2 (75%)	Yes	Yes	**Yes**	420.4
Scenario 2	1 (100%)	No	No	No	–
	2 (75%)	Yes	No	No	–
	3 (50%)	Yes	No	No	–
	4 (50%)	Yes	Yes	**Yes**	367.4
Scenario 3	1 (100%)	No	No	No	-
	2 (75%)	Yes	No	No	–
	3 (50%)	Yes	No	No	–
	4 (50%)	Yes	No	No	–
	5 (50%)	Yes	No	No	–
	6 (25%)	Yes	No	No	–
	7 (0%)	Yes	Yes	**Yes**	0

6.   Conclusions

The disaster response planning simulation platform described in this paper provides decision support based on the interdependencies existing between a power grid and a SCADA system. The platform integrates a PSS Sincal power grid simulator and an ns-2 SCADA network simulator with an I2Sim infrastructure interdependency simulator using software adapters. The platform offers a powerful interactive simulation environment for disaster response planning, enabling planners to evaluate specific scenarios and select the appropriate responses. The platform also supports the use of simulation results for real-time disaster response.

Scenarios involving cascading events that arise from interdependencies existing with other infrastructures can be simulated by extending the platform architecture. This feature will be implemented in future work. The modular approach used in designing the platform supports the implementation of this feature as well as expanding the framework by adding more domain simulators and inter-system adapters.

References

[1] A. Bobbio, G. Bonanni, E. Ciancamerla, R. Clemente, A. Iacomini, M. Minichino, A. Scarlatti, R. Terruggia and E. Zendri, Unavailability of critical SCADA communication links interconnecting a power grid and a telco network, *Reliability Engineering and System Safety*, vol. 95(12), pp. 1345–1357, 2010.

[2] G. Brown and A. Vassiliou, Optimizing disaster relief: Real-time operational and tactical decision support, *Naval Research Logistics*, vol. 40(1), pp. 1–23, 1993.

[3] E. Ciancamerla, C. Foglietta, D. Lefevre, M. Minichino, L. Lev and Y. Shneck, Discrete event simulation of QoS of a SCADA system interconnecting a power grid and a telco network, in *What Kind of Information Society? Governance, Virtuality, Surveillance, Sustainability, Resilience*, J. Berleur, M. Hercheiu and L. Hilty (Eds.), Springer, Heidelberg, Germany, pp. 350–362, 2010.

[4] S. De Porcellinis, S. Panzieri and R. Setola, Modeling critical infrastructure via a mixed holistic reductionistic approach, *International Journal of Critical Infrastructures*, vol. 5(1/2), pp. 86–99, 2009.

[5] D. Dudenhoeffer, M. Permann and M. Manic, CIMS: A framework for infrastructure interdependency modeling and analysis, *Proceedings of the Winter Simulation Conference*, pp. 478–485, 2006.

[6] B. Ezell, Y. Haimes and J. Lambert, Risks of cyber attack to water utility supervisory control and data acquisition (SCADA) systems, *Military Operations Research*, vol. 6(2), pp. 23–33, 2001.

[7] F. Fiedrich, F. Gehbauer and U. Rickers, Optimized resource allocation for emergency response after earthquake disasters, *Safety Science*, vol. 35(1), pp. 41–57, 2000.

[8] A. Ghorbani and E. Bagheri, The state of the art in critical infrastructure protection: A framework for convergence, *International Journal of Critical Infrastructures*, vol. 4(3), pp. 215–244, 2008.

[9] Y. Haimes and D. Li, A hierarchical-multiobjective framework for risk management, *Automatica*, vol. 27(3), pp. 579–584, 1991.

[10] Idaho National Laboratory, CIPR/sim: A comprehensive, real-time critical infrastructure modeling technology, Idaho Falls, Idaho (`www.hsdl.org/?view\&did=21965`).

[11] J. Marti, P. Kini, P. Lusina, A. Di Pietro, V. Rosato, B. Charnier and K. Wang, Inter-system software adapter for decision support by interfacing disaster response platforms and simulation platforms, *Proceedings of the IEEE Global Humanitarian Technology Conference*, pp. 41–46, 2012.

[12] J. Marti, C. Ventura, J. Hollman, K. Srivastava and H. Juarez, I2Sim modeling and simulation framework for scenario development, training and real-time decision support of multiple interdependent critical infrastructures during large emergencies, presented at the *NATO RTO Modeling and Simulation Group Conference*, 2008.

[13] P. Pederson, D. Dudenhoeffer, S. Hartley and M. Permann, Critical Infrastructure Interdependency Modeling: A Survey of U.S. and International Research, INL/EXT-06-11464, Idaho National Laboratory, Idaho Falls, Idaho, 2006.

[14] S. Rinaldi, J. Peerenboom and T. Kelly, Identifying, understanding and analyzing critical infrastructure interdependencies, *IEEE Control Systems*, vol. 21(6), pp. 11–25, 2001.

[15] G. Satumitra and L. Duenas-Osorio, Synthesis of modeling and simulation methods in critical infrastructure interdependency research, in *Sustainable and Resilient Critical Infrastructure Systems*, K. Gopalakrishnan and S. Peeta (Eds.), Springer, Heidelberg, Germany, pp. 1–51, 2010.

[16] J. Sheu, L. Lan and Y. Chen, A novel model for quick response to disaster relief distribution, *Proceedings of the Eastern Asia Society for Transportation Studies*, vol. 5, pp. 2454–2462, 2005.

[17] SimTec, PSS SINCAL Platform, Leobersdorf, Austria (`www.simtec-gmbh.at/sites_en/sincal_updates.asp`).

[18] J. Stamp, V. Urias and B Richardson, Cyber security analysis for the power grid using the virtual control systems environment, *Proceedings of the IEEE Power and Energy Society General Meeting*, 2011.

V

RISK ASSESSMENT

Chapter 14

MISSION-BASED ANALYSIS FOR ASSESSING CYBER RISK IN CRITICAL INFRASTRUCTURE SYSTEMS

Thomas Llanso, Gregg Tally, Michael Silberglitt and Tara Anderson

Abstract   Adversaries with the appropriate expertise and access can potentially exploit the large attack surface provided by the cyber component of critical infrastructure assets to target operations across the various sectors and significantly impact society. This paper describes a family of cyber risk methodologies known as "mission-based analysis" (MBA) that assist system designers in identifying the threats that pose the highest risk to mission execution and in prioritizing mitigation actions against the threats. This paper describes our experiences applying MBA and discusses its benefits and limitations. Also, it describes future enhancements of MBA and compares the approach with other assurance methodologies.

Keywords: Mission-based analysis, cyber security, risk assessment

1. Introduction

The Patriot Act of 2001 defines critical infrastructures as "systems and assets, whether physical or virtual, so vital to the United States that the incapacity or destruction of such systems and assets would have a debilitating impact on security, national economic security, national public health or safety, or any combination of those matters." The dependence of critical infrastructure systems on the cyber component brings both benefits and risks. "Risk" in this context is the product of the impact of a cyber attack on a critical infrastructure mission and the likelihood that the attack will occur. Cyber attacks on critical infrastructures have occurred for decades, but are steadily increasing in scope and frequency. Examples include the Siberian pipeline sabotage in 1982, the Stuxnet attack in 2010, and the incidents at Aramco [13] and at U.S. financial

J. Butts and S. Shenoi (Eds.): Critical Infrastructure Protection VII, IFIP AICT 417, pp. 201–214, 2013.

institutions [4] in 2012. To minimize risks from cyber attacks, it is necessary to identify the vulnerabilities, the likelihood that they will be exploited and their potential impact on the critical infrastructure mission, so that it is possible to identify mitigation actions that increase survivability and resiliency. The 2013 U.S. Presidential Executive Order, Improving Critical Infrastructure Cybersecurity, highlighted the importance of critical infrastructure security and emphasized the need to implement risk-based standards.

At the Johns Hopkins University Applied Physics Laboratory (JHU/APL), we have developed three mission-related risk methodologies that fall under the umbrella of mission-based analysis (MBA). This paper briefly describes our experiences applying MBA and discusses its benefits and limitations in critical infrastructure contexts. MBA is designed to be general enough to analyze cyber threats as well as other threats, such as electronic jamming and physical attacks. However, the primary focus of this paper is cyber threats.

The goal of MBA is to analyze an operational mission, cyber threats to the mission, and information technology systems that support the mission in order to answer four questions: (i) If a threat were to be carried out, what would be the impact to the mission? (ii) What is the estimated level of effort for an adversary to realize a given threat? (iii) What mitigation actions are possible for the so called "hot spots" – threats that have a high mission impact and are relatively easy for an adversary to conduct? (iv) What are the operational costs of the mitigation actions?

The MBA processes share many similarities with NIST risk assessment methodologies [11]. However, one significant difference is the use of likelihood in the NIST methodologies versus the attacker level of effort in MBA. While the NIST methodologies are more generic and abstract, MBA is specifically focused on evaluating the risk of cyber attacks.

To date, MBA has been applied to a number of real-world contexts, primarily within the U.S. Department of Defense. Examples include analyses of Navy ship-board and submarine systems, satellite systems and a homeland security application. These applications have given us experience in optimizing and calibrating MBA, as well as identifying areas for improvement.

At a high level, all MBA variants follow a similar sequence of steps (Figure 1). A set of analytical models are first populated with data from the target problem domain. These models include adversary, mission, system and network models. The models are then scored in order to estimate risk. The scoring typically involves assigning numeric values to the mission impact and adversary level of effort (LOE) corresponding to a threat.

The scoring results are combined to provide an estimate of the risk to the mission due to cyber attack. The results are structured to show a prioritization of threats. Mitigation of threats is then considered, followed by an evaluation of the efficacy of the mitigation actions. The results enable an analyst to develop an action plan that mitigates the highest risk threats first. As threats, missions and cyber systems evolve, it is important to re-evaluate the risk periodically by repeating the steps in the methodology.

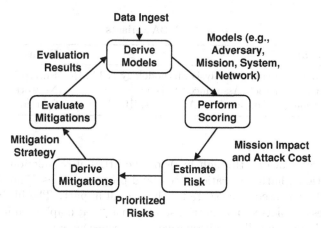

Figure 1. MBA activities.

2. Related Work

Several methodologies have been developed for evaluating the risk to critical infrastructure systems. The practical risk assessment methodology (PRAM) [9] analyzes the risk to safety-critical systems using historical data on accident probability and consequences. The goal is to ensure that new systems are at least as safe as existing systems. However, cyber attacks are fundamentally different from accidents in that the likelihood of occurrence is based on the attacker's skill, resources and motivation, not on random events. It is inappropriate to assume that historical attack data is indicative of future attack methods, frequency or success.

Ralston, *et al.* [12] have proposed risk assessment approaches for SCADA and distributed control systems. McQueen, *et al.* [7] have employed compromise graphs in which the nodes represent attack stages and the edges represent the time to compromise. They discovered that, when this approach was applied to a SCADA system, an 86% reduction in the number of vulnerabilities resulted in only a 3% to 30% increase in the time to compromise, depending on the attacker skill level and target. This methodology could be a useful future enhancement to the MBA process in order to assess the attacker level of effort.

Various mission-focused cyber methodologies have been proposed (see, e.g., [6]). The cyber security risk management (CSRM) methodology [3] uses a risk management approach to qualitatively assess and prioritize cyber security risks. The approach, which is based on NIST 800-30 [11], encompasses four processes: risk management planning, risk assessment, risk mitigation, and risk monitoring and control. It addresses all the phases of the system development lifecycle, using a cost-benefit approach to assess countermeasures that may reduce security risks. The process includes threat assessment and assignment of likelihood values to potential attacks. Threats are identified using a threat database to identify threat categories relevant to the system environment. For a given threat, the analysis estimates the consequence (impact)

Table 1.   MBA variants.

Variant	Focus
Cyber Investment Analysis Methodology (CIAM)	Enterprise
Network Mission Assurance (NMA)	Network
Mission Information Risk Analysis (MIRA)	System

score (on a scale of one through five) for the attributes: mission objectives, system functions, harm, operational cost and programmatics. The assessment uses the highest consequence score for the overall impact. The likelihood and impact scores are plotted in a matrix, similar to a "heat map" used in the MBA process. This process allows alternative countermeasures to be compared for their overall consequence scores that include all five attributes. The CSRM approach appears to be comparable in some aspects to the cyber investment variant of MBA, which is described below.

3.   MBA Variants

Table 1 presents the three variants of MBA. The first variant is the cyber investment analysis methodology (CIAM) [5], which considers risk and mitigation actions at the enterprise level by analyzing forensic data on attacks, vulnerabilities, CVSS scores, protection strategies and protection costs to estimate an optimal investment level by protection type. The second is network mission assurance (NMA) [2], which focuses on the availability of network bandwidth and how cyber attacks that impact network capacity can affect mission. The third is mission information risk analysis (MIRA) [6].

This paper focuses on MIRA because it is highly relevant to critical infrastructure environments. MIRA constructs three main models for the mission, system architecture and adversary. The abstraction level of each model is chosen based on the desired fidelity of the results and the amount of time and resources allowed for the analysis.

The mission model MM is a five-tuple (M, A, B, F, D). M is a set of distinct mission types supported by the target information technology system. A is a set of quantitative mission measures of effectiveness (MOEs) that describe critical performance requirements that must be met to achieve missions in M. B is a set of quantitative system-level MOEs that are required to realize the mission-level MOEs in A. F is a set of mission-essential functions whose invocation directly impacts MOEs in B and transitively in A. D is a set of required information elements that are acted on by the functions in F. In general, there is a many-to-many mapping of MM elements.

The system architecture model SM is a four-tuple (T, N, L, C). T is a set of node types, instances of which are found in the system. A node is defined as an active entity capable of carrying out computation and/or communication operations (e.g., router, switch, desktop, laptop, server or wireless device). N

is a set of node instances in the architecture. L is a set of links between node instances. C is a mapping of data types from D in the mission model to N. A given link represents connectivity, typically in a network or communications context, between two node instances.

The adversary model AM consists of an estimate of the maximum LOE that the anticipated worst-case cyber adversary might muster against the target system. The value ranges from one to ten, where one indicates minimal exertion on the part of the attacker and ten indicates the maximal level of exertion corresponding to the capabilities possessed by a top nation-state attacker.

We now describe the MIRA activities that map to Figure 1. In the Derive Models activity, analysts populate MM, SM and AM. They can do so using a number of techniques, such as reviewing relevant documentation, interviewing mission and system experts, and, if permitted for an existing system, by running automated discovery analytics against operational mission system environments to identify the nodes (N), links between nodes (L), and data types (D) on nodes (C).

In detailing the models, analysts also capture how mission data flows over the system nodes in the context of different mission-essential functions. To characterize the adversary, the analyst considers the mission in the context of different kinds of potential adversaries who might wish to harm the mission.

In the Perform Scoring activity, analysts derive two distinct types of scores: mission impact scores and attack LOE scores. In the most detailed case, a mission impact score is assigned for each viable tuple from (M, A, B, F, D, N, CT) where M, A, B, F, D and N are defined above and CT denotes the type of compromise, e.g., confidentiality (adversary accesses data), integrity (adversary modifies data or service function) or availability (adversary prevents the use of data or a service). A mission impact score is an ordinal value in the range one to five, where one denotes "fully mission capable" (i.e., no mission impact) and five denotes "not mission capable" (i.e., mission fails). An LOE score is assigned to each viable tuple (N, D, CT, AV) where N, D and CT are defined above and AV is the attack vector. Typical attack vectors are network, insider and supply chain implant.

For LOE scoring, analysts have employed the global information grid information assurance portfolio (GIAP) scoring approach that estimates the required cyber attacker capability on an absolute scale ranging from one (script kiddie) to ten (nation-state). Research into platform vulnerability history and threat reports help analysts narrow the estimated capability requirements. Several approaches are available for determining the types of scoring, each with its own strengths and weaknesses. MIRA allows for the use of alternative scoring approaches. One approach we are currently studying involves constructing models of the mission and the related cyber system. A simulated Monte Carlo attacker repeatedly constructs and directs cyber attacks at the system model; the impact of these attacks are automatically assessed by functions that compute MOEs from the system state and mission state. Scoring is a rich area for

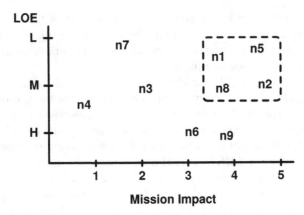

Figure 2.   Heat map.

future research. A more detailed discussion of scoring procedures is omitted in this paper for reasons of space.

In the Estimate Risk activity, analysts create a risk matrix called a heat map (Figure 2). The x-axis of the heat map depicts mission impact scores and the y-axis represents LOE scores, with the highest LOE scores located closest to the origin. In this arrangement, cyber attacks, that are both highly mission impacting and that require a relatively low LOE, appear in the upper right-hand quadrant of the heat map (outlined in Figure 2). These attack contexts represent the highest risk to the mission and become key inputs to the remaining activities.

MIRA currently considers different attack steps/contexts in heat maps individually. An interesting topic for future research is the analysis of combinations of attack steps from an impact/LOE perspective.

In the Derive Mitigations activity, analysts consider different combinations of security controls, such as those described in NIST 800.53 [10], and the effectiveness of these controls at countering the prioritized attack contexts identified in the heat map. Such controls include people, processes and technologies. MIRA enables analysts to prioritize mitigation actions based on the risk reduction achieved. After the mitigation actions have been derived, it is necessary to evaluate the actions.

In the Evaluate Mitigations activity, analysts re-factor the revised system architecture model with the derived mitigation actions and rescore the LOE values of the affected attack contexts. A key goal in this activity is to increase the LOE values via well-placed mitigation actions. Increased LOE values can help reduce the overall mission risk, especially if the recomputed LOE values exceed the estimated capabilities of the cyber adversary in the adversary model AM. Ultimately, analysts produce a set of recommendations based on the overall analysis, including the mitigation actions. For existing systems, penetration testing can provide additional evaluation and validation of mitigation actions after they have been implemented in the cyber architecture.

As stated earlier, of the three variants that make up MBA, MIRA and NMA are most applicable to critical infrastructure systems. CIAM is the least relevant given its general information technology enterprise focus. NMA is useful for critical infrastructure system analysis, especially in cases where network bandwidth and availability are key performance considerations. However, MIRA is the best approach for conducting risk analyses of critical infrastructure systems because of its strong mission/system/data ties. The remainder of this paper focuses on MIRA in the context of critical infrastructure systems.

4.   Applications of the MIRA Variant of MBA

This section briefly describes two examples involving the application of MIRA to critical infrastructure systems, one is a real-world satellite system and the other is a hypothetical scenario involving a railroad control system.

4.1   Satellite Control System

The MIRA analysis of the satellite control system integrates both cyber and electronic warfare attacks, enabling an end-to-end mission risk analysis of the system. The satellite control system consists of purpose-built hardware devices, including ground antennas and special communications processors that are easily represented in the MIRA system model. For reasons of sensitivity, the satellite control system is described at a high level. However, the lessons learned with regard to the application of MIRA to critical infrastructure systems are clear.

The following components are involved in the analysis:

- **Mission Model:** The mission model defines the overall mission objectives of the satellite control system, key mission-level and system-level MOEs, actors or role players engaged with the satellite control system, mission-essential functions and mission data processed by the satellite control system. The satellite control system has a worldwide footprint capable of controlling designated satellites for various purposes on a global basis. The control system provides support for satellite operation, control and maintenance, including functions such as telemetry, tracking and commanding operations, pre-launch checkout and simulation, launch support and early-orbit support when satellites are in their initial or transfer orbits and require maneuvering to their final orbits. Time on the satellite control system is strictly scheduled based on reconciling conflicting, prioritized demands and the availability of ground stations located around the globe.

  The satellite control system mission model captures three primary mission threads with a defined set of quantitative MOEs. An example of a satellite control system mission is: "Help diagnose faults and restore designated satellites to full operation." The MOEs highlight the critical mission requirements needed to obtain mission success. An example of a satellite control system MOE is: "The probability of success in completing a scheduled contact."

Mission-critical functions are then defined for the satellite control system mission set. An example of a mission-essential function is the "Submit updated schedule function." As noted above, the mission areas are analyzed and described as a series of mission threads invoking mission-essential functions. Examples of mission-essential functions defined for the satellite control system analysis are: "Submit satellite communications session request," "Reserve overhead resources for communications fabric," "Submit urgent needs schedule request," "Configure and track link," "Establish communications session" and "Internal and external space operations center communications with satellite."

- **System-Level Model:** The satellite control system is decomposed into node types, node instances and node interconnectivity. The centralized command and control, scheduling and remote uplink/downlink nodes are captured. The resulting system model comprises more than two dozen data types and four dozen computational nodes, such as the schedule data type and the data type indicating the identity and location of the target satellite system.

- **Adversary Model:** The adversary model assumes nation-state level attackers of the advanced persistent threat variety. The threat is applied to the criticality assessment described above to identify hot spots and the level of effort needed to impact mission success and identify system risks.

- **Mitigation Phase:** Specific mitigation actions are recommended as a result of the analysis. Several attacks have a high mission impact but a low estimated level of effort. The results of this analysis enable the identification and prioritization of capabilities, systems, and science and technology needs to align the system with national space policy and U.S. Department of Defense capabilities documents and functional plans.

4.2 Railroad Control System

The second example application of MIRA is in the area of monitoring and controlling train movements through an initiative called positive train control (PTC). The Rail Safety Improvement Act of 2008 requires the implementation of PTC on certain rail lines by 2015 [1]. The analysis presented in this section is based on publicly-available documentation and should not be interpreted as a complete MIRA analysis of PTC.

The major PTC components are [8]:

- **Back Office Server:** This system stores data on speed restrictions, track geometry and wayside signaling.

- **Onboard System:** This system displays train information to the engineer, monitors and controls train movement if the engineer fails to respond to audible warnings, and uses GPS to report train position.

- **Wayside Signal System:** This system comprises traffic signals located along the track that are connected by cellular modems (primarily 220 MHz) to the back office server and onboard system.

- **Communications Network:** This system comprises a redundant wired and wireless communication network that connects a locomotive, cab car, back office server and wayside interface units

The following components are involved in the analysis:

- **Mission Model:** The mission MOEs of PTC are to reduce fatalities, injuries and the cost of damage due to improper train movements. PTC specifically does not attempt to reduce deaths or injuries when people trespass on railroad tracks or vehicles bypass railroad crossing barriers. PTC does not take human operators out of the system, but it does provide a fail-safe mechanism to stop unsafe train movements should the human operator fail to heed alarms and signals from the onboard system.

To improve reliability, PTC is designed to incorporate multiple redundant capabilities. Wayside signals communicate with both onboard systems and back office servers. This ensures that the onboard system receives signal information even if the back office server does not provide the data. The communications network has wired and wireless network connections. Also, since not all geographic areas support accurate GPS measurements, onboard systems have alternative methods to compute location.

Some of the system MOEs for a PTC system are:

- Accuracy of train position reporting (including the track that the train occupies).

- Accuracy of automated train braking (stopping as close as possible to the target without overrunning it).

- Effective throughput of the communications network to ensure timely delivery of the train consist and other data from the back office server to the onboard system.

Some of the mission-essential functions and required information elements include:

- The onboard system reports train position to the back office server via the communications system.

- The wayside signals report the switch status to the back office server via the communications system.

- The back office server reports the signal status to the onboard system via the communications system.

– The back office server sends train consist data, authorizations and restrictions to the onboard system via the communications system.

– The onboard system calculates safe braking parameters based on data from the back office server.

– The onboard system visually and audibly provides information to the engineer.

■ **System Architecture Model:** The major components of the PTC model are described above. Additional components of a PTC implementation include wired and wireless network infrastructure components such as radios, base stations, routers and switches; standard information technology components in the back office server; locomotive and cab car components of the onboard system; and handheld terminals for track work crews.

■ **Adversary Model:** While PTC was mandated in response to accidental train collisions [8], the centralized train dispatching system is also a potential target for adversaries. Passenger train collisions can cause death and injury to large numbers of people. Freight trains pose a potentially greater threat when they carry toxic chemicals and other hazardous cargo that could harm people near the site of a collision or derailment.

■ **Estimating Risk:** According to the system MOEs, the primary concerns are the integrity and availability of the mission functions and information. Confidentiality is a less significant factor in meeting mission objectives, although it is important to protect data regarding future train movements and cargo. For an attacker to achieve the objective of causing a train movement to enter an unsafe area, the train must either violate the assigned authorizations and restrictions, or the data on which the authorizations and restrictions are based must be compromised. In the first case, the back office server would correctly calculate where and when the train should move, but the onboard system would not relay the information to the engineer or execute the required braking actions automatically. In the second case, the back office server would make incorrect decisions because of incorrect train position reporting, train consist reporting or wayside signal reporting.

Further LOE analysis requires information specific to a PTC system. However, the likely targets for attack are the integrity of one or more onboard systems, either directly or through the back office server. The back office server has the potential to provide inaccurate data to an onboard system (causing incorrect braking calculations). It could also impact the integrity of an onboard system through code injection or similar attacks. The attacker LOE would depend on the ability to gain access to an onboard system or back office server. This could be physical access (supply chain, malicious insider or at a train yard) or remote access. Possibilities for remote access include network attacks on a back office server and malicious data injection into the communications network. Since railroads share track sections, PTC is designed to be interoperable across railroads. An infected onboard system could potentially infect the back office server of another railroad when it operates on the same (compromised) line.

- **Mitigation Phase:** The prioritization of mitigation actions is dependent on the LOEs of specific attacks and the impact of the attacks on mission MOEs. Mitigation actions include:

  - Code integrity monitoring in the onboard system with a failstop on integrity violations.

  - Encrypted and authenticated wired and wireless network communications.

  - Isolating the back office server from non-PTC networks.

  - Standard NIST 800-53 [10] controls to protect the integrity and availability of the back office server.

The mitigation actions must be selected so that they do not impact availability and the timely completion of onboard system functions.

4.3 Potential Improvements

Several potential improvements to MIRA are possible that could aid critical infrastructure system evaluations. Our experience applying MIRA has demonstrated the need for automation to support the analysis, particularly during the scoring process. This is especially important for complex, distributed critical infrastructure systems. As a generic example of the need for automation, MIRA analysts work with mission experts to perform mission impact scoring. Unfortunately, manual scoring does not scale to common instances of MM, especially in the case of large critical infrastructure systems. Suppose, for example, that the five MM components have cardinalities of 5, 7, 7, 10 and 20, there are three attack types (confidentiality, integrity and availability) and there are a total of 50 nodes. Then, a total of 7.35 million distinct mission impact scores must be analyzed and assigned, a task that cannot be performed manually. As mentioned above, we are currently researching an approach for automating mission impact scoring.

Methodologies such as MBA produce results that should be independently validated if at all feasible. We have not as yet done this for MBA in the context of critical infrastructure systems, although it is very important given the nature of critical infrastructure systems. A possible approach, albeit potentially costly to execute, is to have independent red teams attack a critical infrastructure system that was previously analyzed and mitigated using approaches such as MIRA and NMA. The independent red team results could help calibrate how well the MBA methods pinpoint important attack types and mitigate against them in the context of the specific critical infrastructure system and in the general case. An alternate approach is to emulate portions of a critical infrastructure system in a testbed or use a modeling environment and attempt to validate the analysis results in these settings with red team techniques.

5.   Principles and Key Takeaways

The following are some principles and key takeaways related to applying MBA to critical infrastructure systems:

- Mitigation actions for critical infrastructure systems should be very sensitive to performance requirements, especially availability requirements. Timing tolerances in critical infrastructure systems are much stricter than those associated with many traditional information technology systems.

- When analyzing critical infrastructure systems, it is important to vary the mission timeline while holding the other attack variables constant. This can assist in worst case analysis. For example, an attack on the integrity of pump settings in a wastewater treatment plant can be far more damaging before the pumps are programmed compared with attacking the settings after the data has been written to log files.

- Since many critical infrastructure systems are fielded for extended periods during which few major upgrades are permitted, it is important that approaches such as MIRA are applied as early as possible in the system development lifecycle when there is still time to follow through on the mitigation actions that are identified.

- Critical infrastructure systems are very tightly coupled to the missions they support compared with general purpose computing systems. Most assurance methodologies do not prioritize the implementation of countermeasures with respect to mission priorities. With its focus on mission assurance, MIRA enables mitigation efforts that prioritize the preservation of critical mission functions with minimal cost and performance impact.

- The segmentation of networks and systems in critical infrastructure environments must be performed with great care compared with non critical infrastructure environments. The separation of business networks from critical infrastructure systems is essential to limit attacks, as demonstrated by the recent targeting of Aramco computer systems [13]. Analysts applying MBA must keep this in mind during their analysis.

6.   Conclusions

As cyber-physical interfaces become more prevalent, especially in critical infrastructure systems, cyber threats are an increasing concern. Mission-based analysis (MBA) is a family of methodologies that allow mission and system owners as well as designers to understand the mission impact of cyber attacks and targeted mitigation strategies in the context of critical infrastructure systems. MBA, in particular the MIRA variant, advances the state of the art in mission assurance for critical infrastructure systems by expanding the analysis beyond the examination of failures and by creating a framework for integrating techniques for modeling missions, adversaries, threat space and impact of successful attacks on prioritized missions. By utilizing MBA, the critical infrastructure protection community can prioritize resource decisions in fiscally-constrained environments to protect against cyber threats that pose the highest risk, thereby reducing the overall risk to critical systems and missions.

References

[1] S. Alibrahim and T. Tse, Signal and Train Control, Federal Railroad Administration Research and Development Program Review, Federal Railroad Administration, Washington, DC, 2008.

[2] C. Burris, J.McEver, H. Schoenborn and D. Signori, Steps toward improved analysis for network mission assurance, *Proceedings of the Second IEEE International Conference on Social Computing*, pp. 1177–1182, 2010.

[3] P. Katsumata, J. Hemenway and W. Gavins, Cybersecurity risk management, *Proceedings of the Military Communications Conference*, pp. 890–895, 2010.

[4] M. Keefe, Timeline: Critical infrastructure attacks increase steadily in past decade, *Computerworld*, November 5, 2012.

[5] T. Llanso, CIAM: A data-driven approach for selecting and prioritizing security controls, *Proceedings of the IEEE International Systems Conference*, 2012.

[6] T. Llanso, P. Hamilton and M. Silberglitt, MAAP: Mission Assurance Analytics Platform, Proceedings of the IEEE Conference on Technologies for Homeland Security, pp. 549–555, 2012.

[7] M. McQueen, W. Boyer, M. Flynn and G. Beitel, Quantitative cyber risk reduction estimation methodology for a small SCADA control system, *Proceedings of the Thirty-Ninth Annual Hawaii International Conference on System Sciences*, p. 226, 2006.

[8] Metrolink, An introduction to positive train control, Los Angeles, California (www.metrolinktrains.com/agency/page/title/ptc).

[9] C. Mokkapati, T. Tse and A. Rao, A practical risk assessment methodology for safety-critical train control systems, *Proceedings of the Annual Conference of the American Railway Engineering and Maintenance-of-Way Association*, 2009.

[10] National Institute of Standards and Technology, Recommended Security Controls for Federal Information Systems and Organizations, NIST Special Publication 800-53, Revision 3, Gaithersburg, Maryland, 2009.

[11] National Institute of Standards and Technology, Guide for Conducting Risk Assessments, NIST Special Publication 800-30, Revision 1, Gaithersburg, Maryland, 2012.

[12] P. Ralston, J. Graham and J. Hieb, Cyber security risk assessment for SCADA and DCS networks, *ISA Transactions*, vol. 46(4), pp. 583–594, 2007.

[13] Reuters, Aramco says cyberattack was aimed at production, *New York Times*, December 9, 2012.

Chapter 15

ASSESSING THE IMPACT OF CYBER ATTACKS ON INTERDEPENDENT PHYSICAL SYSTEMS

Antonio Di Pietro, Chiara Foglietta, Simone Palmieri and Stefano Panzieri

Abstract   Considerable research has focused on securing SCADA systems and the physical processes they control, but an effective framework for the real-time impact assessment of cyber attacks on SCADA systems is not yet available. This paper attempts to address the problem by proposing an innovative framework based on the mixed holistic reductionist methodology. The framework supports real-time impact assessments that take into account the interdependencies existing between critical infrastructures that are supervised and controlled by SCADA systems. Holistic and reductionist approaches are complementary approaches that support situation assessment and evaluations of the risk and consequences arising from infrastructure interdependencies. The application of the framework to a sample scenario on a realistic testbed demonstrates the effectiveness of the framework for risk and impact assessments.

Keywords: Cyber attacks, SCADA systems, impact assessment, testbed

1.   Introduction

The risk of cyber attacks that can compromise the operation of critical infrastructures such as electricity and water distribution systems has increased due to network connectivity and convergence, strong attacker motivation and expertise, and the use of general-purpose and open communication protocols for communications and control. Evaluating the impact of cyber attacks is a complex task due to intra-system interactions and interdependencies. Moreover, interactions between infrastructure components and the infrastructures themselves lead to cascading effects are difficult to model and evaluate.

Supervisory control and data acquisition (SCADA) systems are employed widely in the critical infrastructure to control physical processes. However,

J. Butts and S. Shenoi (Eds.): Critical Infrastructure Protection VII, IFIP AICT 417, pp. 215–227, 2013.

SCADA systems rely heavily on information and communications technologies (ICTs); these technologies exhibit numerous vulnerabilities that can be exploited by cyber attacks, especially those involving malware such as viruses and worms. The often-cited Stuxnet worm [7] that targeted SCADA systems was able to alter the behavior of programmable logic controllers (PLCs). Indeed, despite the adoption of security policies, firewalls and intrusion detection systems across the critical infrastructure, SCADA systems and their networks remain vulnerable as a result on their ICT layer. For these reasons, all impact assessments of faults should also consider cyber attacks [5].

Several research efforts have focused on developing simulation environments that evaluate the impact of malware on critical infrastructure systems. The possibility of modeling and performing cyber attacks in a controlled simulation environment allows SCADA operators to develop and test security standards with the aim of preventing and/or reducing the impact of attacks on physical processes. Due to the difficulty – and danger – involved in performing security tests on real-world SCADA systems [16], SCADA security researchers typically employ hybrid simulation environments that integrate commercial software used in real SCADA systems and simulated components that emulate SCADA networks and devices (e.g., routers and PLCs).

However, most SCADA security testbeds are incapable of modeling and simulating critical infrastructure interdependencies [8]. This paper attempts to overcome this limitation. It describes a SCADA security testbed that engages infrastructure interdependency models in performing impact assessments. The approach seeks to provide SCADA operators with qualitative and quantitative measurements of (near-term) future risk to reduce the decision-making time and effort, and to improve the outcome. The approach is based on the mixed holistic reductionist (MHR) model [2, 3], a general formalism that can describe large, complex systems like critical infrastructures and with their interdependencies and the impact of faults. MHR employs CISIA [4], an agent-based system for modeling and simulating interdependencies. CISIA models each physical component as an agent that exhibits: (i) an operative level, which is defined as the ability to perform the required task; (ii) a set of resources needed by the component to operate; and (iii) a set of faults that can affect the component. The MHR approach has been validated by research conducted under the EU FP7 MICIE Project [20]. It is currently being used in the EU FP7 CockpitCI Project [18] to investigate the real-time impact of cyber attacks on the quality of service (QoS) delivered by targeted critical infrastructure assets.

2.   Related Work

This section discusses research efforts related to SCADA security testbeds and models for analyzing critical infrastructure interdependencies.

Queiroz, *et al.* [16] have designed a testbed for investigating attacks that affect system functionality. The testbed, which is based on a real SCADA network, incorporates a human-machine interface (HMI), remote terminal units (RTUs), and sensors and actuators connected to a corporate network over the

Internet. McDonald, *et al.* [14] have developed a testbed based on a customized simulation framework for analyzing the interactions between a physical process, control devices and a SCADA network. Genge, *et al.* [10] have developed a network emulator environment, which simulates the cyber layer of a SCADA system (e.g. RTUs and process control software) that controls a simplified water purification plant modeled using Matlab. The environment allows the evaluation of the consequences of cyber attacks on the physical process.

In the area of interdependency modeling, Ghorbani, *et al.* [11] have presented a classification and comparison of interdependency modeling and simulation tools for critical infrastructures. The Interdependency Infrastructure Simulator (I2Sim) [17] provides a power simulation environment that models interdependencies between critical infrastructures based on resource requirements and distribution. The core component of I2Sim is a production cell, a functional unit that needs a certain quantity of one or more input resources to produce an output resource. The production cell is associated with a matrix called the human readable table, which encapsulates the behavior of the modeled component by associating input quantities with output quantities. Hierarchical holographic modeling (HHM) [13] facilitates the modeling of complex systems at different levels, including the physical, organizational and managerial levels. HHM has been applied to SCADA systems to evaluate the risk of cyber attacks on controlled critical infrastructures [6].

Agent-based models developed for analyzing complex systems can be applied to critical infrastructure protection. These include NetLogo [21], a multi-agent programming language and modeling framework used to analyze natural and social science phenomena. Another framework is RePast [1], which uses genetic algorithms and neural networks to model the behavior of concurrent agents. Yet another is SimJADE [12], a multi-agent framework based on discrete event simulation that supports generic interaction protocols for agent communications.

Existing SCADA security testbeds have been employed to study the impact of cyber attacks on physical processes, but they do not employ infrastructure interdependency models to evaluate the real-time cascading effects. In contrast, our testbed specifically incorporates interdependency models. This helps evaluate how cyber attacks on SCADA systems can induce cascading effects on interdependent physical processes (e.g., physical and cyber [15]).

This work has been undertaken under the FP7 CockpitCI Project [18]. The project seeks to improve the dependability and resilience of critical infrastructures by providing operators with efficient tools that help prevent cyber attacks and implement consequence containment strategies in the event of attacks. The CockpitCI Project is a follow-up to the MICIE Project [20] that focused on the creation of a distributed alert system for the early detection of cascading physical faults. The alert system to be developed under the CockpitCI Project will: (i) incorporate smart detection agents that monitor potential cyber threats in various networks (e.g., SCADA and IP networks); (ii) identify in real-time the critical infrastructure functionality that is impacted by cyber attacks and assess the degradation of the delivered services; (iii) broadcast alert messages to other

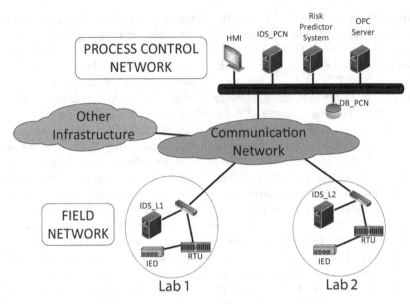

Figure 1. SCADA testbed architecture.

critical infrastructures at different security levels; and (iv) support containment strategies that address the consequences of cyber attacks in the short, medium and long terms.

3.   SCADA Testbed Architecture

The SCADA security testbed engages a typical client-server SCADA network architecture, which incorporates PLCs, RTUs, intelligent electrical devices (IEDs) and an HMI. Two key components are an integrated risk predictor system (IRP) and a set of intrusion detection systems (IDSs). These two components support the evaluation of the impact of cyber attacks on the physical components controlled by the SCADA system. The SCADA network spans two laboratories, one located at the University of Roma Tre and the other at ENEA, also in Rome, Italy. The distribution of SCADA network nodes over the Internet helps model the large geographic scale of real-world SCADA systems.

Figure 1 shows the reference architecture of the SCADA security testbed. The architecture incorporates the following components:

- **Process Control Network:** This network serves as the connection layer for the SCADA equipment. A database (DB_PCN) stores information about field equipment. An HMI provides operators with a facility for visualizing data and information. The data and information can be accessed by other operators via an open platform communications (OPC) server as well as by the IRP, which performs a situation assessment by computing the risk level associated with the state of the considered critical

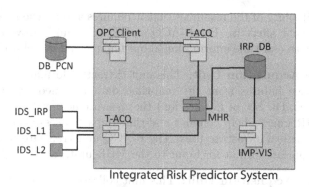

Figure 2. Integrated risk predictor architecture.

infrastructure and evaluating the impact of cyber attacks. Cyber attacks are detected using IDSs associated with the critical infrastructures and relayed to the network (IDS_PCN) whose output is merged into the IRP.

- **Field Network:** This network includes sensors, actuators (IEDs) and RTUs, and supports the acquisition of process field data and the execution of control actions. Two IDSs (IDS_L1 and IDS_L2), one at each laboratory, monitor traffic directed at the RTUs, perform local cyber attack detection and notify the IRP about possible malicious activity to enable it to support global risk assessments. An attacker is assumed to be located in this network and can launch attacks that compromise SCADA system functionality.

- **Communication Networks:** This network uses the Internet to connect the process control and field networks.

4. Integrated Risk Predictor Architecture

Figure 2 presents the modular structure of the IRP. The IRP has six main components: (i) mixed holistic reductionist (MHR) unit; (ii) failure acquisition (F-ACQ) unit; (iii) threats acquisition (T-ACQ) unit; (iv) OPC client; (v) impact visualization (IMP-VIS) interface; and (vi) IRP database (DB_IRP).

- **Mixed Holistic Reductionist Unit:** This unit performs the real-time impact analysis of faults and cyber attacks on a set of critical infrastructures through the execution of an agent-based model. The model represents a network of heterogeneous systems that exhibit interdependencies. The MHR model captures critical infrastructures at different hierarchical levels: holistic, reductionist and service layers. For each critical infrastructure, agents are used to model the production, supply and transportation (or consumption) of tangible or intangible resources: goods, policies, operative conditions, etc. The capability of each agent to provide the required resources depends on its operative condition, which is based on the availability of the resources that it requires and on the severity of the failures that affect it. The F-ACQ and T-ACQ units provide the MHR model with real-time information about failures and attacks, respectively.

- **Failure Acquisition Unit:** This unit extracts information about physical device failures from the real-time data provided by the SCADA database. The set of failures and the measurement values are input to the MHR unit to help conduct real-time impact assessments of the considered critical infrastructures. The F-ACQ unit translates the data into an appropriate format for input to the MHR unit.

- **Threats Acquisition Unit:** This unit collects real-time data from the set of IDSs that provide local and global cyber attack detection assessments. The data includes log data and alert messages produced when malicious attacks are detected. This unit, like the F-ACQ unit, translates data into an appropriate format for input to the MHR unit. Communications between the T-ACQ unit and the IDSs are handled using web service technology: each IDS hosts a web service that accepts requests from web clients hosted by the T-ACQ unit.

- **OPC Client:** The OPC client queries real-time data from the SCADA database (DB_PCN) at a fixed rate. This data, which includes equipment faults and failures and measurement values, is passed to the F-ACQ unit.

- **Impact Visualization Interface:** This unit provides the operator with a graphical user interface (GUI) that shows the real-time status and the predicted impact of failures and attacks on the considered critical infrastructures.

- **IRP Database:** This unit stores the results of MHR model executions. The MySQL database incorporates a historian that maintains all the data for offline analyses.

5.   MHR Modeling

The mixed holistic reductionist (MHR) approach supports the modeling and evaluation of interdependencies existing between critical infrastructures. Interdependency identification relies on the interaction of two different approaches, holistic and reductionist methods.

Holistic models focus on a single critical infrastructure and the evolution of an event within the critical infrastructure, ignoring events in other infrastructures. These models are usually created in collaboration with sector experts and embed complex dynamics related to the single infrastructure (e.g., transient behavior of a power grid when a breaker is opened). In contrast, reductionist models capture elements of multiple critical infrastructures in order to model interdependencies existing between the infrastructures.

Figure 3 shows the MHR modeling technique. The upper boxes represent the holistic approach for two interdependent infrastructures. A situation as-

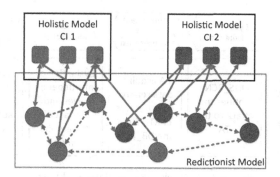

Figure 3. Mixed holistic reductionist modeling technique.

sessment at this level of abstraction is realized by considering several technological and organizational aspects and using techniques and methods specific to each infrastructure. In this context, important services directed towards customers are defined along with the possible impacts due to endogenous faults and threats. An example is the detection of possible cyber attacks on a telecommunications network and the evaluation of the effects on the network. The lower boxes model the reductionist approach, which evaluates interdependencies and propagates faults. At this level, the evaluation of cyber attacks on real equipment is considered, including the equipment responsible for interdependencies such as remote-controlled circuit breakers and switches in a power grid.

6. Attack Scenario

This section focuses on a scenario involving a cyber attack on the reconfiguration service of a power grid, which is controlled by a SCADA system. The scenario incorporates three infrastructures: a medium voltage power grid controlled by a SCADA system via a telecommunications network that connects the control center with the RTUs. Each RTU incorporates a modem connected to a switch; it receives and transmits data in order to open or close the switch. The Modbus/TCP protocol is used for RTU communications. Control actions are implemented by a PLC connected to the HMI. Figure 4 shows the data workflow starting from an attack occurrence to attack impact assessment.

The impact evaluation focuses on the effects of faults and cyber attacks on the services provided by the coupled infrastructures. Note that the services include those supplied to customers (e.g., electricity) as well as those that enable each critical infrastructure to be reconfigured.

6.1 Attack Execution

The scenario involves a man-in-the-middle attack by an attacker located in the process control network or at one of the two laboratories connected to the field devices (see Figure 1). The attacker can eavesdrop on the messages between the two hosts as well as modify messages to send fake data to a host.

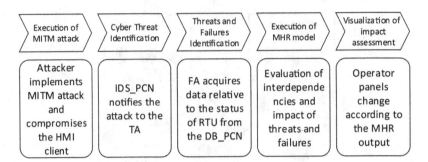

Figure 4. Attack scenario data workflow.

The man-in-the-middle attack exploits a vulnerability in the address resolution protocol (ARP). The attack is commonly referred to as ARP poisoning (spoofing). The attack was performed using Ettercap [19], a packet injector that manipulates ARP tables, enabling the attacker to compromise an RTU (e.g., by manipulating a message or sending fake commands to the RTU).

6.2   Attack Identification

The TCP layer of the Modbus/TCP protocol provides a sequence number that is unique for each session. However, as described in [9], Modbus only accepts the first response received and discards additional responses.

We used Snort as an IDS to detect ARP attacks, unicast ARP requests and inconsistent Ethernet-IP address mappings. In particular, Snort was configured to detect changes in the mappings between valid MAC addresses and IP addresses in order to detect ARP poisoning attacks originating from the SCADA network.

The T-ACQ unit acquires data from the IDSs while the F-ACQ unit acquires data from the real equipment (e.g., HMI). Web service technology is used for connections between the T-ACQ unit and the IDSs: each IDS represents a server and the T-ACQ unit is the client that "polls" the servers to obtain updated information. The connections between the F-ACQ and the real equipment are realized using the OPC client/server architecture.

The T-ACQ and F-ACQ outputs are passed to the MHR model (Figure 5). The outputs of the two units are in the form of XML files with the same structure for both units. A specific XML element specifies the attack type and another element represents the severity of the attack.

6.3   MHR Model Execution

The MHR model was realized using the CISIA agent-based software [4]. The CISIA software models every element (equipment, service, policy or entity) as an agent using a common representation. Each agent is described by its inputs and outputs. Agents exchange resources, such as telecommunication packets, power flows and service levels. Agent behavior is affected by faults

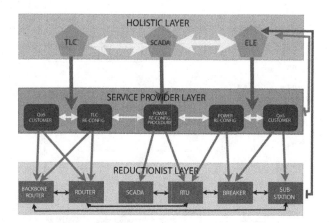

Figure 5. Infrastructure interdependency model.

and failures. The internal representations of agents may be heterogeneous; however, the coupling of the agents with several internal models is achieved using a common exposed interface. Each agent is represented by its operative level or operativeness, the ability of the agent to produce goods and services.

The CISIA simulator uses triangular fuzzy numbers to handle uncertainty. A triangular fuzzy number is expressed using four (crisp) numbers: left, middle, right and height values.

Figure 5 shows the principal agents in the MHR model implementation. Three holistic nodes are shown, one for each critical infrastructure. The services are shown as purple boxes: the quality of service for customers of the telecommunications network and power grid, the automatic telecommunications reconfiguration procedure, and the reconfiguration of the power grid related to the SCADA network and the power reconfiguration topology. The reconfiguration of the power grid needs the SCADA network and the telecommunications network in order to send and receive messages to and from switches via the RTUs. The reconfigured topology of the electric grid is determined based on the ability of each line to feed customers after a power fault. The main objects in the reductionist layer are the telecommunications network routers, the SCADA control center and RTUs, and the switches, breakers and substations in the power grid. To simplify the presentation, Figure 5 does not show the other elements and agents.

6.4   Impact Evaluation

A man-in-the-middle attack can have several outcomes. Surveillance attacks collect information about the SCADA system and RTUs and the messages they exchange, or they read requests issued by the HMI to RTUs. More serious attacks modify reply messages (e.g., randomly or using a "NOT" operator, which would close a circuit breaker instead of opening it). Other attacks change messages transmitted between the HMI and RTUs. These attacks can compromise

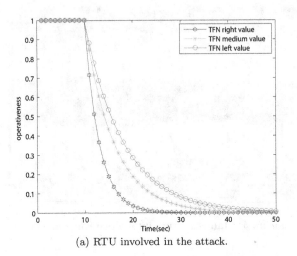

(a) RTU involved in the attack.

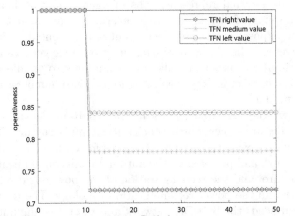

(b) Reconfiguration service in the power grid.

Figure 6. CISIA operative levels.

the functionality of the SCADA system by altering the control strategy and ultimately affecting the physical system.

The implemented attack changes the values of messages sent from the HMI to the RTUs, which are connected to circuit breakers and switches. Figure 6(a) shows the behavior of an RTU under attack (computed using CISIA). The behavior exhibits an exponentially-decreasing trend starting at the attack start time ($t = 10$). Note that the RTU should execute commands from the HMI only in the event of a fault in the power grid.

The reconfiguration service in the power grid involves operator-initiated procedures that change the topology of the power grid after a fault has occurred.

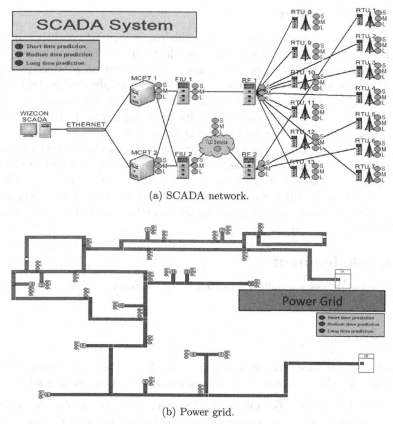

(a) SCADA network.

(b) Power grid.

Figure 7. Operator panels for the SCADA network and power grid.

These procedures are implemented by the HMI sending commands to selected RTUs to open or close switches. The reconfiguration procedures cannot be executed if one or more RTUs are affected by the attack. Figure 6(b) shows the operative level of the power grid reconfiguration service. Note that in Figures 6(a) and 6(b), three values (i.e., left, middle and right values) are used to represent triangular fuzzy numbers. The y-axis values are between 0.7 and 1.0; the height values are not shown because these values are always equal to 1.0.

Figure 7 shows the operator panels, which present the system behavior to operators in a simple and effective manner. The panels show system snapshots with the possible impact in the near future using colored circles to express the severity of equipment faults.

The operative level of each element is specified using a red cross if the element is not working (e.g., a load in Figure 7(b)). A circle near an element denotes the prediction of its operative level during the next iteration. Note that S denotes a small time prediction (during the next step), M a medium time prediction (during two time steps) and L a large time prediction (during three time steps).

7.　Conclusions

The experimental testbed described in this paper supports real-time impact assessments of cyber attacks on interdependent critical infrastructures. The sample scenario focused on the evaluation of the impact on services provided by a SCADA system that controls a power grid. The physical layer and the services provided by the two infrastructures were modeled using the CISIA agent-based tool. The experimental results involving a man-in-the-middle attack on a SCADA RTU demonstrate the utility and effectiveness of the testbed as a means for providing infrastructure operators with the current status as well as the predicted impact on key infrastructure components and services.

Our future research will continue to refine the testbed and the modeling framework. Also, it will investigate more complex attacks on interdependent critical infrastructures, including stealth attacks that modify packet content in SCADA-RTU communications.

Acknowledgement

This research was partially supported by EU Project Cockpit-CI FP7-SEC-285647/2012.

References

[1] N. Collier, RePast: An extensible framework for agent simulation, *Natural Resources and Environmental Issues*, vol. 8(1), article no. 4, 2001.

[2] S. De Porcellinis, G. Oliva, S. Panzieri and R. Setola, A holistic-reductionistic approach for modeling interdependencies, in *Critical Infrastructure Protection III*, C. Palmer and S. Shenoi (Eds.), Springer, Heidelberg, Germany, pp. 215–227, 2009.

[3] S. De Porcellinis, S. Panzieri and R. Setola, Modeling critical infrastructure via a mixed holistic reductionistic approach, *International Journal of Critical Infrastructures*, vol. 5(1/2), pp. 86–99, 2009.

[4] S. De Porcellinis, S. Panzieri, R. Setola and G. Ulivi, Simulation of heterogeneous and interdependent critical infrastructures, *International Journal of Critical Infrastructures*, vol. 4(1/2), pp. 110–128, 2008.

[5] G. Digioia, C. Foglietta, S. Panzieri and A. Falleni, Mixed holistic reductionistic approach for impact assessment of cyber attacks, *Proceedings of the European Intelligence and Security Informatics Conference*, pp. 123–130, 2012.

[6] B. Ezell, Y. Haimes and J. Lambert, Risks of cyber attack to water utility supervisory control and data acquisition (SCADA) systems, *Military Operations Research*, vol. 6(2), pp. 23–33, 2001.

[7] N. Falliere, L. O'Murchu and E. Chien, W32.Stuxnet Dossier, Symantec, Mountain View, California, 2011.

[8] C. Foglietta, G. Oliva and S. Panzieri, Online distributed evaluation of interdependent critical infrastructures, in *Nonlinear Estimation and Applications to Industrial Systems Control*, G. Rigatos (Ed.), Nova Science, New York, pp. 89–120, 2012.

[9] W. Gao, T. Morris, B. Reaves and D. Richey, On SCADA control system command and response injection and intrusion detection, *Proceedings of the eCrime Researchers Summit*, 2010.

[10] B. Genge, I. Nai Fovino, C. Siaterlis and M. Masera, Analyzing cyber-physical attacks on networked industrial control systems, in *Critical Infrastructure Protection V*, J. Butts and S. Shenoi (Eds.), Springer, Heidelberg, Germany, pp. 167–183, 2011.

[11] A. Ghorbani and E. Bagheri, The state of the art in critical infrastructure protection: A framework for convergence, *International Journal of Critical Infrastructures*, vol. 4(3), pp. 215–244, 2008.

[12] D. Gianni, Bringing discrete event simulation concepts into multi-agent systems, *Proceedings of the Tenth International Conference on Computer Modeling and Simulation*, pp. 186–191, 2008.

[13] Y. Haimes and D. Li, A hierarchical-multiobjective framework for risk management, *Automatica*, vol. 27(3), pp. 579–584, 1991.

[14] M. McDonald, G. Conrad, T. Service and R. Cassidy, Cyber Effects Analysis Using VCSE, Promoting Control System Reliability, Sandia Report SAND2008-5954, Sandia National Laboratories, Albuquerque, New Mexico, 2008.

[15] A. Nieuwenhuijs, E. Luiijf and M. Klaver, Modeling dependencies in critical infrastructures, in *Critical Infrastructure Protection*, E. Goetz and S. Shenoi (Eds.), Boston, Massachusetts, pp. 205–213, 2008.

[16] C. Queiroz, A. Mahmood, J. Hu, Z. Tari and X. Yu, Building a SCADA security testbed, *Proceedings of the Third International Conference on Network and System Security*, pp. 357–364, 2009.

[17] H. Rahman, M. Armstrong, D. Mao and J. Marti, I2Sim: A matrix-partition based framework for critical infrastructure interdependencies simulation, *Proceedings of the Electric Power and Energy Conference*, 2008.

[18] The CockpitCI Project, CockpitCI, Selex Systems Integration, Rome, Italy (www.cockpitci.eu).

[19] The Ettercap Project, Ettercap (ettercap.github.io/ettercap).

[20] The MICIE Project, MICIE, Selex Communications, Rome, Italy (www.micie.eu).

[21] S. Tisue and Wilensky, Netlogo: A simple environment for modeling complexity, presented at the *International Conference on Complex Systems*, 2004.

Printed in the United States

By Bookmasters

Printed in the United States
By Bookmasters